Boatbuilding
Manual

3rd edition

Boatbuilding Manual

Robert M. Steward

International Marine Publishing Company
Camden, Maine 04843

Published by International Marine Publishing Company
21 Elm Street, Camden, Maine 04843
(207) 236-4342

Typeset by The Key Word, Belchertown, Massachusetts
Printed and bound by BookCrafters, Chelsea, Michigan

10 9 8 7 6 5 4 3 2 1

Library of Congress Catalog Card Number 87-2626
International Standard Book Number 0-87742-236-2

Contents

Foreword   *vii*

Preface   *ix*

Preface to the First Edition   *xi*

1   General   *1*

2   Plans   *10*

3   Tools   *16*

4   Woods   *27*

5   Fiberglass and Other Hull
    Materials   *43*

6   Fastenings   *54*

7   Lines and Laying Down   *77*

8   Molds, Templates, and the
    Backbone   *101*

9   Setting Up   *122*

10   Framing   *131*

11   Planking   *145*

12   Deck Framing   *172*

13   Decking   *180*

14   Deck Joinerwork   *188*

15   Interior Joinerwork   *201*

16   Miscellaneous Details   *213*

17   Safety Standards   *254*

Recommended Reading   *259*

Equivalents   *263*

Index   *267*

FOREWORD

The lights often showed bright late in the evening at the Mizzentop in Huntington, New York, and continue to do so at Anchordown here in Darien. I have enjoyed a lifetime influenced by the talk of small boats—their design, their building, and their use. Most rewarding of all aspects, perhaps, are the letters that come along—letters extolling the grand experience encountered in the building of a boat!

There has always been great satisfaction—a justified feeling of accomplishment—related to making things with one's own hands. In this age of specialization I believe boatbuilding can offer even more satisfaction—as well as relaxation and a challenge to individual ability and ingenuity. Few things involve the many skills required in building a boat, each essential for its successful completion. Possibly nothing else is as rewarding.

Further, nicely fashioned, well-built boats are growing more and more expensive. To build your own may well be a practical solution—as well as rewarding. Surely the joys of being afloat are manifold, and those experienced aboard a boat you have built with your own hands are immeasurable.

Bob Steward, being exceptionally well qualified by his long experience in the "world of small ships," has produced a clearly written text of merit and great worth. After years as an apprentice he worked in several small boat yards before joining the highly respected office of naval architect Philip L. Rhodes, where he spent many years engaged in designing and planning numerous power and sailing yachts, as well as commercial boats. The period of World War II found him in an engineering capacity working between various yards and design offices. Far more pleasant work was resumed at war's end involving yachts—and Bob accepted a position with a West Coast firm as superintendent of yacht repair and construction. Sometime later he returned to the East Coast where a number of yacht designs were produced, ranging from 22 to 73 feet, which required his experienced supervision of lofting and construction. The warmer clime beckoned, with its slower pace and easier living, and

Bob moved to Florida to continue his work involving the designing and supervision of numerous yachts. Presently he is semiretired, but is still called upon to design small boats or to make half models.

Bob Steward's classic work has been heartily received from the time it was first published. In this latest edition, Bob has made numerous revisions relating to new materials and present regulations and standards in addition to providing more of his wonderfully clear drawings. Surely this comprehensive and practical material, so well presented, will provide the amateur boatbuilder and the professional with a world of valued and valid information. Indeed, scarcely a week passes when, in writing letters to boatbuilders all over the world, I do not suggest *Boatbuilding Manual* as a source of knowledge.

John Atkin, S.N.A. & M.E.
Anchordown
Darien, Connecticut

PREFACE

It is indeed difficult to realize that 17 years have passed since International Marine Publishing Company went into business and acquired the copyright to *Boatbuilding Manual*, which was to become the first IM publication. It has been a happy marriage, but there have been two sad occurrences during that time: Boris Lauer-Leonardi, the small boatbuilder's staunch friend and longtime editor of *The Rudder* magazine when it was beloved and respected by true boatlovers worldwide, and Phil Rhodes, one of the greatest and most versatile naval architects, have both sailed over the horizon and are missed by countless friends.

I have been exposed to many more people since the 1980 revision of *Boatbuilding Manual* and it has been gratifying to meet or hear from so many who have read and learned from the book. In addition, the two yacht design schools in the U.S. continue to use *Boatbuilding Manual* as text material. YDI Schools (formerly the Yacht Design Institute) in Blue Hill, Maine, uses the complete book, while the Westlawn School of Yacht Design, Stamford, Connecticut, reprints portions of the book as two of the course lessons.

Throughout this book, you will find the names and addresses of firms that carry tools and materials or firms that provide services of value to boatbuilders. Such mention is not to be construed as advertising for the products or services offered. Rather, I believe that the reader will benefit from my research of the sources, possibly saving time in finding suitable boatbuilding materials. Contact the firms directly and tell them what you need.

In addition to the photo and illustration credits given in the earlier edition, I wish to thank the following sources: Seemann Plastics, Inc., Huckins Yacht Corporation, and Gougeon Brothers, Inc., for the use of photos in this revised edition; and Torin, Inc., for both photos and sketches.

I cannot close without mentioning the small craft designers and both amateur and professional boatbuilders for the enthusiasm that encourages me to continue extending the scope of this book. Thank you all, near and overseas.

Robert M. Steward
Jacksonville, Florida

PREFACE TO THE FIRST EDITION

During a meeting a number of years ago with Boris Lauer-Leonardi and the late Andy Patterson, Editor and Business Manager respectively of the fine old *Rudder* magazine, it was decided that I should write some articles about boat construction aimed at the amateur and, hopefully, of some value to the beginning professional. This decision resulted in a series of 20 consecutive monthly pieces that were so well received that they were made into a book. The reception of this, too, was enthusiastic, and soon after it was introduced, the book was published abroad in French. Letters of approval were received from afar. One that lingers in my mind was from a Turkish naval officer who not only bought the book, but also built a boat from my plans. Then again Olin Stephens, famed yacht designer, told me how the French edition was of value to him on an inspection trip in Europe when the book illustrations served to break a language barrier between him and a builder. Things like this are heartfelt, because in so small a field the monetary reward must, unfortunately, be secondary.

As time went on, the number of requests for the book showed that a revision was in order. So now we have *Boatbuilding Manual*, again done with the enthusiasm of Boris as a prime mover, although there have been times, when the midnight oil was burning low, that I was not so happy with his prodding, since he charmed me with his silver tongue to sandwich a number of how-to-build plans and articles into the program at the same time. The new book has been rewritten, but includes a little of the old, as well as techniques I have picked up in the interim, and new materials that have been accepted.

Do not think that this or any other book can teach all there is to know about boatbuilding. The best I can hope for is to give some guidance to those with the urge to build a boat—an urge that usually is very rewarding. I trust that this book, plus a good set of plans from an understanding and experienced designer, will lead to the realization of a dream for many who otherwise could not enjoy boating and the sea.

Assuming he has the ability with woodworking tools, and is armed with plans and the elements of boatbuilding set forth in this book, there is no reason why an amateur cannot turn out a creditable boat, but he is cautioned not to be too pretentious at first. Better to start with something small, like a dinghy, to acquire the feel of boat construction, and then go on to a larger craft.

The author wishes to thank Philip L. Rhodes for the use of some photographs; Fred Bates for telling of his experience with strip planking; Joe Schabo of Fort Lauderdale for tracking down the remarkable photo of the Gulfstream 42 in frame; William G. Hobbs for the use of the same photo; and my family for patience on days when I was drawing or writing when we should have been fishing or sailing.

Robert M. Steward
Jacksonville, Florida

Chapter 1

GENERAL

During the past several decades, more and more people have learned how to use skillfully both hand and power tools for household chores and improvements, making furniture, outbuildings, and the like, and they often turn out very creditable jobs. Such people are good candidates for boatbuilding. Yet, many are intimidated by the thought of making something that is not all square corners; bending wood or other flat material to form curved shapes discourages them. And when they look into boatbuilding and see that it usually starts with a lines plan and the attendant table of offsets that dimensions the curves—well, that's *that*. These people are unnecessarily depriving themselves of a very fascinating and satisfying pastime.

Constructing the first boat, however small, is an experience not to be soon forgotten. Watching a hull grow from flat paper drawings and flat material into a shapely form provides hours of fun and is excellent therapy after a stressful day. When the job is carefully done, the finished vessel is a source of great pride to the builder. And unlike a piece of furniture, which is often put in a corner and soon forgotten, a boat is used over and over for pleasure through the years.

A number of lucky people with the desire to learn boatbuilding have been able to take courses in various parts of the United States, principally in the Northeast and Northwest. Unfortunately, all too few of these courses are located so that the great number of would-be boatbuilders can take advantage of this splendid opportunity to learn the craft, so there is still ample reason for books on boatbuilding.

The purpose of this book is to introduce boat construction by explaining the elementary problems involved from starting the hull until water first laps at the keel. I don't purport to teach all the skills of an expert boatbuilder.

It is impossible to cover briefly all the information needed to build every type of boat. If you are fortunate enough to live in a boatbuilding area, you can learn a great deal from observation. When it comes down to building the kind of boat you want, you should bear in mind that a good set of plans is not only insurance against disappointment, but is also a source of construction details. In this book, I assume

1

that you have acquired the ability to use ordinary carpentry tools—not much more is needed to build some boats—and, of equal importance, that you know how to keep your tools sharp. Nothing is worse or more discouraging than trying to make progress by hacking away with dull tools; there is no excuse for doing so. If you are victim of dull edges, better take a week off in order to learn how to sharpen tools.

Along with the many modern products imported from Japan have come an increasing number of hand tools that are anything but modern, and made with steel that really sharpens well. In one mail order catalog there is a story told by an American tool buyer of a Japanese woodworking shop in which the apprentices do nothing but sharpen tools for six months. So don't fret when you have to spend a few minutes bringing the edge of a chisel up to grade. Incidentally, I can attest to the effectiveness of Japanese water stones for honing.

If the project is to build a boat of a material other than wood or fiberglass, then another field has been opened, namely the cutting, shaping, and welding of metal. Builders of metal boats utilize many of the basic wood boatbuilding techniques, but for book-learning about metal hull construction, refer to Recommended Reading at the end of this book.

A person considering the building of a boat very likely has been exposed to boats and boating, either for pleasure or for commercial purposes, and may have a pretty good idea of what he wants—sail, sail and power, or pure power. Yet, I have received mail about boatbuilding over the years from people with no boating experience and nothing more to go on than a hope of being waterborne in the future. Somewhere along the line they must choose a certain type of hull after deciding what their requirements are.

There are three basic hull types: flat-bottomed, v-bottomed, and round-bottomed. Sawn in two at mid-length, sections through these hulls appear as shown in Figure 1-1.

The flat-bottomed hull in cross-section consists of straight lines running across from side to side. The bottom may also be a straight line when viewed from the side (such as in a scow or barge), or the profile of the bottom may be curved, or "rockered." In any event, the flat-bottomed hull is the easiest to build, has a minimum of beveled or twisted parts, and, if properly designed, can be a useful craft. Flat-bottomed skiffs are found the world over; flat-bottomed dories have a long heritage. Then there are pram dinghies, garveys, etc., that all have their places. In general, though, boats with flat bottoms are best used on sheltered waters. A lines drawing for a flat-bottomed skiff is shown in Figure 7-4.

The arc-bottomed boat is a variation of the flat bottom and a close cousin to the v-bottom. Probably the best known arc-bottomed design is the Star class sloop. These 22-footers are still sailed worldwide, though they were designed in 1911. Both the flat and the arc-bottomed hulls require the minimum of layout work prior to building, as will be seen later.

The frames for a v-bottomed boat are made from a full-size drawing of the hull sections and then set up and left in the hull as permanent members of the structure. While this involves less work and less money for materials than framing a round-bottomed hull, it still calls for careful fitting. The chine pieces, or corners in the sections, of a v-bottomed hull must be carefully worked to achieve bevels that continually change from bow to stern. The frames, too, are all beveled and each is made up of as many as seven carefully fitted and securely fastened parts.

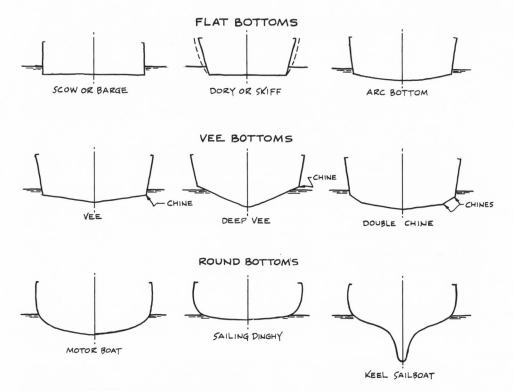

Figure 1-1. *Sections at mid-length of typical flat-, v-, and round-bottomed hulls.*

A round-bottomed hull has curved transverse frames that are sometimes called ribs. These are shaped by steaming or soaking them in boiling water until they are supple enough to be bent either directly on the hull framework or over forms in the shop, and then located in the hull after they have cooled and set. Most boats of the size a beginner would build have frames bent right in the hull; the bevel necessary to have them conform to the hull shape is twisted in during the bending process. Do not let this scare you. When working with relatively light material, the bending is not unduly difficult and can be mastered after a few attempts. In fact it can be a great deal of fun. The process will be described in more detail further along during a discussion of framing.

Bending wood by steaming or boiling is not restricted to round-bottomed construction alone, as it is entirely possible that certain parts of v-bottomed boats, such as the forward ends of bottom planks, will not bend on the boat cold and must be made limber for them to fit the shape of the hull.

Figure 1-2 is a lines drawing for a small round-bottomed hull. Lines drawings are discussed in detail in the chapter on lofting, which is the making of full-size hull drawings and templates for the various parts.

The relative merits of the hull types are argued far and wide, but just about everyone will admit that there will never be a v-bottomed hull as handsome as a well-designed round-bottomed boat, especially for a sailing craft.

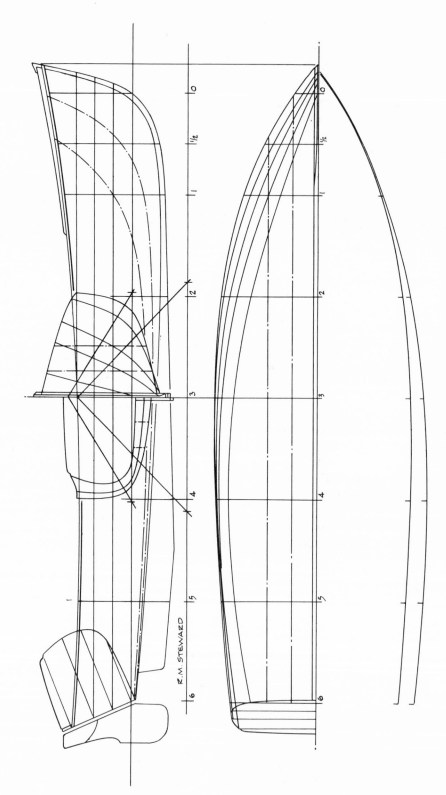

Figure 1-2. *17' 7" round-bottomed wooden launch that has been built by numerous backyard and professional builders.*

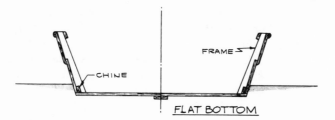

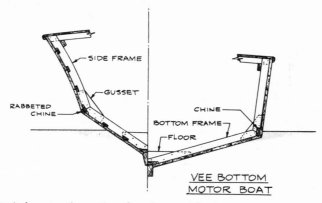

Figure 1-3. *Typical construction sections through v- and flat-bottomed boats.*

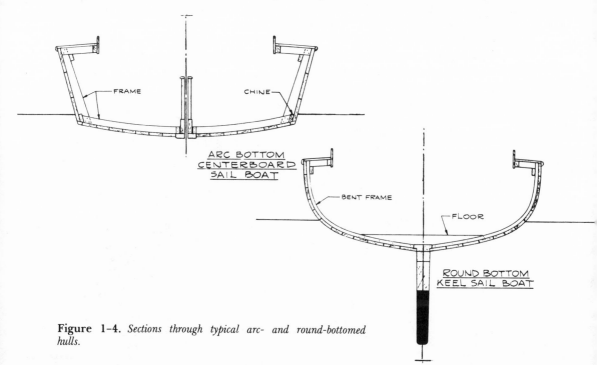

Figure 1-4. *Sections through typical arc- and round-bottomed hulls.*

Figures 1-3 and 1-4 show the essential differences between the framing of flat-, v-, arc-, and round-bottomed hulls. Although the lower ends of the frames in the round-bottomed boat are shown butted against the keel, it is sometimes possible, depending on the hull shape, to install them in one piece, exending from the deck on one side to the deck on the other side. In contrast, note the number of pieces that make up a frame for a v-bottomed boat. On the other hand, frames are spaced farther apart than in a round-bottomed boat, so the frames are fewer in number.

Figure 1-5 is a section through a rather normal sailboat of the cruising or classic ocean racing type. The construction is typical of either the so-called deep keel or combination keel-and-centerboard type boats, the latter being of moderately shallow draft, greater than an unballasted centerboarder but less than the deep keel type. This type of boat is not recommended for the amateur's first attempt at boatbuilding unless he has helped on a similar job or has watched enough of this kind of construction that he will not become discouraged when on his own. The framing is more difficult due to reverse (S) curves in many of the frames, the planking is a tougher job than on a simpler hull, and there is a lot of heavy work getting out the backbone and deadwood.

The time needed to build a hull can be reduced if the hull shape is such that it can be covered with large pieces of flat material such as plywood. If a hull shape does not have compound curvature it is called "developable" and can be formed from flat sheet. There are ways of designing a hull with developable surfaces, either graphically on the drawing board or with a computer program. The surfaces are cylindrical, conical, or a combination of both, and the designer must be content with the limitations of these curves.

Figure 1-6 shows the lines for a 52-foot hull that was designed with the aid of a computer. This boat was built of large fiberglass sheets: one for each side, one for each half of the bottom, one for the transom, and a number of joined strips for the wide chine surface on each side. On the other hand, the v-bottomed hull in Figure 1-7 cannot be built in this manner, for there are concave sections in both the sides and bottom. Flat sheets cannot successfully be bent in two directions at the same time.

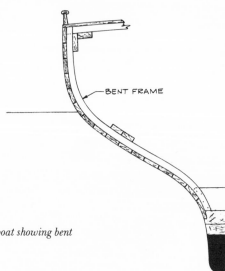

BENT FRAME

Figure 1–5. *The midship section of an auxiliary sailboat showing bent frame with reverse curve.*

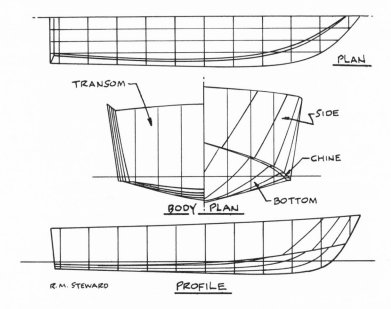

Figure 1-6. *A 52-foot fiberglass commercial fishing boat hull having developable surfaces.*

Most of the figures in this chapter have been labeled with the names of some of the principal hull lines, and the beginner must become familiar with this nomenclature. For instance, the top edge of the hull viewed in profile is the sheerline, while the same line viewed in plan is the deck line, or deck at side. A chine is obviously the intersection between the side and bottom of a v-bottomed hull. Other lines in the surface of a hull will be explained later. Since both sides of a boat are usually the same, a designer only draws the lines for one side of a hull.

For hundreds of years, wood was the primary material used for building hulls, but matters are different now. As this is written, boats of fiberglass-reinforced resin have been manufactured for 35 years, and now fiberglass boats dominate the standardized boat market, with hulls and other parts produced in volume from expensive molds and tooling.

However, wood is not dead. Many pleasure and commercial boats are still built of wood in the United States and elsewhere. Wood is being used in hulls in the conventional manner, some are built with plywood planking, and other hulls are made with multiple layers of relatively thin wood glued together and then often covered with fiberglass cloth and resin.

The techniques of wooden boatbuilding are extensively employed in the construction of tooling for fiberglass boats and parts. Wood is used for the interior joinerwork in the better quality fiberglass boats to avoid the cold, antiseptic appearance of the molded plastic and "mica" finishes that have become a logical extension of molded fiberglass hulls and cabins.

When demand is limited, such as for yachts 65 feet and longer, welded aluminum alloy construction or a welded steel hull with superstructure built of the light alloy is the choice of most of the larger builders. But here again, wood is usually chosen for

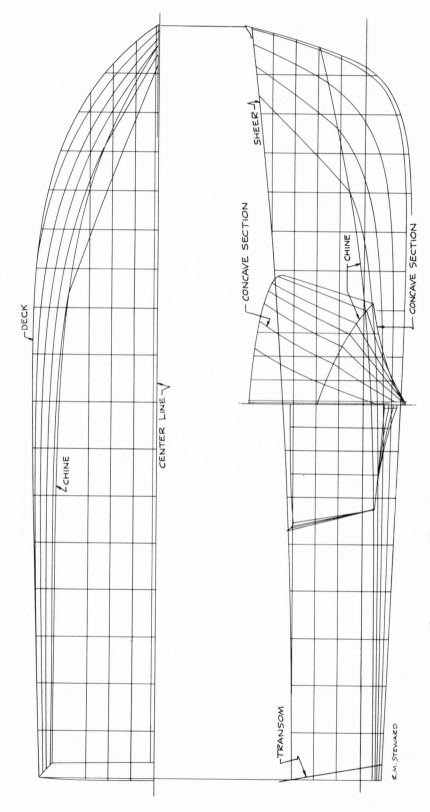

DECK

CHINE

CENTER LINE

SHEER

CONCAVE SECTION

CHINE

CONCAVE SECTION

TRANSOM

K.M. STEWARD

Figure 1-7. *A 32-foot wooden v-bottomed powerboat used as a specimen-collecting boat by the University of Florida.*

Figure 1–8. Susan, *a flat-bottomed rowing skiff, 11' 3" in length, designed by the author in 1952. Over 100 have been built, mostly as first boats for beginners.* (Photo courtesy Missy Hatch, The Rockport Apprenticeshop.)

the finish in the quarters because it provides a feeling of warmth that can never be achieved by the synthetics.

It is possible to gain an introduction to boatbuilding by purchasing and assembling a "kit" boat. There are a number of kits for v-bottomed motorboats and sailboats, usually with plywood planking. Most of these are furnished with beveled parts that require but reasonable care to set up the frames accurately to form the hull. Also available are full-size paper patterns and templates for parts, with all the wood provided by the builder from local stock. Then there are firms that supply a bare fiberglass hull as part of a kit. Here is where an amateur must be careful to be sure that guidance is provided or available to locate components such as engines and fuel and water tanks. The weights of such items can be quite large, and the amateur should not bite off more than he can chew.

Making a kit boat does not give the same sense of accomplishment as building a boat from scratch, but the scheme does make sense for those with limited spare time or for those who want a particular model of boat that is available in kit form. Listings of kit boat manufacturers are found in boating magazine ads and in the *Boat Buyers Guide*. In addition, a good number of fiberglass hull builders advertise in *National Fisherman*. See the Recommended Reading at the end of this book.

Chapter 2

PLANS

A set of plans is needed for a boatbuilding project unless you have decided to build a kit boat. Seldom does one want to build just any boat—rather there is an urge to own a certain type, either power or sail, and usually there is an idea about the size suitable for the intended use. There are several sources for plans, and ample time should be spent on the search for a design to make sure the boat will meet your requirements.

Knowledge of arrangements feasible for various lengths of boats can be obtained by scanning the design sections of the monthly boating magazines. These small drawings are ample for study of what is offered by the design, and the designer or naval architect can be contacted for further information. Some of the boating magazines and some of the monthly do-it-yourself magazines for the home mechanic offer for sale a choice of power and sailboat plans that have been run as "how-to-build" articles over the years. The plans they make available are to a larger, more practical scale than those in the original articles. The same magazines carry ads of several firms that specialize in plans for the backyard builder, and in some cases they also offer full-size patterns for hulls.

At the end of this chapter is a list of sources for small craft plans. In addition, *Boat Buyers Guide*, whose address appears under Recommended Reading, gives many other plan sources.

Regardless of their source, try to determine whether the plans that interest you are sufficiently detailed for you to completely understand the vessel's construction. It cannot be emphasized too strongly that good plans are well worth their price, because their cost is but a fraction of the total cost of the boat. The cost of the plans might be considered as insurance that the finished boat will be a success. When designers do not draw the profusion of details that the novice builder would like to have, this book should be very helpful in filling in some of the missing information.

I would warn you against making changes in the hull lines, heights of superstructures, or locations of major weights. Such procedures can result in

10

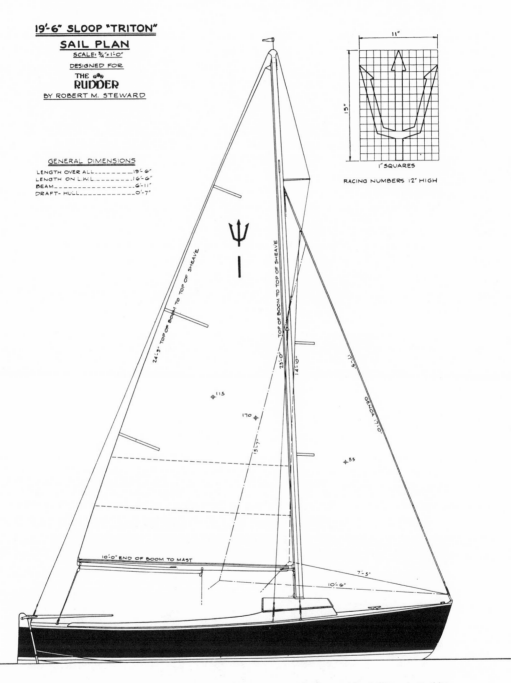

19'-6" SLOOP "TRITON"

SAIL PLAN
SCALE: ¾"=1'-0"
DESIGNED FOR
THE
RUDDER
BY ROBERT M. STEWARD

GENERAL DIMENSIONS
LENGTH OVER ALL _____ 19'-6"
LENGTH ON L.W.L. _____ 16'-6"
BEAM _____ 6'-11"
DRAFT- HULL _____ 0'-7"

1" SQUARES
RACING NUMBERS 12" HIGH

Figures 2-1, 2-2, 2-3. *These plans were drawn by the author as part of* The Rudder's *"How to Build" series and appeared in the February 1948 issue of that publication. Large-scale blueprints were offered by* The Rudder *for use by home builders and are available from* WoodenBoat *(address given at the end of the chapter).*

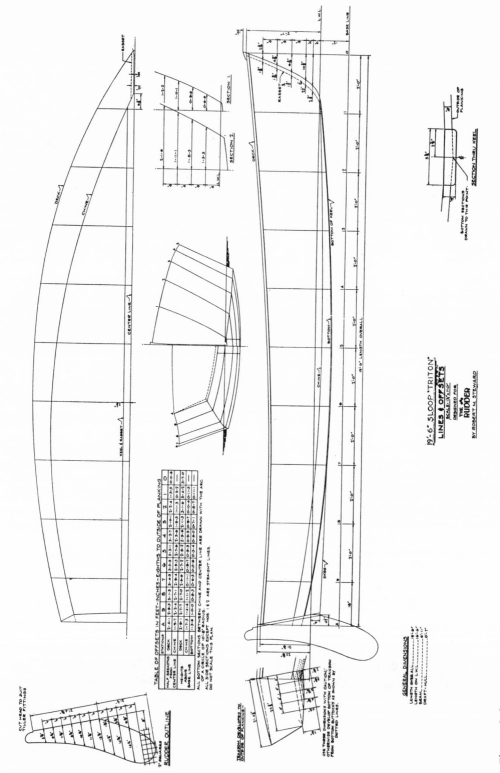

Figure 2-2.

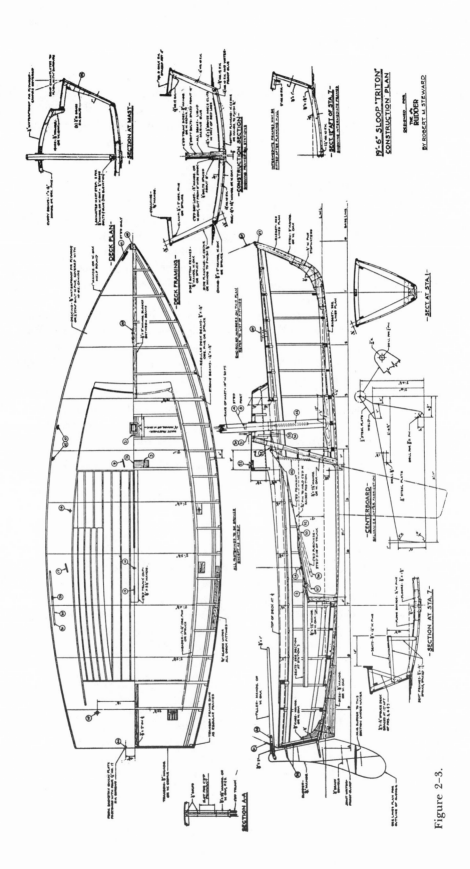

Figure 2-3.

unsatisfactory performance at the least, or even downright reduction of seaworthiness. Consult the designer before making any major changes, and if he advises against them, you will be better off using plans that will give you what you want without departing from the drawings.

Plans for Boats Carrying Passengers for Hire

Every year there is a great number of boats built to carry six or more fare-paying passengers, whether it be for sightseeing, dinner and dancing, or, more likely, fishing. If you are contemplating building such a craft, you should be aware that, in the interest of safety, the construction and equipment of passenger-carrying boats is regulated by the U.S. Coast Guard. The regulations are not unduly strict, but you should not start construction without at least obtaining approval of the hull construction. The routine is fairly simple if you take the time to consult with the closest Marine Inspection Office of the U.S. Coast Guard. In general, an application is made for the inspection of the boat, the service, the route, and the number of passengers to be carried. If there is a complete set of plans, it should be submitted; otherwise, if construction is to be started quickly, general arrangement drawings are necessary and also details of the hull. The Coast Guard has a book of regulations that spells out the design and equipment requirements and lists the plans that must be submitted for approval. They no longer offer the book for free, but they can tell you the location of a government bookstore that stocks the publication.

Restoration

Restoring old wooden boats and even early fiberglass boats has gained considerable popularity during the past decade. This is easily understood since many of the older designs have more appeal than the look-alike plans turned out today. Much restoration is done by amateurs, but a good many professional shops are kept busy catering to those who prefer the older, sometimes classic boats, both sail and power, and can afford to have others do the restoration.

An amateur planning to restore a boat that has caught his eye should be wary of one that has deteriorated beyond his ability to repair it, or one that will require too much time and money—even if money is not important, an excessive amount of time can destroy his enthusiasm before the job has been completed. Hardly a month goes by in which a boating magazine does not carry a classified ad reading "1945 Classic mahogany runabout, partially restored. . . ."

In any event, the situation is not unlike choosing plans from which to build your dream boat—first be absolutely certain the design is exactly what you want, and then, if you are not personally capable of making an accurate judgment of the boat's condition, hire a surveyor for the job. And don't use just any surveyor: get one that is unquestionably familiar with the type of construction employed in the craft being considered.

Sources for Plans (Small Craft)

WoodenBoat (a magazine), Box 78, Brooklin, ME 04616. Catalog available.

International Marine Publishing Co., 21 Elm Street, Camden, ME 04843. Books of study plans; free monthly catalog of standard references and new releases.

Bruce Roberts, 35 Bellview Drive, Saverna Park, MD 21146

Charles W. Wittholz, 100 Williamsburg Drive, Silver Spring, MD 20901.

John Atkin, Box 3005, Noroton, CT 08620.

Glen-L Marine Designs, 9152 Rosecrans, Bellflower, CA 90706.

Motor Boating & Sailing (a magazine), 224 West 57th Street, New York, NY 10019.

Texas Dory Boat Plans, P.O. Box 720, Galveston, TX 77553. Plans for a considerable number of simple boats, many with flat bottoms.

Harold H. ("Dynamite") Payson & Co., Pleasant Beach Road, South Thomaston, ME 04848. Plans for "instant" boats of plywood planking using "tack and tape" method of construction—worth study by the first-time boatbuilder.

Chapter 3

TOOLS

The selection of tools needed to build a boat depends upon the type of project being undertaken. Generally it is best to start with a small craft to get the feel of the work—that is, to appreciate the difference between boatbuilding and common carpentry. A beginner's first choice will often be a plywood-planked open small boat. Such a hull requires a minimum of tools, most of which are usually found in a homeowner's tool chest—hammers, hand saws, planes, chisels, screwdrivers, a brace and auger bits, an "egg-beater" type hand drill and twist bits, etc. There very likely is a ¼" electric drill in the kit as well.

Other hand tools such as a draw knife, spokeshave, bullnose plane, rabbet plane, and round-bottom plane are out of the ordinary and can be added as the need arises.

One hand tool that is unmatched for planing end grain or plywood edges is a low-angle (20 degrees) block plane. Once you have become familiar with one of these with a well-sharpened blade you'll put aside for good the regular block plane.

In addition, let's not overlook wood rasps—flat and oval—or metal files—flat, square, and round.

Layout Tools

Essential tools for layout work and useful from start to finish are a 24" carpenter's framing square, a level at least 24" long, a pair of dividers, a chalk line, a carpenter's pencil compass, a six-foot folding rule and, for larger craft, a 25- or 50-foot measuring tape of steel or fiberglass.

A tool that should be classed as an aid to layout is a sliding T-bevel such as the Stanley No. 18, used for transferring bevels from the drawings to the lumber and for picking up bevels in many ways.

Another type of bevel, almost indispensable, is a small one shown being used in

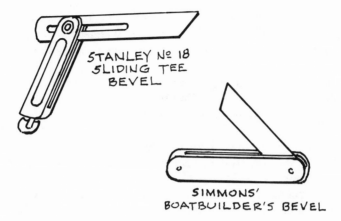

Figure 3–1. *Bevels are extremely handy for layout work.*

Figure 8-10. I have one made with wooden cheeks and a brass blade, very old and source unknown. I once asked a tool company if it would make some, sending my bevel for examination, but it was not interested. However, Walter Simmons makes and sells at a reasonable price an all-brass "boatbuilder's bevel," ³⁄₁₆″ thick x ½″ wide x 3″ closed length. There is no substitute for this tool in tight quarters. Simmons' address is given at the end of this chapter.

Clamps

One might have a C-clamp or two in his kit but when building a boat this is merely a start. There never seem to be enough clamps of the C-type.

The shorter versions of the bar-type clamps do much the same job as the C-clamps

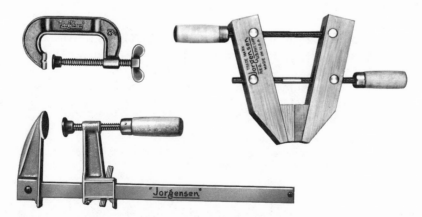

Figure 3–2. Top: *A "C" clamp, the most useful all-around clamp, and a handscrew clamp shown holding tapered pieces.* Bottom: *Bar clamps are made with capacities of 12″ to 36″.*

and also have a place of their own in the longer lengths. Jorgensen bar clamps have a unique "clutch" to regulate the clamping length; Wetzler bar clamps, on the other hand, have a more conventional method of adjustment. I would not turn down a gift of either kind.

I have a number of Pony spring clamps that are useful at times. In the larger sizes it takes a strong squeeze to open these but the pressure is in proportion. I have tried lower-priced spring clamps made in the Far East that have very weak springs. Cheap, but no good!

Handscrew clamps as illustrated are handy at times too, and a few of the woodworker's tool shops sell the steel parts so you can make your own clamps using a hardwood like maple.

Figure 16-7, Chapter 16, shows bar clamps and handscrews being used to apply pressure to the glued joints of a hollow wooden spar under construction. Note the number of clamps employed!

Lapstrake or clinker planking of hulls is discussed in Chapter 11. Should you ever get to building one of the beautiful small craft possible with this type of construction, then very likely you will appreciate the custom lap or planking clamps made by Walter Simmons (see the end of this chapter for his address); I know of no other source for these specialized clamps at this time.

Circular Table Saw

There are many choices in both bench and free-standing types. Buy the best tilting-arbor saw you can afford—8, 9, or 10″, with a rip fence that adjusts along a tube or bar (not just a shape integral with the table edge)—and fit it out with carbide-tipped blades.

With the rip fence out of the way and the blade raised just slightly more than the stock thickness, long and gentle curves can be cut using this tool.

Bandsaw

My shop has a 12″ Craftsman (Sears) bandsaw but I wish I had a 14″ Delta (Rockwell) and not only for the extra depth of throat. The Delta table tilts in two directions, 45° right, 10° left.

Walter Simmons recommended Olsen-brand bandsaw blades to me some time ago and I have been using them happily ever since. They can be bought direct from The Olsen Saw Company, Bethel, CT 06801.

Portable Circular Saw

This is the next best thing to a bench saw and can perform a variety of tasks. It can be used for cross-cutting, straight-line ripping (with a strip of wood tacked in place as a guide), and also for cutting easy curves as described above for the bench saw. There are numerous makes on the market, the old standby being a Skilsaw (Skil).

Figure 3-3. *A 14" bandsaw, Delta International Machinery Corp., shown with rip fence on table.*

Portable Jig Saw

Again, there are many choices. A variable speed model is good for cutting either wood or metal with the appropriate blade. This type of tool is used for curved cuts in plywood panels, for cutting away a plywood deck in way of hatch openings, and for cutouts such as portholes, sink openings in galley counters, and the like.

Tools for Making Holes

A great many holes have to be made during the construction of a boat—small holes for hundreds of fasteners, larger holes for through-hull and deck fittings. Most will be made with twist drill bits driven by rotary devices ranging from the common eggbeater drill for small jobs to ¼"-, ⅜"-, and ½"-capacity drill motors, preferably of variable speed.

When buying twist drills the high speed steel ones are more economical in the long run than carbon steel because they do not burn as quickly when drilling hardwood or metals. Extra long bits are not hard to find—look for "electrician's" or "aircraft" drill bits.

I have seen old-hand boatbuilders grind twist drills to a tapered point, the profile becoming similar to that of a wood screw. The resulting hole gives the screw good holding power, and is faster than having to drill first a tight hole for the screw shank and then a second, smaller one for the threaded length. There is much more about tapered drills and holes for fasteners in Chapter 6.

If your kit includes a traditional hand-operated ratchet brace and a set of Jennings- or Irwin-brand auger bits, these work nicely in boatbuilding.

In anything but the smallest hulls there will be long holes to be bored such as for floor timber fastenings, and others that will be discussed later on. These can be made with long twist drills or augers, lengthened if necessary by welding on an extension. Boatbuilders prefer the "barefoot" type of auger which is easier to keep on a straight course and also is easier to withdraw for clearing away chips than a conventional auger having a threaded lead screw. Augers should be driven by a powerful slow-turning electric drill, preferably reversible.

Hole saws are made in sizes ranging from 9/16" through 6" in diameter, but their short length limits the thickness of the material they can cut and generally dictates that they be used for openings sized to suit through-hull fittings for water inlets, toilet and engine exhaust discharge fittings, and similar purposes. A size can be found to come very close to the outside diameter of pipes but sometimes a rasp must be used to get the hole just right. The accompanying photograph shows an arbor that mates with

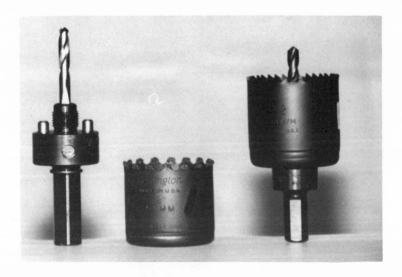

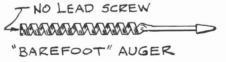

NO LEAD SCREW

"BAREFOOT" AUGER

Figure 3-4. *Hole saws and the old "barefoot" auger for long holes.*

and drives the saw using a power drill. A single arbor will not accept all sizes of saws. In the Morse-brand line, for instance, three sizes of arbors are needed to use the full range of saws. The arbor pilot bits are replaceable. Morse also makes a 12″ extension.

Although small craft can be built in a shop without a drill press, there are times when this tool is very helpful. Chuck capacity should be ½″, the minimum being ⅜″. A press is particularly valuable when holes must be plumb to the surface.

Jointer

Used mostly for edging, one 4″ or wider is a useful tool but is not essential for the small boat builder.

Electric Plane

I resisted buying a power plane for myself for a long time although I knew from boatyard experience that it saves much labor when properly handled. Now I have one with a 3¼″-wide blade and have found it to be increasingly helpful. In one yard we had repairs to make on an Alden schooner that had tangled with a stone jetty in a fog at night. A lightweight 3″ Skil electric plane was used to smooth jagged gouges in the lead ballast keel at the cost of breaking the toothed drive belt a few times over a period of six hours. It was the perfect tool for the job.

Electric Screwdriver

This tool becomes important when hundreds or more wood screws must be driven to secure hull planking. There are a number of makes on the market. Electric screwdrivers are not new; they are powerful, not overly heavy, and can be fitted with bits for different types of screw heads.

Cordless Tools

Yes, indeed! I have a Skil cordless screwdriver with a reversible bit for slotted and Philips-head fasteners and a Black & Decker cordless with a chuck that accepts either drill or screwdriver bits. As long as you don't expect too much from these tools they become almost habit-forming. There are numerous makes available with various duty ratings.

Thickness Planer

This machine has always been the most costly piece of equipment in a small shop. But the story has changed in recent years and some planers of limited capacity have

Figure 3–5. *Electric drill and screwdriver in action. There are nine C-clamps visible keeping plank in place for fastening to frames. Note that hull has been tilted to make bottom more accessible.*

become comparatively affordable. A planer is not essential in that milling can always be done off-site, but it really is a nice machine to have in the shop. One example of small planers now on the market is the Ryobi Model AP-10, which will handle stock up to 10″ wide and 5″ thick, but will of course perform better on smaller dimensioned stock. Current consumption of 13 amps at 115 volts A.C. requires no special wiring.

Sanders

There are a number of portable and stationary sanders available. The most common stationary type is one with a vertical disc and adjustable tilting table, as well as a belt that pivots from horizontal to vertical. This tool is ideal for sanding small parts, if you can afford one and have the shop space.

A portable disc sander is great provided you learn how to control one. This tool can easily spoil any workpiece with unwanted gouges. Practice on something other than your hull!

A portable belt sander is used for smoothing planks, or any long stock. This tool

Figure 3-6. *Makita 1900 BW 3¼" electric planer.*

too can damage your work but is easier to master than a disc sander. Keep the belt moving to avoid cutting a valley.

A relative newcomer to the field is the "finishing" or "palm" sander. The most popular size for small craft takes a quarter sheet of standard 9″ x 11″ abrasive paper and is easy to control. I have used mine with paper from 40 grit (be careful!) to 220 grit for an acceptably smooth surface and the latter grit for the rapid sanding of varnish between coats. Note that during most sanding operations it is prudent to wear a dust mask. In Chapter 16 there is a discussion of abrasive papers and some sanding aids.

Figure 3-7. *Ryobi Model AP-10 surface planer.*

Figure 3–8. *Makita BO 4510 finishing sander.*

Portable Lumber Support Rollers

If you normally work alone another person must be called to help when sawing long stock unless the shop has portable supports adjustable to the heights of the saw tables. There are many varieties of these to be seen in boatbuilding shops, most of them homemade. In my case the shop area calls for equipment that occupies a minimum of space when not needed. The accompanying sketch shows supports I built and named "My Wife" because she no longer had to be called upon to help me.

For the rollers I used hardwood rolling pins with free-turning handles having plastic bearings; the rest of the support parts are plywood and a few scraps of lumber. The roller unit is slipped over the crossbar of a saw horse. The upper set of holes sets the roller at the height of a bandsaw table while the lower set suits the height of the bench saw table. If the shop floor is uneven the plywood roller cheeks can be held at the desired height using clamps rather than the carriage bolts with wing nuts as shown.

Since making my supports I came upon a substitute for the rolling pins—so-called infeed and outfeed rollers, 14″ long with steel rods protruding from the ends. These are pictured in the catalog of Woodworker's Supply of New Mexico (address below).

Some of the tool houses now sell lumber supports through their catalogs. Beware of the cheap versions sold, as a rule, in warehouse-type home improvement stores; one unit I saw was so light it required ballasting at its base.

Sources for Tools

The firms listed here stock good tools; some of them stock for both woodworking and metalworking. Largest in this list is of course Sears Roebuck and Co., which publishes

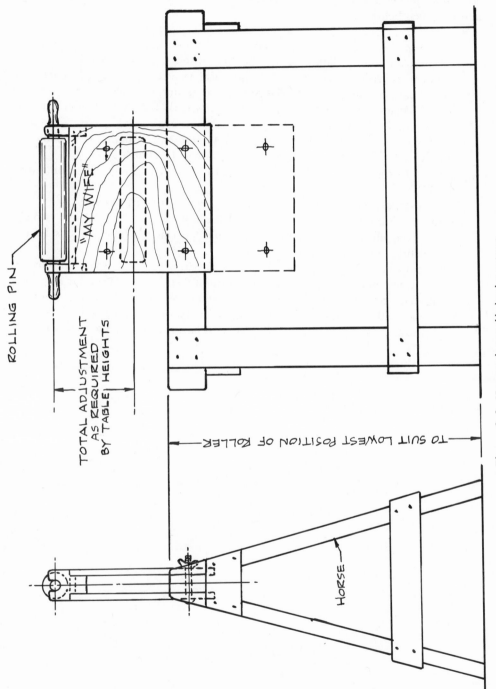

ROLLING PIN

"MY WIFE"

TOTAL ADJUSTMENT
AS REQUIRED
BY TABLE HEIGHTS

TO SUIT LOWEST POSITION OF ROLLER

HORSE

Figure 3-9. Homemade portable lumber support.

an annual power and hand tool catalog available at its bigger stores or from the address given below.

Adjustable Clamp Co., 417 N. Ashland, Chicago, IL 60622. Manufactures a complete line of clamps under the "Jorgensen" and "Pony" brands.

Craftsman Wood Service Co., 2727 South Mary Street, Chicago, IL 60608.

The Fine Tool Shops, 20 Backus Avenue, Danbury, CT 06810.

Garrett Wade Co., Inc., 302 Fifth Avenue, New York, NY 10001. Their catalog is beautifully illustrated.

Highland Hardware, 1034 N. Highland Avenue N.E., Atlanta, GA 30306.

Sears, Roebuck and Co., Sears Tower, Chicago, IL 60684.

Seven Corners Ace Hardware, Inc., 216 West 7th Street, St. Paul, MN 55102.

Trend-Lines, Inc., 375 Beacham Street, Chelsea, MA 02150-0999.

Walter Simmons, Duck Trap Woodworking, R.F.D. 2, Cannan Road, Lincolnville Beach, ME 04849. Planking lap clamps, boatbuilder's bevel, riveting tools, other marine hardware.

Wetzler Clamp Co., Inc., Rte. 611, Box 175, Mt. Bethel, PA 18343. Produces a complete line of clamps, but sold through distributors. Write for catalog.

Woodcraft Supply Corp., 313 Montvale Avenue, Woburn, MA 01801. Another house with a well-illustrated catalog; all items quoted postpaid.

Woodworker's Supply, Inc., 11200 Menaul N.E., Albuquerque, NM 87112.

Chapter 4

WOOD

Wood is one of the easiest materials out of which the amateur can build a boat, and it remains a favorite of many professionals, despite the great growth in synthetic materials. Not all woods are suitable for boatbuilding, however, so as we go along, there will be comments on those kinds that have proven durable—one of the most desirable qualities sought—and have the necessary strength.

It is beyond the scope of this book to more than scratch the surface on the subject of wood, even when limited to the trees found in the United States alone, so I will limit our discussions to the small number of commonly accepted boatbuilding woods and how the lumber is manufactured from logs. A few reasons for the elimination of certain woods from boatbuilding are brittleness, softness, weakness, susceptibility to decay, and shortness of growth. On the other hand there are time-tested woods available that have the necessary qualities, but these types can seldom be found in an ordinary lumberyard. Fortunately almost every area where boats are built has a yard that fully understands the needs of the boatbuilder, and the amateur is advised to seek the aid of such a supplier to obtain the high grade lumber needed for long hull life. There should be no compromise in the matter of lumber quality, for when the labor of the builder is considered, the extra cost and trouble of good material is of little consequence.

Sawing of Lumber

Grain is formed by the angle of the annual rings with the face of a board, and its orientation has much to do with the suitability of the lumber for use in boats. The grain's orientation in boards depends upon how the lumber is cut from logs. After a tree has been felled and trimmed, it is easy for the lumberman to run the log through a saw and cut it into boards as shown in Figure 4-1A. This is called plain sawing, and all but one or two of the boards sawn from the log in this manner are called slash grain

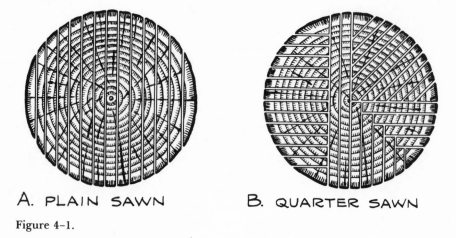

A. PLAIN SAWN   B. QUARTER SAWN

Figure 4-1.

or flat grain. A more expensive and more wasteful method of cutting up the log, B in Figure 4-1, is called quarter sawing, and the resulting boards are known as rift, vertical, or edge-grain boards. It can be seen from Figure 4-2 that a few boards from the middle of a plain-sawn log have rift grain just like quarter-sawn lumber, but the majority of the plain-sawn boards are not desirable for boatbuilding, as will be shown.

Seasoning

Wood for almost any purpose at all must be dried or seasoned to reduce the moisture content present when the tree is cut, at which time the content may be as much as half

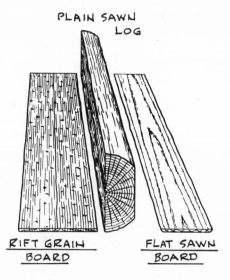

Figure 4-2. Courtesy Forest Products Laboratory, USDA Forest Service.

or more the weight of the log. There are two ways that wood contains moisture, absorption by the cell walls and absorption into the cell cavities themselves. When the wood has taken on as much as the cell will hold, the wood is said to be at the fiber saturation point. In this condition the moisture content of the wood averages about 25 percent, and no shrinkage takes place until this percentage is reduced. Seasoning is the process of reducing the moisture content to about 15 percent, an acceptable level for boatbuilding material, and this is when the wood shrinks. After it seasons to whatever level is wanted, wood shrinks further if more moisture is removed and swells if more moisture is taken on. Shrinking or swelling is greatest in the direction of the annual rings (tangential), about one-half as much as *across* the rings (radial), and but little in the length of a board. Distortion from shrinkage is shown in Figure 4-3, and it can be seen that slash-grain boards cup more than rift-sawn. Shrinkage of rift-sawn lumber tends more toward reducing thickness than width, producing boards with greater dimensional stability than flat-grain ones, and for this reason rift-sawn lumber is desirable for planking, decking, and other boat parts.

The tendency to cup should be considered when planking. For example, when planking the bottom of a simple boat like a skiff the annual rings should curve against the chine. See A in Figure 4-3. The cupping tendency shows up in time when planks are wide.

There are two methods used for seasoning wood, and the mention of the merits of one versus the other just might start up an argument in the local boat shop. There are those who will accept only air-dried lumber, a process that can take several years, depending upon the thickness of the pieces. It is generally accepted that air-dried wood is the best for boatbuilding, and on numerous occasions I have seen this being done right in boatyards. On the other hand, modern production cannot wait too long for material, so the lumber is placed in a kiln to be dried in a number of days. Drying boat lumber by this method must be done with care, because the normal product of

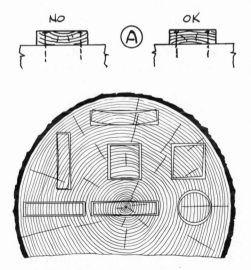

Figure 4-3. *Characteristic shrinkage during seasoning of pieces sawn from a log.* (Courtesy Forest Products Laboratory, USDA Forest Service.)

the kiln will have a moisture content as low as eight percent, whereas time has shown that regardless of the drying method, the moisture content of boat material should be between 12 and 16 percent, with many accepting 15 percent as ideal. Moisture content, incidentally, is expressed as a percentage of the lumber weight when oven dry.

Drying in a kiln speeds up the evaporation of moisture, causing fast drying on the surface and slow drying inside, and is said to affect both the strength and elasticity of the wood. Lumber for boats must not be too green or it will shrink and check excessively during the building period, nor must it be too dry or it will absorb moisture and swell unduly. In the case of some types of planking the latter condition could be very serious.

There are meters made for determining the moisture content of wood, and they must be used properly for correct results. The best procedure for the amateur is to leave the selection of the wood to the experts who understand the requirements of boatbuilding. These people also know that boat lumber should not have large knots and checks, decay, or nondurable sapwood.

Kinds of Wood

In the northeastern part of the United States, where many like to think boatbuilding in this country was born, the practice of using certain available native woods was established long ago, and time has proven its worth. Through the years, lumber from other parts of the country, as well as material from foreign lands, has been added to the list of suitable woods, with substitutions of local products being made in certain areas as a result of satisfactory experience with these woods for boatbuilding. As a typical example, frames would be of oak in most localities, but keel, deadwood, and other backbone members might be yellow pine in the South, white oak in the Northeast, or Alaska cedar or Douglas fir on the West Coast. As long as it is proven, the choice of wood makes little difference, but a boat involves too much work to gamble with untried materials that may rot in a short time or be brittle or not hold fastenings.

As a guide, I give here a list of good woods, together with principal properties and approximate weights per board foot (one foot square by one inch thick) at 12 percent moisture content.

White Oak

Weight about 4.2 pounds (heavy). Durable, stiff, strong, and holds fastenings exceptionally well. Easily steam-bent, thus excellent for frames, but for this purpose the oak should be green, not seasoned. Also used extensively for all backbone members such as keel, stem, deadwood, etc. Good white oak grows in New England southward through the Appalachian area, and it is axiomatic that the most durable oak is from trees felled during the winter when the sap is not flowing. (See Winter Cutting vs. Summer Cutting following the description of Alaska cedar.) It should be noted here there is a much greater supply of red oak than white oak. The red variety is weaker and less durable than white oak and is to be avoided when it is at all possible to find white oak.

Douglas Fir

Weight about 2.9 pounds (medium). Strong and straight-grained, useful for stringers, clamps, sometimes for spars as a substitute for Sitka spruce when light weight is not of utmost importance, and for planking when rift-sawn. Grows in Oregon, Washington, and California. Logs are large, from which veneer is peeled for manufacture into plywood panels. Douglas fir is often called Oregon pine, and it is available—as are Western red cedar, Sitka spruce, and meranti (a mahogany-like wood)—as ⅛" veneers for cold-molded hull construction.

Yellow Pine (Longleaf)

Weight about 3.4 pounds (heavy). Strong, very durable, and straight-grained. Used for stringers, clamps, and for planking if weight is not a factor, also as a substitute for white oak keels, deadwood, etc. May be available in good long lengths in some localities. Has been reported as not durable in fresh water, but I cannot substantiate this. Grows in Southern United States in Atlantic and Gulf states.

White Pine

Weight about 2.1 pounds (light). Genuine northern white pine, enormous quantities of which were used in the construction of sailing ships years ago and for spars in the British Navy's sailing warships, and often later for laid decks in yacht building, is seldom seen nowadays. White pine is mentioned here because the wide, clear boards available make it a tempting material for the amateur, but the dubious durability of many varieties makes this wood undesirable for boat construction, except for interior joinerwork.

White Cedar, Northern and Atlantic

Weight about 1.9 pounds (light). Northern white cedar grows from Maine southward along the Appalachian Mountain range. Atlantic white cedar, which grows near the Atlantic coast from Maine to northern Florida and westward along the Gulf coast to Louisiana, is also known as juniper, southern white cedar, swamp cedar, and boat cedar. It is not strong, but its uniformity and resistance to rot make it excellent for planking. Soaks up moisture rapidly, but shrinkage is low, both of which qualities are especially good for light lapstrake-planked boats that are alternately in and out of the water. Sapwood layer is usually thin. Almost always supplied as "flitches," that is, plain-sawn boards with or without bark on the edges. These "boat boards" (or "round edge" or "live edge" boards) taper in width just as the tree trunk does and can be advantageously used for hull planking.

Port Orford Cedar

Weight about 2.4 pounds (light). Moderately strong, clear, and straight-grained. Heartwood very resistant to rot. Used for planking and bright finished decks. Grows in southern Oregon and northern California and is a material familiar to the layman as the wood from which vast numbers of venetian blind slats have been made. Has a distinctive spicy odor.

Western Red Cedar

Weight about 1.9 pounds (light). Highly resistant to rot and available in good widths and lengths for planking. This wood, however, is soft and weak, thus not the best material for this purpose.

Cypress

Weight about 2.8 pounds (medium). Moderately strong, heartwood very resistant to rot. Used for planking where weight is not a factor because it soaks up water to a great extent, making for a heavy boat after a short time in the water. Grows in southern low swamplands of the United States. If you want to use cypress in a boat, find a supplier who understands this material because I have been told that the supply of stock of boatbuilding quality is "sorry."

Sitka Spruce

Weight about 2.4 pounds (light). Moderate shrinkage, high strength for its weight, and availability in long, clear lengths make it ideal for spars. Grows on Pacific Coast in a narrow strip from northern California to Alaska. Not particularly resistant to rot, but this is not detrimental when spars have proper care. Still available in aircraft quality, because believe it or not, there are always plenty of amateur-built wooden aircraft under construction. One dealer's stock list (1986) shows lengths of 30 feet and up.

Spruce (Northern White)

Weight about 2.4 pounds (light). High strength for weight, not very resistant to rot. Used for deck and interior joinerwork framing where weight-saving is the primary consideration. Grows in New England.

Philippine "Mahogany"

Weight about 3.0 pounds (medium). This is the market name for woods known as *lauan* and *tangile* in the Philippine Islands that are extensively used for planking and trim in this country. It is decay-resistant and an excellent material for planking and is used by the finest of builders for this purpose. When selected for color and grain it is attractive for cabin sides and trim. Somewhat more difficult to finish than true mahoganies. Hardness and color vary considerably. Holds fastenings well and is relatively inexpensive considering its qualities. According to one large importer, the best grade is known as "firsts and seconds" and the better boatbuilders prefer the more expensive, darker red variety.

Other Mahoganies

Weights vary from medium to heavy. Honduras, Mexican, and African mahoganies have all been used for planking, exterior finish, and interior joinerwork of fine yachts. They are heavier than the so-called Philippine mahoganies, are better looking, easier to finish, and more expensive. Honduras or Mexican mahogany is a favored first-quality planking and finish material. According to Abeking and Rasmussen of Lemwerder, Germany, builders of some of the finest yachts in the world, suitable African mahoganies are *Khaya ivorensis, Sipo utile, Sapeli aboudikro* and *Niangon nyankom*, and if this firm uses these kinds they should be acceptable to anyone. In the past Abeking and Rasmussen stated that there are other kinds of African mahoganies that are *not* suitable, so here again it is a case of dealing with a reliable supplier of woods.

Teak

Weight about 3.5 pounds (heavy). Not as strong as people think, but extremely durable. Has a natural oil that excludes moisture and thus has minimum shrinkage. The acceptable kind is grown in Burma or Thailand and is so expensive in the United States that its use is reserved for decks and trim. Teak decks are not coated as a rule; they are scrubbed periodically to a whitish finish that, in the opinion of many, has no equal, or treated periodically with one of the dozen or more "teak oil" finishes on the market. Varnished teak trim has a rich appearance. Worms are not fond of teak, so this wood is often used to sheath the bottom of a keel as protection in case some of the toxic anti-fouling bottom paint is rubbed off. Teak also contains a gritty substance that dulls tools quickly, adding somewhat to the cost of working it.

White Ash

Weight about 3.4 pounds (heavy). Straight-grained, strong for its weight, and very durable. Used for deck beams as a substitute for oak where reduction in weight is desirable. Suitable for steam-bending and used for small boat frames; also a favorite for sailboat tillers and an old standby for oars.

Hackmatack

Weight about 3.1 pounds (medium), also called larch or tamarack. Tough and durable. Only the roots, from which natural crooks are made, are used for boatbuilding. Stems for small boats and knees are cut from these crooks. On the other hand, Abeking and Rasmussen once told me that larch was their second choice (behind African mahogany) for single-planked hulls.

Alaska Cedar

Weight about 2.6 pounds (medium). Straight-grained, moderately strong, heartwood very resistant to decay. Minimum shrinkage when seasoned. Good for planking and used for keels in areas where it is grown, southeastern Alaska to southern Oregon. Heartwood is bright yellow, sapwood usually narrow.

Winter Cutting vs. Summer Cutting

In the remarks about white oak it was noted that in the opinion of most, if not all, of the old hands in boatbuilding, the most durable wood comes from trees felled in the winter; therefore it was something of a jolt to come across the following paragraphs in *Wood: A Manual For Its Use As A Shipbuilding Material, Volume I,* U.S. Navy Bureau of Ships, 1957.

"An old belief still given wide currency is that winter-cut lumber is more durable than summer-cut lumber. The belief is based on the erroneous assumption that in winter, 'the sap is down,' while in the summer, 'the sap is up,' in the living tree. Actually, tests have demonstrated conclusively that standing trees contain about as much sap in winter as in summer.

"The only sound objection to summer-cut lumber is that logs are more likely to deteriorate if left exposed to high summer temperatures that may accelerate checking and attack by insects and decay fungi. Reasonable precautions, particularly prompt sawing after felling, and good piling and seasoning methods, remove the danger of such damage to summer-cut material."

Strength vs. Weight

Because a comparison of strengths is of interest, the woods mentioned above are listed below in order of strength, with the weight per board foot again shown.

Species	pounds	Species	pounds
White ash	3.4	Cypress	2.8
White oak	4.2	Sitka spruce	2.4
Yellow pine	3.4	Northern white spruce	2.4
Douglas fir	2.9	Port Orford cedar	2.4
Teak	3.5	Alaska cedar	2.6
Hackmatack	3.1	White cedar	1.9
Honduras mahogany	2.9	White pine	2.1
Philippine "mahogany"	3.0	Western red cedar	1.9

It is recommended that those who want to learn more about wood acquire the *Wood Handbook* of the Forest Products Laboratory, U.S. Department of Agriculture, listed under Recommended Reading in this book.

ABS Design Stresses for Wood

The strength of a few of the foregoing woods are listed in the *Rules for Building and Classing Reinforced Plastic Vessels*, a 1978 publication of the American Bureau of Shipping, the American counterpart of Lloyd's Register of Shipping. ABS specifies that the wood be of best quality, well seasoned, clear, free of defects adversely affecting its strength, and with grain suitable for the purpose intended, and lists *allowable design stresses* in pounds per square inch as follows:

Species	Extreme Fiber in Bending	Compression Parallel to Grain
Ash, white	1866	1466
Cedar, Alaska	1466	1066
Fir, Douglas	2000	1466
Mahogany*	2330	1333
Oak, white	1866	1333
Pine, longleaf yellow	2000	1466
Spruce, Sitka	1466	1066
Teak	1500	1200

* 35 pounds per cubic foot minimum weight

Plywood

Panels composed of layers of wood veneers glued together were used for many years for items that were to be protected from the weather, but their use for marine purposes awaited the development and application of completely waterproof adhesives. This touched off a boom of plywood hull building. Plywood is still used for this purpose, but mostly by amateurs on a one-off basis, because the stock boat manufacturers have gone almost totally to production line building of fiberglass hulls. There is still a place for plywood in the marine field for such parts as decks and superstructures for limited-production fiberglass boats, and it is extensively used for structural bulkheads and interior joinerwork in hulls of all construction types.

Being made of thin layers of wood securely bonded to each other, plywood panels are stiffer than boards of equal thickness and have advantages over regular lumber, even for some parts of boats made completely of wood. Due to the stiffness of plywood panels, weight can be saved—a matter that can be of importance in both powerboats and sailboats—and working with panels instead of a number of small pieces can save a lot of time.

Although there are exceptions, it is not theoretically possible to plank a hull with plywood panels unless the designer has specially shaped the hull for such construction. As mentioned in Chapter 2, plywood cannot be bent in two directions at once to fit on a surface that has compound curvature. However in reference to the exceptions mentioned above, it has been found that the bottom planking of certain arc-bottomed hulls can be made of plywood with the use of strategically located clamps and fastenings. Only experience can help you with this.

If you should happen to have a set of plans for the boat you want and get the notion that it should be planked with plywood in large pieces (rather than in narrow strips), even though the designer has specified otherwise, check with him first to see whether it is feasible. This procedure may save you a major heartbreak.

Plywood is made by laying up thin layers of wood with the grain at right angles to each other, and the number of layers is always odd so that the grain of the face plies is always parallel. The number of plies and their thickness are important. Cheap ⅜" plywood, for instance, might have two thin faces and a relatively thicker inner ply, whereas a better grade will have five plies of wood, each of about equal thickness. It can readily be seen that with right angle construction, the three-ply panel will be relatively weak when bent parallel to the grain of the inner ply.

The most common and inexpensive kind of plywood is made of Douglas fir. To obtain the fir veneer for making plywood panels, the logs are placed in a lathe and turned against a knife edge that peels the veneer at its desired thickness; thus most of the grain is flat grain, called wild grain, and in fir it is indeed difficult to tame sufficiently for a smooth paint finish. Fir also checks badly so that a paint finish develops hairline cracks that become greater in number as time goes on. This situation is at its worst when the plywood is exposed to the elements, but even when the plywood is used in interior joinerwork, checking can make it difficult to achieve a first-class paint job. Such checking can be substantially reduced by coating the fir with a sealer before painting, using a plywood sealer made by one of the marine paint manufacturers. My favorite is International Paint Company's Interlux 1026 Wood Sealer Clear. Fir plywood is acceptable for interior work that is to be covered with either one of the modern vinyl wall coverings or with one of the durable high-pressure laminates such as Formica-brand. It can also be used for planking and decking that is to be covered with a synthetic cloth, such as fiberglass and resin, in which case do *not* seal the surfaces to be covered.

Plywood Grading

Previous editions of this book carried data furnished by a large marine plywood manufacturer that has since closed its mill. For this edition I am indebted to The Harbor Sales Company, 1400 Russell Street, Baltimore, MD 21230, and to Boulter Plywood Corporation, 24 Broadway, Somerville, MA 02145 for the updated plywood information. Both of these firms sell to individual boatbuilders as well as to the large producers.

Marine and exterior grades of plywood are both laminated with waterproof glue, the difference being in the quality of the veneers. Marine grade panels made in the U.S. are, in my opinion, *not* what they used to be from post-World War Two through the 1950s. Current grading is to U.S. Product Standard PS 1-83, effective December 30, 1983. At one time marine grade panels were always made with both faces of A-grade veneer; however, PS 1-83 shows marine grades A-A, A-B, and B-B. With few exceptions I doubt you can readily buy anything but A-A panels, so from here on I'll confine remarks to the panels stocked by the firms mentioned above, as well as by Maurice L. Condon Company, 250 Ferris Avenue, White Plains, NY 10603, a boatbuilding lumberyard that ships orders. All of the above firms issue catalogs and price lists upon request.

PS 1-83 calls for the use of only Douglas fir or Western larch in marine panels. The marine grade A faces are limited to a total of nine repairs in a 4 x 8-foot panel, with inner plies of B grade or better veneers. The specification for the B grade is stated and if you are sufficiently interested I suggest you obtain a copy of PS 1-83 from your dealer or from the American Plywood Association, P.O. Box 11700, Tacoma, WA 98411.

The wild grain of Douglas fir that makes panels almost impossible to paint without hairline cracks developing later resulted in the introduction of Medium Density Overlay (MDO) panels. Dealers stock these panels in a good variety of sizes. They are exterior grade with medium-density resin-impregnated fiber fused to one or both sides of the panel. The wood in the panel faces is B grade veneer, with C grade inner plies. Used for interior joinerwork, MDO panels are ideal for a first-class paint finish.

Plywood Panel Sizes

Some of the suppliers named in the foregoing discussion carry A-A grade Douglas fir marine panels as follows:

¼, ⅜, ½, ⅝, ¾, 1, and 1⅛ inches thick x 48 inches wide x 8 to 24 feet long.

Lengths above 10 feet are usually scarphed. Boulter and Harbor can make scarphed panels, the latter firm making them up to eight feet in width and 50 feet in length.

The MDO panels are available overlaid one or both sides in most of these sizes:

⁵⁄₁₆, ⅜, ½, ⅝, ¾, 1, 1⅛, 1¼ inches thick x 48 and 60 inches wide x 8 to 10 feet long.

Foreign Marine Plywood Panels

I believe the suppliers mentioned above will confirm that specifications for marine panels manufactured in Europe are higher than for those manufactured in the U.S.; due to increased demand these European panels are now stocked in the U.S. All of the imported panels appear to be of hardwood and are thus much easier to finish than domestic fir panels.

Foreign-made plywood panels are laminated to metric thicknesses. Listed below are the equivalents to U.S. measurements:

Inch	mm.	Inch	mm.
⅛	3	⅜	9
⁵⁄₃₂	4	½	12
³⁄₁₆	5	⅝	15
¼	6.5	¾	18–19

Here are some examples of imported stock that can be obtained, usually to British Standard BSS 1088 WBP:

AA grade rotary-cut or ribbon-sliced lauan (Philippine "mahogany") or meranti, a similar wood; also rotary-cut khaya, a durable African hardwood, ¼ through ¾ inch thick x 4 feet wide x 4 through 24 feet in length. (When panels are to have a clear finish bear in mind that there is a difference in grain between rotary-cut—the way Douglas fir veneers are made—and sliced, which means the veneers are slice-cut from a fixed rather than a spinning log.)

The Dutch have been making really fine marine grade panels for some time under the brand name of Bruynzeel. The same species of wood is used throughout the panels and two kinds of wood are offered. One, the heavier, is of African Regina mahogany; the other, lighter by about 30%, is of occume (or okoume), an African hardwood not as durable as the Regina but used by those seeking to save weight wherever possible. The Bruynzeel Regina is stocked in the U.S. in thicknesses of ⁵⁄₃₂ through 1 inch thick x 4 feet wide x 8 to 16 feet in length. The Bruynzeel occume range of sizes is not quite as extensive.

Other foreign manufacturers of high quality panels that are stocked in the U.S. are Bowa, Denmark; Isoroy, France; and Mallinson Denny, England.

For the teak lovers there are many choices of teak-faced panels, most with *very* thin face veneers (1.0 mm, or only a fat ⅓₂"!). Boulter Plywood, however, lists marine panels with ¹⁄₁₆ inch teak on both faces of the panels.

There are also panels faced with teak strips about 2½ inches wide separated by narrow strips of very light wood to simulate laid decking. These are used for cabin soles. For exterior use as, for example, a fiberglass deck overlay, there are panels made by Bowa in which the teak strips are separated by inlaid black silicone rubber "caulking."

Cutting Plywood

Due to the thin veneers that make up a panel, plywood tends to splinter on its underside when sawed, and fir is one of the worst in this respect. A piece of solid lumber clamped on the underside of the panel will eliminate this splintering. Cuts should always be made by a fine-toothed crosscut saw with the face-side of the plywood up. Lightweight portable circular saws are handy when much plywood is to be cut, and there are blades with fine teeth made for just this purpose. The edges of plywood panels are best smoothed with a low angle, sharp block plane set for a fine cut and held at an angle to the edge rather than parallel to it.

Bending Plywood

Plywood can be bent to curvature either dry or after it has been steamed. If the latter method is used, the panel must be dried before another part can be laminated to it. Sometimes it is advantageous to dry-bend two panels each of half the desired finished thickness. The following chart is a guide (not the gospel) to the minimum radius around which a dry panel should be bent. Panel thickness and bending radii are in inches.

Panel Thickness	Axis of Bend Across Grain	Axis of Bend Parallel to Grain
¼	24	60
⁵⁄₁₆	24	72
⅜	36	96
½	72	144
⅝	96	192
¾	144	240

Laminating Wood

Glued parts of laminated solid wood or plywood can be used in boat construction because of the availability of waterproof adhesives that cure at room temperature. Lamination often allows curved parts to be made with minimum waste of material and means that large parts can be made of small pieces of wood readily obtained and easily handled. Cold-molding and strip planking, as described later, are both forms of wood laminating, as are hollow spars. Laminated parts are not necessarily cheap due to the time that must be taken to prepare the form and the material, but the parts are strong, particularly laminated solid wood assemblies of parallel grain construction, such as deck beams, that would have cross grain in them if sawn from solid stock. Laminations are much less likely to check and split than non-laminated parts, and although laminating does not increase the strength of the wood itself, the strength of an assembly such as the stem shown in Figure 4-4A is greater than if it were made of solid pieces jointed in the conventional manner.

Builders with an interest in laminating become quite ingenious at concocting forms for laminating parts that, if built from one piece or from jointed pieces, would be less strong or less durable.

Figure 4-4B shows the lamination of a tiller. A part like this would have cross grain if sawn from one piece of wood. A form for a part such as a tiller can be made either by steam bending a strip of wood and fastening it to cleats secured to the bench or floor

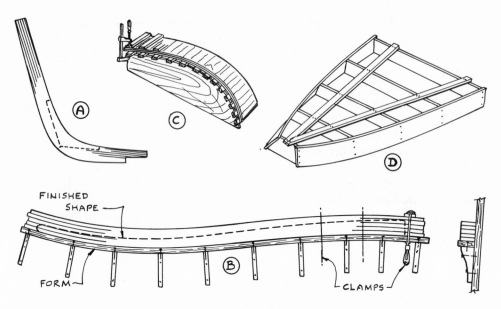

Figure 4–4.

to the designated shape of the tiller, or the form can be sawn from a board about 1½″ thick. Clamps to hold the shape of the lamination must be spaced closely to prevent voids in the lamination.

Another type of form is shown in C, and it can be used for laminating either solid stock or plywood. Fir plywood ⅛″ thick can be bent quite sharply to laminate such parts as deckhouse roof corners, cockpit coaming corners, and the like. D is a sketch of a form used to glue up right- and left-hand parts with twist, such as the bulwark rails at the bow of a boat.

No matter how the form is constructed, there is one thing that must be remembered: the form must be covered with waxed paper to prevent it from becoming glued to the part being laminated.

There is no rule for the thickness of the lamination strips except that they must be thin enough to take the required shape easily. If they are not sufficiently thin, you will have a hard time holding them in place while clamping.

Scarphing Lumber and Plywood

When lumber is not obtainable in long enough lengths for the job at hand, shorter lengths can be joined with glued flat-scarphs having a ratio of length-to-thickness of 8 or 10 to 1. Boards can be tapered by a hand or electric plane using a rig as shown in Figure 4-5, and a similar rig can be devised to do the planing with a router. However, scarphing a wide plywood panel this way takes a lot of patience, especially if you have to set up the rig for just one or two scarphs. Consequently a tool called the "Scarffer" put out by the boatbuilding firm of Gougeon Brothers, Inc., 706 Martin Street, Bay City, MI 48706, is indeed of interest to the amateur and professional alike. As shown

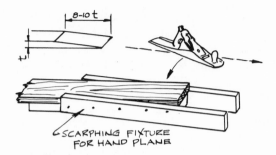

Figure 4–5.

in the photograph, Figure 4-6, the "Scarffer" is an attachment for a portable circular saw. Used with a saw blade of good quality, it is said to cut a clean scarph with a single pass of the saw.

Sources for Boatbuilding Lumber

Fortunately, the problem of finding good boatbuilding wood has been reduced somewhat by suppliers named herein who sell specifically (but not exclusively) to boatbuilders, and by the advertisements published in periodicals like *WoodenBoat, Small Boat Journal* and *National Fisherman*.

Builders who wish to build a cold-molded wooden hull (more about this method later) are fortunate to have suppliers of ⅛″ thick veneers of different kinds of suitable wood. Some of these woods are vertical grain Western red cedar, vertical grain

Figure 4–6. *The Scarffer, put out by the Gougeon Brothers firm, simplifies cutting scarph joints in plywood sheets.*

Douglas fir, vertical grain Sitka spruce and vertical grain red meranti, which is similar to Philippine mahogany. This material is stocked in good widths and lengths by The Dean Company, P.O. Box 426, Gresham, OR 97030; Maurice L. Condon Company, 250 Ferris Avenue, White Plains, NY 10603; and Genwove U.S. Ltd., P.O. Box 310, Indian Trail, NC 28079.

Prevention of Wood Decay

The first step in the prevention of decay is to select woods that have proven durable in boats, and it should be remembered that the heartwood of a log is the most resistant to rot. Decay is caused by fungi that feed on the cellulose between the cell walls of wood. For the fungi to grow, certain conditions of moisture, temperature, and air must be present. The moisture content must be on the order of 25-30 percent, the temperature 75-90 degrees F., and the air stagnant. Wood that is always dry does not rot because of the lack of moisture, and wood that is continously wet does not rot because there is no air present.

There will be more later on the importance of building to avoid leaks in deck and cabin, where water can enter and be trapped, just waiting for the right temperature for the fungi to grow.

In addition to the natural decay resistance of some woods and the precautions against leaks that can be taken by the builder, chemicals can be used that are toxic to fungi and marine borers. These preparations are cheap, easy to apply, and they reduce the chances of decay.

Copper naphthenate has been used by boatbuilders as a wood preservative for many years. Two brand names are Cuprinol and Woodlife. Be sure to read and heed the instructions printed on the containers.

The preservatives are easy to apply by brushing or dipping, the larger parts being brushed and smaller pieces, such as planking butt blocks, short deck beams, and the like, being dipped in a container of the preparation.

Scantlings

The dimensions of the hull timbers in wooden boatbuilding are called scantlings. For instance, a list of scantlings includes the size and spacing of frames, planking thickness, keel depth and width, stem width, and sizes of clamps, stringers, deck beams, etc. The actual dimensions may be given as the "siding," generally the smaller dimension, and the "molding," usually a vertical dimension. As an example of this, referring to Figure 12-1A, a deck beam would be sided 1½" and molded 2½", while a clamp would be sided 1½" and molded 4". The dimensions of frames are an exception to the above, because the fore-and-aft dimension is the siding, and the athwartship dimension is the molded size. The terminology is peculiar to boatbuilding, and the builder quickly becomes adjusted to its usage.

It has been noted that quite a few designers, apparently tiring over the years of hand lettering the words "sided" and "molded" on their drawings, simply abbreviate these words to S and M. This could be very confusing to the first-timer, but now you know.

Chapter 5

FIBERGLASS AND OTHER HULL MATERIALS

Wood has been the traditional material for boatbuilding and it remains so because of the relative ease with which it can be worked. However, depending upon the skill and ingenuity of the builder, there are other materials to be considered, sometimes in combination with wood.

Wood and Fiberglass

When the type of wood hull construction is suitable, there is much to recommend covering the wood with resin and fiberglass or other such cloth. The hull planking should preferably be of a stable type, such as strip planking, double or triple diagonal planking, or plywood. Normal carvel planking swells and shrinks with moisture changes, and this might cause the covering to crack. However, there are those who do not hestitate to cover old carvel-planked hulls with fiberglass, but the covering is made quite thick and is mechanically fastened to the hull.

When the hull is suitable, the use of covering adds strength, prevents rot, minimizes leaks and weight gain from absorption of water, and protects against the attack of worms and borers. The latter by itself is a great advantage, for it reduces the worries that can be brought on by delays in hauling out for bottom cleaning. The weight of the covering does not add much to the overall weight of the boat, and when it is planned for in the design, the wooden structures can be reduced in size to compensate for the weight of the covering. In anything but very fast boats the added weight does not count for much anyway.

The fabric is usually fiberglass cloth, but polypropylene and Dynel are also used. The resin can be either polyester or epoxy. The latter is more expensive and more time-consuming to use, due to slower cure at room temperatures, but its adhesion to wood is superior.

Covering is also recommended for plywood decks, cabin tops, and the like, and the covering of joints in cabin sides, etc., to prevent leaks is a genuine boon to the builder when the joined work is to be painted rather than varnished. Taped joints can be sanded to feather edges and made invisible under a paint finish.

Hulls are covered with fiberglass cloth weighing (without resin) between 6 and 20 ounces per square yard, depending upon size and service, and often doubled in areas of strain such as at the chines of v-bottomed boats. Ten-ounce cloth is about right for covering vertical cabin sides of plywood. The accompanying table indicates approximately how much weight is added by covering a surface with fiberglass cloth and polyester resin; common fiberglass reinforcements besides cloth are included. Since weights are in direct proportion to thickness, materials other than those shown are easily interpolated.

I won't attempt here to give any of the many sources. There is a polyester resin known as general purpose; for minimum sagging and running while working overhead or vertically there is also a high-viscosity, thicker resin.

Anyone who dabbles with boats will sooner or later want to cover old wood, and there are certain precautions that must be taken for a good job. All old finish must be cleaned off the wood, and the wood must be dry. In the case of a plywood hull, for instance, the boat must be hauled out of the water and put under cover, the old finish stripped, and the wood allowed to dry for several weeks before covering. Epoxy resin is strongly recommended for old wood. Take note, however, that epoxy resin by the gallon may be more than double the cost of an equivalent amount of polyester resin.

New wood or old, oil base fillers must not be used over the heads of fastenings, because they will be softened by the resin. For filling cracks and smoothing gouges use either a polyester automobile body putty, which is very fast drying and can be sanded

APPROX. WEIGHTS PER SQ.FT. OF FIBERGLASS REINFORCEMENTS INCLUDING POLYESTER RESIN			
	DESIGNATION	WT. OZ./ SQ.FT.	THICK-NESS (INCH)
CHOPPED STRAND MAT	3/4 OZ. / SQ. FT. 1 1½ 2	3 4 6 8	.028 .033 .050 .067
GLASS CLOTH	6 OZ./ SQ. YARD 8 10	1.33 1.8 2.25	.011 .016 .018
WOVEN ROVING	14 16 18 24	3 3.5 4 5.25	.022 .025 .028 .038

Courtesy of Torin, Inc.

Figure 5-1.

soon after use, or make a mixture of epoxy resin and a material like Cabosil proportioned to produce the consistency of putty.

For many years Defender Industries, Inc. has catered to the needs of the home boatbuilder and they carry a large selection of polyester and epoxy resins, fiberglass and other synthetic fabrics, such as polypropylene, Dynel, and Kevlar, and a complete selection of resin fillers, tools, etc. The address of Defender is 255 Main Street, New Rochelle, NY 10802-0802.

Molded Fiberglass Hulls

The shiny, commercially produced fiberglass hulls are usually made from a female mold. This requires that a wooden male plug be made, just as though you were building a wooden hull, using strip-planking or plywood, whichever is suitable for the hull shape. The plug is then covered with glass cloth and resin and is worked to a very smooth finish, for every blemish will be reproduced when the female mold is made. When the plug is finished as desired, a release is applied so that the female will not stick to it. Then glass cloth and mat and polyester resin are laid up successively until a strong, rigid mold has been made. Rather than rely entirely upon shell thickness to hold the mold's shape, the shell is reinforced on the outside with a network of rough wood and sometimes steel. If a particular hull shape is such that it cannot be withdrawn vertically, the mold is made to split on the centerline.

Some builders decrease the time needed to build stiffness into the mold by using sandwich construction. After a portion of the fiberglass laminate has been laid up against the plug, they use a core material followed by more fiberglass. The mold stiffness is thus increased greatly by spreading the glass skins apart, the core material acting in much the same manner as the web of an I-beam that separates the flanges.

Suitable core materials are cellular foams and end-grain balsa. If the plug from which the female hull mold will be made is not constructed to be later used as a boat then price dictates the choice of core material for the plug.

When the female mold for the production of a hull has been removed from the plug, it is polished and waxed and any blemishes are repaired. It is then ready for laying up a hull. Sometimes a partial disc of wood or steel, larger in diameter than the beam of the boat, is added to the outside of the mold near each end so the mold can be rolled from side to side while laying up the fiberglass and resin. When the hull is anything larger than dinghy size, this minimizes the amount of time the builders must spend actually working in the hull while laying up and makes the work mostly downhand. The more you can stay out of the sticky resin the less distasteful the job will be. This presumes that the hull will be made by laying up the laminates by hand and applying the resin with roller and brush. When hulls are produced in large quantity, resin and chopped glass fibers can be applied with specialized spray equipment, but these hulls are not as strong as those laminated with fiberglass cloth.

The high gloss finish on the outside of molded hulls or other similarly constructed parts of the boat results from first spraying a gel coat of resin on the surface of the mold. The gel coat can be of any color desired, and contrasting stripes at the waterline and other accent stripes can be sprayed as well when you know what it is all about. After the gel coat has been applied, the hull is laid up with fiberglass fabrics (cloth, woven roving, and chopped strand mat) until the necessary thickness has been reached.

How does one make a mold and lay up a fiberglass hull if detailed instructions are not available? Watching others do these things is the best way, but if this is not possible, there are books that spell out the techniques. The laminate schedule—information detailing the composition of the fiberglass hull laminate, such as the weight and type of glass reinforcement, number of layers, etc.—should be outlined in the plans of the boat. As experience is gained, the builder may develop his own ideas about laminates, but guidance is needed for the first attempt at this type of boatbuilding.

"One-Off" Fiberglass Hulls

It was inevitable that builders would come along and figure out a way to build a fiberglass hull without having to spend the time and money to construct a female mold. Seemann Fiberglass, Inc., P.O. Box 13704, New Orleans, LA 70185 not only devised a method but also invented and patented C-Flex "planking," which consists of parallel rods made of fiberglass-reinforced polyester alternating with bundles of continuous roving, with each "plank" being held together by a webbing of two layers of lightweight, open-weave fiberglass cloth.

The construction method is fairly simple. A hull form is framed with sectional molds and sometimes stiffened with longitudinal strips let into the molds. Smaller hulls are most conveniently built upside down, as shown in the accompanying photograph, but the larger sizes are best built right side up. The molds must be spaced so that the C-Flex "planking" will not sag between them, the spacing varying with the weight of the C-Flex. The C-Flex, which bends longitudinally and sideways, is then laid over the molds and conforms to the hull shape with little fitting. On the framework for a round-bottomed hull one edge of the planking is usually shaped to the sheerline and secured; then each additional "plank" is carefully butted to the adjacent width (Figure 5-2). For a v-bottomed hull, the C-Flex is applied to the chine and the covering is continued to the sheer and, on the bottom, to the centerline. When the frame has been completely covered with the C-Flex planking it is wet out with resin, either polyester or epoxy, and then lamination is continued with conventional fiberglass materials until the desired thickness has been reached.

By the nature of its construction, the C-Flex is very strong in the direction of the rods. It is made in two weights, 0.33 and 0.5 pounds per square foot, is 12" wide, and comes in 100' and 250' rolls. Like any similar construction, the amount of finishing time depends upon the care taken to have a fair layup and the degree of smoothness desired. Seemann has just patented a method of using C-Flex construction for sheathing to prolong the life of wooden hulls, and will furnish detailed information to anyone interested in this approach.

One-off fiberglass boatbuilders frequently use a technique known as sandwich construction, where the laminate consists of a core between fiberglass skins. This type of construction has several advantages over single-skin construction. Probably the

Figure 5-2. *A roll of C-Flex being laid down. Note that the widths laid down earlier (being held in place by ice picks) are carefully butted against one another.*

biggest advantage is its favorable stiffness/weight ratio. A sandwich laminate is significantly stiffer than a single skin of the same number of laminations, and with a lightweight core such as balsa or foam, the weight of the sandwich is not much greater than the single skin. This fact presents the designer using sandwich construction with options: he can keep the same thickness and weight laminate as for a similar single-skin hull and end up with a thicker, much stiffer hull; he can reduce the thickness and weight of the glass skins and have a cored laminate with strength equal to the single skin; or he can use a sandwich laminate designed to both save weight and increase stiffness.

Other than stiffness and light weight, sandwich construction offers additional benefits. The interior sweating for which single-skin fiberglass hulls are notorious is minimized or non-existent in a sandwich hull. Noise and vibration are also reduced, and the absence of the transverse framing sometimes used in single-skin fiberglass hulls gives more usable space inside the hull.

Another comparison that should be made between single-skin and sandwich construction is what happens in the event that the hull is punctured, particularly under the waterline. In such circumstances, the single-skin hull will admit water, but this is not so of a sandwich hull unless both skins and the core are punctured— something that advocates of sandwich construction feel is unlikely during the normal life of a boat. It follows, of course, that if a cored laminate should be completely punctured the result of such an accident is no worse than for a single-skin hull. As a safeguard against impact, the outer skin of a sandwich is often made thicker than the inner skin, up to a ratio of 6:4. The repair of a sandwich laminate is no more difficult than for a single skin, unless the core material has been damaged, in which case a piece of the core will need to be inserted if the hull is to be repaired in the same way it was constructed. Otherwise, the damaged section of the outer skin is ground away with abrasive tools, feathered into the adjacent undamaged skin, and the void is filled with fiberglass and resin the same as for single-skin fiberglass repair.

To build a sandwich hull, a framework of transverse section molds and longitudinal strips (called ribbands or battens) is needed to define the shape of the hull, and it makes sense to build upside down. Figure 5-3 shows the forward end of a male mold for an 86-foot powerboat hull.

Using foam core as an example of one-off construction, the sheets are fitted against the mold (using a heat lamp to make the foam pliable where necessary or using "contoured" core material instead) and held in place with nails driven through plywood scrap "washers" until the foam can be held in place with screws through the ribbands from *inside* the mold into the foam (Figure 5-4). The foam is then covered with the specified thickness of the fiberglass outside skin (Figure 5-5).

Careful workmanship is required to ensure a complete bond between the core material and the glass skins. Interruptions in the bond will hasten delamination of the sandwich when the lamination is loaded to deflect between supports and this will weaken the affected part of the hull. When there is a good bond between the skins and the core, some of the burden of the laminate strength falls upon the core itself. For this reason the laminate designer must carefully investigate the available core materials

Figure 5-3. *The male mold for an Airex-cored, 86-foot powerboat. Note how closely spaced the ribbands are.*

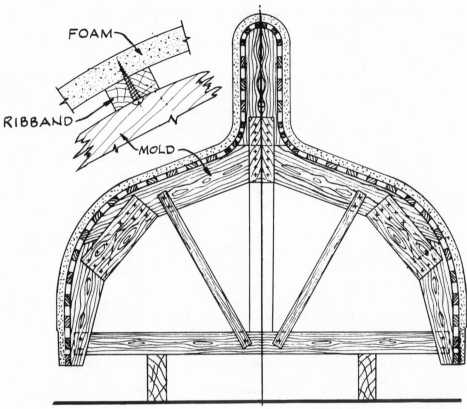

Figure 5-4.

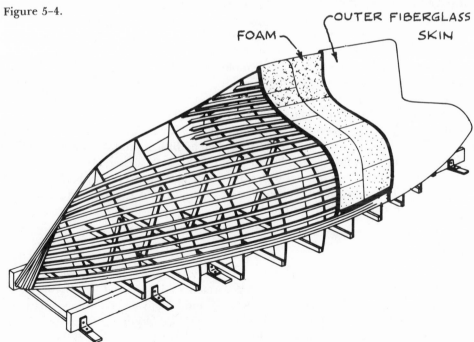

Figure 5-5.

for use in boat hulls. Obviously, a material that resists crumbling upon impact and that does not absorb water is desirable.

Some of the most popular cores are:

Airex (closed-cell 100 percent polyvinyl chloride foam), marketed in the U.S. and Canada by Torin, Inc., 9 Industrial Park, Waldwick, NJ 07463. Torin can provide pertinent guides to laminate/core/laminate thicknesses.

Termanto and *Termino* (closed-cell polyvinyl chloride-based foams), also marketed by Torin, Inc.

Klegecell (closed-cell foam, partly polyvinyl chloride), manufactured by American Klegecell Corp., 204 North Dooley St., Grapevine, TX 76051.

Contourkore (end-grain balsa wood), manufactured by Baltek Corp., 10 Fairway Court, Box 195, Northvale, NJ 07647.

I cannot go into all the construction details here; suffice it to say that while the hull is still upside down the outside fiberglass skin should be smoothed to the extent desired while it is still possible to work downhand. If you wish more information on sandwich construction, the core manufacturers can supply you with it.

Overturning a cored hull is a trying procedure because the shell is quite limber before the inner fiberglass skin is added to the laminate to complete the sandwich. One method used by several builders of hulls with Airex foam cores is shown in Figure 5-6. This involves the use of a holding cradle fitted to the upside-down hull to support the hull as it is overturned and which the hull sits in while the construction of the boat is completed.

Although the aforesaid is a "one-off" method of hull construction, the mold can be used for additional hulls. It is a matter of economics to calculate how many hulls can be produced before the cost of a female mold is justified. Female molds that have been built for the production of single-skin fiberglass hulls can also be used for molding a sandwich hull. The laminate is simply changed to include a core.

The use of an existing hull as a male mold—either with permission if necessary, or without conscience if plagiarized— is yet another method of making a hull shape.

Still another one-off fiberglass hull system is based on wooden transverse molds, a centerline shape, and a considerable number of fairly light fore-and-aft battens to support a unique steel wire mesh called Str-r-etch Mesh, a product invented by Platt Monfort and sold by his Aladdin Products, Inc., RFD 2, Wiscasset, ME 04578. The ½" mesh is constructed so it drapes with remarkable fairness over a properly prepared grid mold. This must be one of the fastest of the various one-off methods. More details are available from Aladdin.

Steel

When you stop to think about it, steel is a remarkable material. It is strong, very inexpensive when compared with other metals, and with proper equipment, it can be worked to almost any shape desired. The relative ease of joining pieces by electric welding makes it a suitable material for small craft with a saving in weight over old-

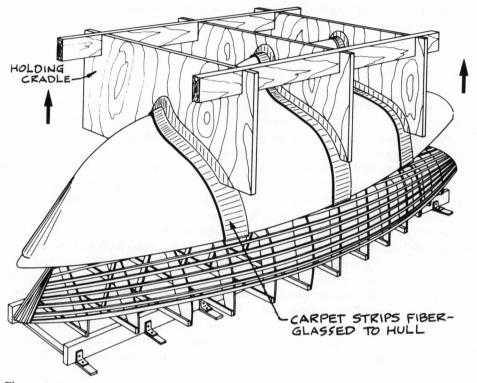

HOLDING CRADLE

CARPET STRIPS FIBER-GLASSED TO HULL

Figure 5–6.

fashioned riveted construction. One disadvantage of steel is its low resistance to corrosion by sea water. Fortunately, the years have brought about improved coatings to protect steel against corrosion, but the coatings must be constantly maintained. An advantage of steel construction (and aluminum construction as well) is that inner bottom integral fuel and water tanks can be built in, using the hull for one side, enabling larger capacities to be carried than in wooden hulls.

Steel is not a material for the average beginner by any means, but without reflecting for too long I can remember two good-sized auxiliary sailboats of steel built by people who had not built a boat before. However, they did have metalworking experience and the necessary equipment. The worst fault of these boats was the humps and hollows in the hull plating, and both builders said that they had gained experience so that if they did it again the hulls would not be so rough.

Rough plating of steel hulls is often disguised by skillful application of trowel cement, probably because it is cheaper to do this than to expend the labor needed to smooth plating by heating and quenching. The roughness of the plating is caused by stresses set up when welding the plating to the frames and one plate to another. The sequence of welding is of importance in this respect.

Here in northern Florida there are several builders of full-bodied steel sailboat hulls using a system of framing and plating that results in better-than-average fairness.

Even though steel is an old material, research technicians have invented new alloys of higher strength so that steel hulls can be built lighter today than ever before.

Aluminum Alloys

A few of the many aluminum alloys, notably alloy 5086 in the United States, are satisfactory for boatbuilding. These alloys are relatively high in strength and corrosion resistance and can be satisfactorily welded. A fair amount of this metal is consumed by yacht builders, but by far the most of it has been used to build a large fleet of offshore oil field crew transports and platform supply vessels.

In general terms, alloys of aluminum reduce construction weight over that of steel. This permits the carrying of more deadweight or an increase in speed, or the possibility of achieving speed with less horsepower.

Several builders of pleasure boats either build only in aluminum or have a line of aluminum boats in addition to those of other materials. Small craft such as dinghies and runabouts of aluminum are made by stretch-forming sheets over male molds to produce a large part or an entire half out of one piece of metal. Otherwise, regular transverse or longitudinal framing is used and covered with plating as in steel construction. Aluminum construction is more expensive than steel construction, for not only does the aluminum itself cost more per pound than steel, the actual welding also costs more. This more than makes up for the fact that the weight of aluminum involved in a particular project will always be less than the weight of the steel required.

Many builders of steel boats have converted to aluminum construction with little need to change equipment except for welding, but like steel, it is not a material for the beginner. One very important problem area encountered with aluminum construction is galvanic corrosion. This occurs between the aluminum hull and dissimilar metals found in such fittings as sea cocks, propellers, shafts, rudders, etc., and also occurs when the aluminum hull is exposed to stray electrical currents in anchorages. This can be prevented, and the methods for doing so should be spelled out in the plans and specifications for the boat. If you lack this information, the marine departments of the aluminum manufacturers can be consulted for help.

Welding and the preparation of the finished surface are also areas that require care. Welding aluminum is quite different than welding steel. It is imperative that weld areas be absolutely clean if good welds are to be made. If you are in need of information about welding, the aluminum manufacturers can provide assistance. When it comes to painting the surface, the marine paint makers have special systems for coating aluminum and instructions for cleaning it before coating. The highest quality hull takes a lot of labor; a really smooth yacht finish on the topsides of a welded aluminum yacht hull requires fairing of the surface with fairing compounds.

Ferrocement

Some years back there was a wave of enthusiasm about constructing hulls of ferrocement. Essentially, the system consists of a framework of concrete reinforcing rod interlaced with wire, with cement applied to it so that the steelwork is completely embedded and not exposed to the atmosphere. It is understood that great care must be taken to eliminate voids in the cement, and that the basically heavy weight of the construction makes it impractical for hulls under 30 feet in length.

Exotic Hull Materials

There have been a number of materials developed recently that have higher strengths and lower weights than wood and fiberglass-reinforced plastic, and development in this area is bound to continue. Graphite, in fiber form, has been used in super-lightweight fishing rods and in highly stressed areas of racing sailboat hulls. It is three times stronger and five times stiffer than steel. Likewise, S glass, which is twice as strong as the common E glass from which the standard boatbuilding glass fabrics are made, is much stronger and is stiffer for its weight than is steel. Kevlar fabric, made from Dupont aramid fibers, is another lightweight high-strength material.

Exotic materials have also found their way into bulkheads. Years ago, the introduction of relatively stiff marine plywood bulkheads was a giant step forward in strength as compared to the bulkheads made of vertical wood staving or decorative panels. Now, plywood as a bulkhead material has been surpassed by at least two other materials that are stiffer and much lighter. Panels of both these materials come with fiberglass skins, and they are used in large transport aircraft. One type of core is end-grain balsa and the other is a honeycomb made of a Dupont material called Nomex, which is used in helicopter blades.

Although such exotic materials can work out well, especially where light weight is a consideration, there are other factors to consider. If they are to be used properly these materials require specialized techniques and knowledge. Another consideration is their high cost. For example, S glass is twice as expensive as E glass. As for Kevlar, a builder of high-speed powerboats who uses this material once told me that, pound for pound, a Kevlar/resin combination was as much as seven times more expensive than the standard mat/woven roving/resin combination. Since these exotic materials are not used throughout a hull, but only as a substitute for strength-contributing laminate material, it is hard to make a general comment about the cost of building hulls using exotic fibers, for laminate designs differ from boat to boat. About all that can be said, then, is that the use of such exotic materials will certainly lead to an increase in cost.

The state of the art is constantly changing. New materials will always be developed, and there are always those who will try to apply them to boatbuilding, just as surely as there are always those who seem not to care about the cost of yachts that appeal to them.

Chapter 6

FASTENINGS

Compared with the heavily constructed wooden boats of the old days, almost all modern craft can be considered to be lightly built. Thus the innumerable fastenings holding the parts together assume extra importance as a primary contribution to a tight, seaworthy boat. All fastenings should be sized according to their task and located with thought by the designer and builder. They should always be driven in carefully drilled holes of proper size to ensure maximum holding power.

Galvanized Iron

The builder of a wooden boat can save a considerable amount of money by using galvanized iron hull fastenings. Old-timers have passed down the word that galvanized-fastened boats will last a lifetime, and indeed there are hulls here and there that seem to prove this point. On the other hand, I examined a wrecked shrimp boat, beached about 10 years after it was built, that proved just the opposite.

Although the above would appear to offer contradictory evidence regarding the durability of galvanized fastenings, it doesn't. The galvanized fastenings of today simply are not the galvanized fastenings of yesterday. In the first place, the old-timers used galvanized iron, whereas the fastenings available today are most likely of mild steel. When bared of their protective coatings, fastenings of mild steel do not have nearly as much resistance to corrosion as do iron ones. Second, the old-time iron nails and rods were always coated by hot dipping in molten zinc. Many "galvanized" fasteners today are zinc coated by electroplating, which results in a relatively thin coating that cannot be compared to coating by hot dipping. In fact these "zinc-plated" fasteners have no place in a boat.

Here is what Independent Nail, Inc., a manufacturer of special-purpose nails, has to say about the zinc coating of fasteners:

"'Galvanized' has turned out to be generally a poorly understood adjective. The best type is a hot-dip, whose surface is, for practical purposes, pure zinc. Tumbler, hot-tumbler, hot-galvanized each refer to a tumbler process from which the coating may be contaminated with iron right on the surface. Electro and mechanical galvanizing each generally produce very thin zinc coatings serving for appearance more than for performance."

Galvanized boat nails and galvanized wood screws have often been used to fasten planking to frames. A frame should be at least 1½" thick if a nail is to be buried in it without going through the frame. With lighter frames, the nail goes through the frames and is clinched over on the inside. When poor nails are used, the zinc will separate from the nail where it is bent, exposing the bare metal. Many boats have had to be refastened because corrosion started at the end of such nails and progressed throughout the length of the fastening. Renailing is an expensive job, and the necessity to do so is a good sign that the fastenings were inferior or inadequate to start with.

In the case of the smaller-sized hot-dipped galvanized wood screws, the threads are frequently clogged with zinc when they are dipped, and when driven, they tear the wood around the hole, reducing holding power.

Even if he has had some good experiences in the past with galvanized fastenings, the builder is advised to be sure of his fastenings by using a better metal for fastenings that are to be constantly in water. Although more expensive initially, the best fastenings are cheap in the end.

Brass

If a decision is made against using galvanized fastenings it might seem that a good alternative would be brass fastenings, but the use of brass for fastenings exposed to salt water cannot be advised against too strongly. Brass as furnished for the manufacture of screws and bolts is very high in zinc content, perhaps as much as 30 percent, and in an electrolyte such as sea water, the zinc leaves the alloy. What remains is a spongy copper so reduced in strength that the fastening is practically useless. This is called dezincification and can be expected when a copper alloy is used that contains zinc in excess of 16 percent. There are mechanical disadvantages, too. The high zinc brass alloys are not particularly strong; it is easy to break off screws being driven into hard woods. Brass is all right for the fastening of interior parts such as joinerwork, but care should be taken not to use it in the hull.

Silicon Bronze

For every structural fastening in a boat it is hard to beat a copper silicon alloy sometimes called Everdur. It is about 96 percent copper and is so strong that fastenings are seldom wrung off when being driven, and of major importance, it is highly resistant to corrosion from sea water. The use of this metal removes the risks involved with the brasses and galvanized steel fastenings and is well worth the difference in cost. A point to be remembered is the higher resale value of a bronze-fastened boat.

Using a 1½″ No. 8 flathead wood screw for comparison, a 1987 price sheet lists silicon bronze of this size at 18% more than brass. In my opinion it is wise to spend the difference.

Monel

This nickel copper alloy ranks above silicon bronze in strength and corrosion resistance, but the cost of screws and bolts made from it is much too high for most people to afford. It can be used in conjunction with silicon bronze without fear of much galvanic action between the metals. For instance, Monel is often used for fastening bronze propeller shaft struts, and Monel shafts have bronze propellers in direct contact. The strength and stiffness of Monel make it very satisfactory for Anchorfast boat nails, a popular fastening for some purposes because of the labor saving it offers over driving screws. (*See* Threaded Nails.) Monel as a metal has many uses in boat construction and will be mentioned further.

Copper

Copper has excellent corrosion resistance, but because of its softness it is suitable mostly for fastenings in the form of flathead nails that are used as rivets or for clout nails sometimes used in hulls with light lapstrake planking.

Stainless Steel

There are many alloys under this common heading. It is recommended that these metals not be considered for hull fastenings unless you are guided by someone who has vast experience and satisfactory proof of corrosion resistance and freedom from galvanic action with other materials being used in the same boat. Without such assurance, the use of stainless steel should be limited to applications above water. It is the best metal for fastening aluminum alloy deck hardware, stanchions, and aluminum alloy window frames, for it avoids corrosion of the alloy parts. Of the many stainless steels, the one known as Type 316 seems to be the most corrosion-resistant in a salt atmosphere, but finding fastenings of this alloy may take some doing. One or two of the high-quality yacht builders have, in the past, special-ordered Type 316 wood screws to secure stainless steel half-oval rub strips to minimize "bleeding" of the screw heads. If you can find one of these builders, he might be happy to reduce his stock of such fastenings.

Other than as a fastener material, stainless steel is being used more and more for boat parts, notably deck hardware, sailboat specialty hardware, stanchions and pulpits, engine exhaust system parts, and propeller shafting. Stainless is also used for wire rope rigging and rigging fittings on spars. As with many materials that might be used in a boat, it is best to leave experimentation to others, using it yourself only when you know the application has been proven.

I do not believe that fasteners of 316L stainless steel are available off the shelf. If so, these would be the best of the 18-8 (18% chromium, 8% nickel) alloys. 316L as well as 304L (with a carbon content of less than .03%) were developed to provide austenitic steels with superior corrosion resistance. I have used 316L in plate form for a number of years to make fabricated high-speed rudders.

Mixture of Metals

The loosely used term "electrolysis" is applied by the average boatman to the corrosion and erosion of metals by electrolysis, cavitation, or galvanic action; usually the destruction of metals is blamed on electrolysis, due to lack of knowledge of the other causes. Except for discussing galvanic action between fastenings, the subject is beyond the scope of this work.

Sea water is an electrolyte that will cause an electric current to flow between dissimilar metals when in contact or close proximity to each other. When this occurs, current will flow from the anode to the cathode, that is, the anodic fitting or fastening will be attacked and gradually destroyed by what is properly termed galvanic corrosion. The intensity of the attack will vary according to the relative positions of the metals in the galvanic series and also the relative areas or masses of the metals. The positions in the galvanic series in sea water of some metals follow:

Anodic or Least Noble

Zinc
Galvanized steel or galvanized wrought iron
Aluminum alloy 5456
Aluminum alloy 5086
Aluminum alloy 5052
Aluminum alloy 356, 6061
Mild steel
Wrought iron
Cast iron
18-8 Stainless steel Type 304 (active)
18-8 Stainless steel Type 316, 3% molybdenum (active)
Lead
Tin
Manganese bronze
Naval brass (60% copper, 39% zinc)
Inconel (active)
Yellow brass (65% copper, 35% zinc)
Aluminum bronze
Red brass (85% copper, 15% zinc)
Copper
Silicon bronze
Cupro-nickel (90% copper, 10% nickel)

Cupro-nickel (70% copper, 30% nickel)
Composition G bronze (88% copper, 2% zinc, 10% tin)
Composition M bronze (88% copper, 3% zinc, 6½% silicon, 1½% lead)
Inconel (passive)
Monel
18-8 Stainless steel Type 304 (passive)
18-8 Stainless steel Type 316, 3% molybdenum (passive)
Titanium

Cathodic or Most Noble

It might be possible to use only one metal, notably silicon bronze, for all of the fastenings in a wooden hull, but where a mixture is the most practical, the metals used should be ones that are reasonably close together in the galvanic scale, such as copper, silicon bronze, and Monel. All of these metals are used to manufacture fasteners of one sort or another.

Note that stainless steels are shown in the series above in two different positions. As I understand it, the surface of the steel is passivated by chemical treatment to hasten the formation of oxide. This can be done after all machining and working has been finished, and after the steel has been thoroughly cleaned and degreased. The passivated surface is more resistant to corrosion. Without passivation, the corrosion resistance is severely reduced, and it is best to avoid the use of these metals for underwater fastenings. If the surface has been treated, but the treatment has been destroyed or altered, the metal's corrosion resistance will be uncertain; it is best to treat such metals as if they were not passivated.

I know of a case where, due to ignorance, a bronze stern bearing casting was fastened with galvanized iron lag screws—a perfect example of setting up galvanic corrosion. The dissimilar metals were in contact in sea water; first the zinc disappeared, and then the iron was attacked until the bearing finally came loose.

Many boats with bronze hull fastenings have been built with cast iron ballast keels, but in this case the comparatively huge mass of anodic material, the iron keel, would show only slight signs of attack due to its bulk. The bolts securing the keel can be of hot-dipped galvanized wrought iron or Monel. The outside of the iron should have several coats of a marine vinyl-type anti-corrosive paint to act as a nonmetallic barrier to galvanic action.

Needless to say, only the least expensive steel fasteners should be used in the construction of molds, jigs, plugs for fiberglass parts, bracing, etc., that will never be part of a boat. It may seem ridiculous to even mention something like this, but I have seen boatyard employees use bronze and Monel fasteners in throw-away work rather than visit the stockroom for steel nails and screws.

Screw Bolts

These are ordinary machine bolts with square or hexagonal heads and nuts, and they are made in silicon bronze, stainless steel, Monel, and "galvanized" steel. Longer bolts can be homemade by threading a piece of rod on both ends, screwing a nut as a head on one end, and peening over the end of the rod to prevent the head nut from turning. Washers of the same material are used under the head and nut. Drilled holes should be the same diameter as the bolt. Screw bolts are used for fastening many backbone parts and have the advantage over drift bolts of being able to be tightened when the wood shrinks.

Well-equipped professional builders sometimes head their own long bolts. They have a die, usually for a flat head, and the end of the rod is heated and forged to shape.

Drift Bolts

When bolts must be very long and a through-bolt is not practical or necessary, a drift bolt can be used. They are made from a piece of rod and driven like a large nail. One end is pointed slightly by hammering; the other has a washer or clinch ring under a driving head formed by riveting the end of the rod. The clinch ring (see Figure 6-14) is thick, flat on the under side, and has an edge rounded up to a countersunk hole as for a flathead wood screw. This takes the end of the rod peened to shape. One source for clinch rings is Mr. Z's Products, 22322 Bassett Street, Conoga Park, CA 91303. The hole is bored between one and two diameters shorter than the bolt to be driven and should have smooth sides. The size of the hole must be less than the diameter of the bolt for a tight, driving fit. Be careful not to bend the bolt above the timber when driving it. When a pair or a series of drift bolts is called for, it is best to drive them at an angle (Figure 6-1) which locks the parts together and enables them to resist strains. Drift bolts are usually made of silicon bronze or galvanized steel.

Quite often drift bolts must be driven through narrow stock like floors, rudders,

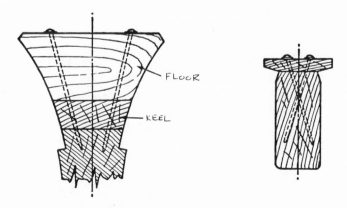

Figure 6-1. *Drift bolts are driven at an angle in order to lock the parts together.*

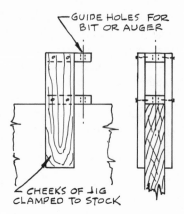

GUIDE HOLES FOR
BIT OR AUGER

CHEEKS OF JIG
CLAMPED TO STOCK

Figure 6–2. *A homemade jig.*

and centerboards, all of which will be discussed later, so keeping the hole on course is imperative. A homemade jig, Figure 6-2, is useful for this purpose.

Carriage Bolts

These are screw bolts with a round button head and a square neck on the shank just under the head that keeps the bolt from turning in the wood, provided the hole for the bolt is the same size as the shank and also smooth. There is a chance a carriage bolt head will spin in a rough-sided sloppy hole, thus defeating the purpose of using a carriage bolt in the first place. These bolts are used in many parts of the structure such as to fasten frames to floors, stringers to clamps, and frames and deck beams to clamps or shelves, and are made in silicon bronze, galvanized iron, and stainless steel.

Fin Head Bolts

The best all-around type of bolt for wooden boatbuilding is the fin head type shown in Figure 6-14. I have never seen one for sale in any chandlery or catalog, but I often saw them in use in at least two of the best boatbuilding yards in the U.S.; the bolts would have been made-to-order in bronze. Such a bolt can be hammered flush with the wood surface, or be countersunk and plugged without leaving a cavity. I'll guarantee that the floors-to-frames fasteners in the Nevins-built auxiliary shown in Figure 6-15 were fin head bolts although the label indicates the more conventional carriage bolt.

The noted designer L. Francis Herreshoff, writing about fin head bolts, said in part that "pressure should be brought to bear on manufacturers to produce them . . . With Everdur bronze or Monel this type could be cold-headed and I believe it would be one of the cheapest to produce for there is no slot to be cut." Enough said.

Special Note on Bolt Threads

Fastenings are used to hold parts together and keep them from moving; therefore, they must be tight in their holes. This is not possible if the bolts have what are called *rolled threads*. Bolts of this type are common today because threads formed by rolling instead of cutting are cheaper to manufacture. The unthreaded shank of these bolts is smaller in diameter than the outside of the threads, so the shank cannot possibly be tight in the hole. Bolts of this type are all right when the fastening is in tension only, but this is seldom the case in the hull structure, so rolled-thread bolts should not be used.

Wood Screws

Flathead screws are used extensively in wooden boatbuilding for fastening planking and decking and many other parts. They are available from stock made of galvanized iron, brass, or silicon bronze, and are also produced of Monel and stainless steel. All are made with slotted heads, many with the Phillips or similar type heads which some builders prefer in order to minimize screwdriver bit slippage and thus the possible scarring of adjacent wood.

Tests have shown that screws with sharp, thin threads develop the greatest holding power in tension. The threads of hot galvanized wood screws in the smaller sizes are bad in this respect. However, withdrawal resistance of screws used as plank fastenings is theoretically not too critical; the most important function of fastenings is not to keep the planks from springing off, but to prevent them from "working" past their neighbors in a fore-and-aft direction when the hull is being driven through seas. (Such working is the cause of leaking seams in a conventional single-planked hull.) Indeed, the primary job of hull fastenings is to hold the parts in place. Here the area of the wood that bears against the fastenings is very important; a thick fastening puts more wood to work resisting stresses than a thin one. This is a strong argument for using screws instead of nails as planking fastenings, because for a given length, a screw can be used that is thicker than a nail. The accompanying table shows the screw sizes that have been accepted over the years for planking and decking, and if you compare the gauge of any one of the screws with an ordinary boat nail of the same length, the greater screw thickness will be obvious. Unlike common boat nails, however, Monel Anchorfast nails and Stronghold bronze nails are available in heavy gauges suitable for planking fastenings, but they usually must be made to order.

Some will consider the screw sizes in Figure 6-3 to be on the heavy side, but the table is meant for hulls that will be subject to rigorous service, such as ocean cruising. The sizes may be reduced by a gauge or so for powerboats and other boats of light construction built for sheltered waters. When building from plans, be guided by the fastening sizes specified.

The size of a drilled hole for a screw affects the screw's holding power to an appreciable extent. A general rule to follow for determining the lead hole size is 90 percent of the diameter at the root of the screw threads in hardwoods and 70 percent in softwoods. The lead hole drill sizes in the table are a guide for hardwood, such as oak, because the threaded part of a screw used for fastening planking is sunk into the

PLANK THICKNESS	SCREW LENGTH & GAUGE[1]	SCREW DIAM.	BODY DRILL	LEAD DRILL[2]	PLUG DIAM.
3/8"	3/4" No. 7	.150"	9/64"	No. 44	NONE
1/2"	1" No. 8	.163"	5/32"	No. 40	NONE
5/8"	1 1/4" No. 9	.176"	11/64"	No. 37	3/8"
3/4"	1 1/2" No. 10	.189"	3/16"	No. 33	1/2"
7/8"	1 3/4" No. 12	.216	13/64"	No. 30	1/2"
1"	2" No. 14	.242"	15/64"	No. 25	1/2"
1 1/8"	2 1/4" No. 16	.268"	17/64"	No. 18	5/8"
1 1/4"	2 1/2" No. 18	.294"	9/32"	No. 13	5/8"
1 1/2"	3" No. 20	.320"	5/16"	No. 4	3/4"

FLAT HEAD WOOD SCREWS FOR PLANKING

[1] MAY BE REDUCED ONE GAUGE FOR DECKING.
[2] FOR HARDWOOD

Figure 6-3.

frame, but it is best to check the table sizes by driving a few screws in samples of the wood to be used. Most builders use just one drill for screws in mahogany or white cedar planking and oak frames and this is satisfactory if the plank does not split in way of the unthreaded screw shank. If splitting does occur, you should drill through the *plank only* using a body drill that is *slightly* under the actual screw diameter. The sizes for these are also shown in Figure 6-3. It is recommended that either laundry soap or beeswax be rubbed in the threads of screws, especially when driving into hardwood. This acts as a lubricant and reduces the driving labor.

In the best yacht practice the screw holes in 5/8" planking and over are counterbored and plugged (Figure 6-4) with plugs of the same kind of wood as the planking, while the heads of screws in thinner planks are set slightly below the surface, with the heads puttied over to make the fastenings invisible on the finished hull. Marine hardware suppliers sell plugs of mahogany, teak, or oak, or you can buy a plug cutter for a drill press and make your own from scraps of the same kind of wood you will be plugging.

The depth of counterbore for the plugs should be about one-third of the plank thickness. The plugs are dipped in thick paint, waterproof glue, or varnish (the latter recommended for wood that is to have a natural finish), set in the counterbored holes with the grain parallel to that of the planking, and lightly tapped home with a hammer. If hit too hard, the plug may be crushed and it may swell later, possibly breaking the paint film or at least presenting an unsightly look. Give the bond a day or so to harden, then cut the plugs flush with the surface using a sharp chisel. Do not try

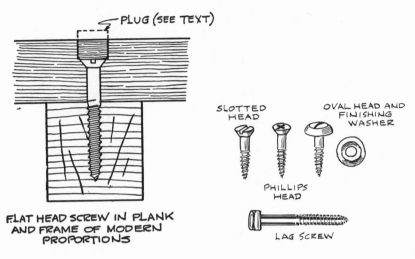

Figure 6-4.

to flush off the plug with one cut of the chisel. Rather, take light cuts to determine run of the grain; then you will not chip off the plug below the surface of the plank and have to start all over again.

Drilling proper holes for wood screws can be done with separate bits or with bits that combine the operations. There are patented countersinks that drill the lead hole followed by the countersink for the screw head and patented counterbores that drill the lead followed by the hole for the plug. The latter is used most because it is unnecessary to countersink for a flathead screw that is to have a plug over it.

Plugs can sometimes become crowded where planking strakes are narrow, particularly near the strakes' ends, where the plank width is least. This can be overcome either by carefully staggering the holes if the width of the frame will permit it or by reducing the gauge of the screw just enough to use a plug of the next smaller size.

Some years ago I began to use tapered drills for wood screw holes. From a maximum diameter matching that of the screw body (which reduces the risk of splitting the plank) the drill is ground to taper to a point, thus conforming to the wood screw shape. The bit is used with a countersink that is adjustable for the length of the screw. This countersink drills for a flathead fastener; when an adjustable stop collar is used, it also counterbores for a plug to the depth desired. In addition the countersink can be used with an untapered drill bit to drill and counterbore for a machine-screw type fastener. The diameter of the counterbore is proper for a plug larger in diameter than the screw head. Stock sizes of these countersinks are shown in Figure 6-5.

Much superior to a common twist drill for making clean holes in wood is the brad point bit. It is also easily centered for starting a hole where it belongs.

Shown in Figure 6-6—but not to relative scale—are a tapered drill with countersink and stop collar (positioned for a shallow plug), a brad point bit, and a plug cutter.

W.L. Fuller, Inc., 7 Cypress Street, Warwick, RI 02888 has been supplying

STOCK SIZES OF FIG. 6-4A C'T'RSINKS		
SIZE SCREW	DRILL DIAM. ✱	COUNTERBORE (PLUG. DIAM.)
NO. 6	9/64"	3/8"
8	11/64"	3/8"
10	13/64"	1/2"
12	7/32"	1/2"
14	1/4"	1/2"
16	1/4"	5/8"

✱ STRAIGHT OR TAPERED DRILL.

Figure 6–5.

countersinks, counterbores, plug cutters, and tapered drills to the boatbuilding industry for many years. These items may be difficult to find locally, but they frequently appear in many tool catalogs.

There are only a few places where round-head screws are used in boats, but, for example, they are the logical fastening for securing rigging tangs to wooden masts, since the thin metal of which a tang is made will not permit a countersunk hole. Oval-head screws are only used in light joinerwork where fastenings must show and for securing panels that are removed from time to time for access to such things as steering gear and other items located behind joinerwork. In these places oval-head screws are used with finishing washers so that screw holes do not become too worn from repeated use.

Stainless steel screws labelled 18-8 have become easily available in the standard configurations of flat, round, and oval head wood screws. It is possible that these will be sold for less than silicon bronze screws; therefore they should be considered for fastening joinerwork, but I am reluctant to use them below the waterline until I have greater experience with them. Stainless steel "tapping" type screws are also easy to

Figure 6–6.

find. These are basically sheet-metal fasteners but can be used in fiberglass parts. Normally they are threaded for the entire length of the shank, so they are best in tension rather than for bearing loads.

Lag Screws

Lag screws, sometimes called lag bolts, are large wood screws with a square head that are turned in with a wrench. Periodic tightening of a lag screw can wear the threads in the wood until the holding power of the screw is gradually lost; therefore lags are only used where through-bolts are not possible or practical. A hole of the same diameter as the lag screw is bored for the length of the unthreaded shank and the hole for the thread should be sized the same as for a regular wood screw. Lag screws are made in galvanized iron, brass, and silicon bronze, the latter being preferred.

Hanger Bolts

These are lag screws having the upper or head end of the shank threaded for a nut. They are used principally for fastening propeller shaft stuffing boxes and stern bearings and for holding down engines to beds. By backing off the hanger bolt nut, these parts may be removed for repair or replacement without disturbing the screw in the wood. Hanger bolts are turned in with a wrench applied either to a nut run down to the end of the threads or to two nuts locked together on the threads. They are usually made of brass and silicon bronze, the latter being preferred.

Copper Wire Nails

Copper nails are made in the form of common wire nails with flat heads. They are used almost exclusively as rivets for fastening frames to floors, stringers to frames, planking laps to one another in lapstrake construction, and planking to frames where both the planking and frames are light in size. The hole for the nail should be drilled as small as possible without it being so small that the parts split or the nail bends while it is being driven. Drive the nail all the way in to draw the parts together; then the head must be backed up with an iron while a copper burr is driven over the point of the nail. A burr is simply a washer and it is important that it be a driving fit over the nail or else it will dance all over the place when the rivet is being formed. The burr is driven up against the wood with a set, which is nothing but a length of steel rod with a hole in the end slightly larger than the diameter of the nail. With nippers, cut off the point of the nail so that a length equal to one to one and a half times the diameter of the nail is left for riveting. Again with the head of the nail backed up with the iron, do the riveting with many light blows with the peen end of a machinist's hammer. Heavy blows will bend the nail inside the wood. A bent rivet tends to straighten under stress, resulting in a weak, loose fastening. Light blows form the head and draw the wood together.

Copper rivets are excellent for light work but are rather soft. Screws should be used for fastening planking when the size of the frame will permit them to be completely sunk. Nails are also thinner than screws for the same job, a point discussed under Wood Screws. See Figure 6-7 for sizes of copper wire nails.

Galvanized Boat Nails

As mentioned before, these are cheap fastenings and not too much life can be expected from them. The nails are forged, have a peculiar button head, rectangular

NON-FERROUS NAIL SIZES				
	COPPER WIRE		ANCHORFAST & STRONGHOLD	
LENGTH	SHANK DIAM.	APPROX. NUMBER PER LB.	SHANK DIAM.	APPROX. NUMBER PER LB.
5/8"	.065"	1380	.065"	
3/4"	.065"	1160	.065"	
	.072"	956	.109"	462
7/8"	.072"	808	.065"	825
			.109"	393
1"	.072"	704	.072"	775
			.109"	350
1 1/4"	.083"	424	.083"	525
			.109"	280
			.134"	
1 1/2"	.109"	208	.109"	210
			.134"	135
			.165"	90
1 3/4"	.109"	180	.134"	120
	.120"	144	.165"	76
2"	.134"	106	.134	105
	.120	130	.165"	68
2 1/4"			.165"	64
2 1/2"	.134"	86	.165"	58
2 3/4"			.165"	53
3"	.148"	56	.165"	48
3 1/2"	.165"	40	.165"	25

Figure 6-7.

shank and either a blunt or a chisel point. In frames up to about 1¼″ thick, chisel-pointed nails are driven so that the points project about ½″ to ⅜″ through the frames and are clinched against the frame with the grain. To prevent splitting the frame, the nail is driven with the chisel edge across the grain. A nail of acceptable quality will clinch without cracking either the nail or the zinc coating. Blunt-pointed nails are used in heavier frames and are buried entirely within the frame. Whether or not the holes are counterbored for plugs, the heads of either type nail must be driven below the surface of the planking with a nail set and an attempt must be made to prevent cutting the coating of zinc by using a set shaped to fit over the entire head of the nail.

Threaded Nails

Another type of fastening for a boat hull is a nail with a unique annular thread. As the nail is driven, the grooves on the shank shape the wood fibers into countless minute wedges that grip the shank to resist withdrawal. (See Figure 6-8.) It is claimed that it takes 65 percent more force to pull this threaded nail than an unclinched galvanized boat nail, 31 percent more than a clinched boat nail, and 3 percent more than a wood screw. As these nails are available in non-ferrous material, the objection to nails because of corrosion has been overcome. Some boatbuilders have used these nails for their planking, and figures show that some yards have reduced their plank fastening labor by one quarter.

There are quite a few kinds of threaded nails on the market, including some made abroad. Tests have shown the importance of the thread form and one of the best is rolled on the nail by the people that make Anchorfast nails—Independent Nail Inc.,

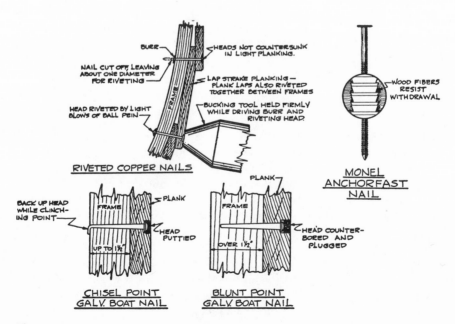

Figure 6-8.

SCREW GAUGE VS. NAIL DIAMETER		
SCREW		NAIL
SHANK DIAM.	GAUGE No	WIRE DIAM.
.086"	2	.083"
		.095"
		.109"
.125"	5	.120"
.138"	6	.134"
.164"	8	.165"
		.180"
.190	10	
		.203"
.216	12	.220"
.242	14	.238"
		.265"
.268	16	
		.284"
.294	18	.300

Figure 6–9.

Bridgewater, MA 02324. The name Anchorfast is owned by the International Nickel Co. and is used only when the threaded nails are made of Monel. Anchorfast nails can be identified by an anchor stamped on the head of the nail. Independent also makes nails of other materials and calls them Stronghold, but if Monel is not used it is recommended that the second choice be limited to those made of silicon bronze. The Monel nails are stiffer than the silicon bronze, making them more resistant to bending when driven.

For fastening planking, nails should be the same diameter as the screws they replace, or else more of them should be used. Pilot holes as recommended by the manufacturer should be drilled for all but the smallest sizes. The pilot hole size recommended is 50-70 percent of the nail diameter, depending upon the hardness of the wood, and about 80 percent of the nail length.

THREADED NAILS		
PLANKING & DECKING (NOT PLYWOOD)		
WOOD THICKNESS	NAIL SIZE LIGHT DUTY HULLS	NAIL SIZE HEAVY DUTY HULLS
1/2"	1 1/4" x .083"	
5/8"	1 1/2" x .134"	1 1/2" x .165"
3/4"	1 1/2" x .134"	1 1/2" x .180"
7/8"	1 3/4" x .165"	1 3/4" x .220"
1"	2" x .165"	2" x .238"

PLYWOOD PLANKING & DECKING			
PLYWOOD THICKNESS	NAIL SIZE	NAIL SPACING	
		ALONG EDGES	PLANKING BATTENS & DECK BEAMS
1/4"	7/8" x .109"	1 1/2" - 1 3/4"	3" - 4"
3/8"	1 1/4" x .109"	2 1/2" - 3"	4" - 5"
1/2"	1 1/2" x .134"	3" - 4"	4" - 5"
5/8"	2" x .165"	4"	5"
3/4"	2 1/4" x .165"	4"	5"

STRIP PLANKING (SEE TEXT)		
WOOD THICKNESS	NAIL DIAM.	APPROX. SPACING
5/8" - 3/4"	.083"	4"
7/8" - 1"	.109"	5"
1" - 1 1/4"	.134"	6"

Figure 6-10.

In Figure 6-7 are shown the sizes of Monel Anchorfast and Stronghold silicon bronze nails usually found in the stocks of distributors. Figure 6-9 is a comparison of standard nail and screw gauges as a guide for those wishing to substitute nails for screws, and in Figure 6-10 nail sizes for various types of planking and decking are tabulated. These sizes, of course, must be used with discretion, as they do not necessarily apply to every case.

Unusual Nail Fasteners

Other than the copper wire nails used as rivets, as mentioned earlier, there are two other copper nails that have a place in boatbuilding. The most common of these unusual nails is the square-cut copper "clout" nail. These can be used in light construction for fastening planking to thin, flat frames such as seen in canoes, for fastening the laps of clinker planking up to about ½″ in thickness, and for "quilt" fastening the layers of double diagonal planking between frames.

In the case of the latter, where the layers of planking are glued together and the nails are used only to ensure a good bond, some builders drive the nails against a heavy iron held against the inside of the planking by a helper. When the iron is held properly, the point of the nail turns 90 degrees and is flush with the wood. It takes teamwork to know where the next nail will be driven, but once the routine is established, the nails are clenched at a fast rate.

The point of the nail is turned back into the wood when clout nails are used as primary fasteners without adhesives. This works all right in the laps of softwood planking and with softwood frames like those of canoes, but when used with hardwoods, a rivet is more reliable than a clenched nail.

For clench-nailing, first drill a snug hole as described earlier for riveting copper wire nails. As the nail is driven through, the point is turned over by holding an iron against the point and forming it into a hook. When the point is about to enter the wood the iron is held against the hook and the man outside completes driving the nail until the head is flush with the wood. This all takes practice and some trials to determine how much longer the length of the nail should be compared to the thickness of the parts being fastened together. Figure 6-11 shows the elements of the clenching process, and Figure 6-12 the riveting process when traditional square-cut boat nails are used in conjunction with dished "roves."

The holding power of a square-cut copper nail is a great deal more than a round wire nail, but the customary use of square nails is as rivets. As with copper wire nail rivets, a snug hole should be drilled and heading should be done with light blows of the peen hammer. The dished rove is noteworthy: it functions like an ordinary "burr," but the dished shape grips the wood and tensions the rivet. The heads of nails shown in Figure 6-12 may be left "proud" or countersunk into the planking; in either case, the bucking iron must be suitably shaped.

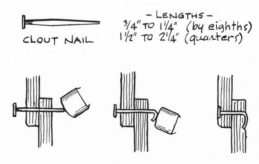

CLOUT NAIL

– LENGTHS –
¾″ TO 1¼″ (by eighths)
1½″ TO 2¼″ (quarters)

Figure 6-11. *Clenching a copper clout nail.*

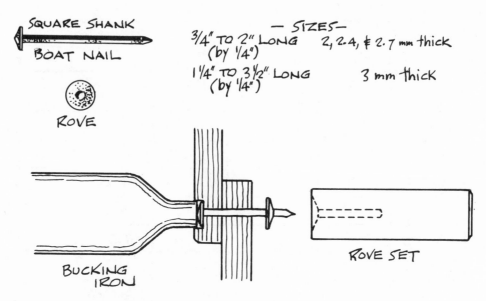

Figure 6-12. *Traditional square-shank boat nails.*

Other square-cut copper boat nails (and dished roves), both domestic and imported, may be obtained with different head configurations, including flat heads and countersunk flat heads.

Copper clench nails are available from The Copper Nail, Box 936, Sacramento, CA 95804; Duck Trap Woodworking, RFD #2, Cannan Road, Lincolnville, ME 04849; and Strawbery Banke Inc., Box 300, Portsmouth, NH 03801.

Square shank boat nails for riveting are available from William Cannell Boatbuilding Co., Inc., Box 900, Camden, ME 04843; The Copper Nail; Duck Trap Woodworking; and Tremont Nail Co., 21 Elm Street, Wareham, MA 02571.

A source for all types of marine fasteners for backyard as well as professional boatbuilders is Jamestown Distributors, 28 Narragansett Avenue, Jamestown, RI 02835. For metric fasteners of all types try Metric & Multistandard Components Corp., 128 Saw Mill River Road, Elmsford, NY 10523.

Miscellaneous Fasteners

There are a few other types of fasteners that have some uses in boat construction when they are made of proper non-corrosive materials. Machine screws are bolts and are useful as through-fasteners for light work. Usual sizes are from Number 6 (a fat ⅛") up through ¼" in diameter. Figure 6-13 is a table showing hole sizes for clearance and for tap drills, etc.; there will be times when you will find this very handy. Machine screws are made with flat, round, and oval heads, and in brass, chrome-plated brass, bronze, and stainless steel.

Staples, applied with hand, electric, or air-operated guns, can be used to hold thin pieces of wood when laminating, positioning fiberglass or other woven materials, and

SIZE	DIAM. INS.	THREADS PER INCH	TAP DRILL	CLEARANCE DRILL
NO. 6	.138	32	NO. 36	NO. 28
NO. 8	.164	32	NO. 29	NO. 19
NO. 10	.190	24	NO. 25	NO. 11
NO. 10	.190	32	NO. 21	NO. 11
NO. 12	.216	24	NO. 16	NO. 2
NO. 12	.216	32	NO. 13	NO. 2
1/4"	.250	20	NO. 7	17/64" OR 9/32"
5/16"	.3125	18	F	21/64" OR 11/32"
3/8"	.375	16	5/16"	25/64" OR 13/32"
1/2"	.500	13	27/64"	33/64" OR 17/32"

BODY & TAP DRILLS FOR U.S. STANDARD MACHINE SCREWS & BOLTS

Figure 6-13.

for many other such jobs. If the staples are to be removed later, they can be of inexpensive steel; otherwise bronze, Monel, or stainless steel must be used. The ultimate staple that I have seen is a rather long Monel wire staple with coated legs that defy withdrawal. Driven with an air gun, the staple head will sink below the surface of

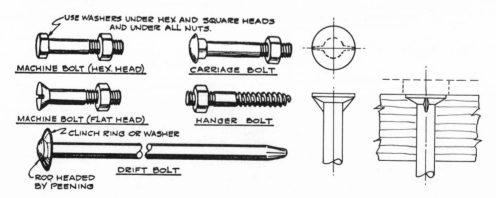

Figure 6-14. Left: *Bolts commonly used in boatbuilding.* Right: *Fin head bolt has many applications in wooden hull structure.*

Figure 6-15. *The frame of a fine auxiliary yacht, illustrating the uses of bolts mentioned in the text.*

fir plywood. These staples have been used to fasten plywood decking that is glued to beams and around the edges and many other similar plywood parts. Stapling is the fastest method of securing parts and is quite satisfactory when used in conjunction with an adhesive.

For many years riveting remained a method of fastening used only by professional metalworking shops, but due to the invention of "pop" rivets, minor riveting jobs can now be done by the amateur. Most hardware stores carry these rivets and hand-operated riveters. This kind of fastening is a one-man job, because pop rivets are inserted into a drilled hole and secured from the same side without the need for any back-up. Pop rivets are extensively employed in production fiberglass boatbuilding. A typical application is in securing a molded deck that fits over the hull, the rivet holding together the deck, hull, and rub rail. The latter is usually an aluminum alloy extrusion and the rivets are of a similar alloy. Their use should be limited to above the water, and generally for fastening thin parts, say an assembly having a total thickness of no greater than ⅜". Those who make their own metal enclosures, such as aluminum alloy cases for electrical switchboards, will find that pop rivets make the job go a lot easier and faster.

Metric Fasteners

Because the metric system of measurement is standard elsewhere in the world, it is quite possible that a person in the U.S. will be confronted with the problem of drilling a properly sized hole for a metric bolt. Accordingly, Figure 6-16 tabulates clearance drills for some common metric sizes that may be encountered.

NOMINAL DIAM.		CLEARANCE DRILL (U.S.)
MM	INCH	
M 3	.118	NO.31 OR 1/8"
M 3.5	.138	NO.28 OR 9/64"
M 5	.197	NO. 8 OR 13/64"
M 6	.236	1/4"
M 8	.315	21/64"
M 10	.394	13/32"
M 12	.472	31/64"
M 14	.551	9/16"

Figure 6–16.

Fastening Metal Fittings

To avoid galvanic corrosion, fasten bronze underwater parts such as shaft logs, stern bearings, rudderposts, seacocks, and propeller shaft struts with silicon bronze. On deck, fasten stainless steel trim and hardware with stainless steel, bronze fittings with silicon bronze, galvanized fittings with hot-dipped galvanized fastenings, Marinium fittings with stainless steel or Monel, and aluminum alloy fittings with stainless steel.

Adhesives

Adhesives, used either alone or in conjunction with mechanical fasteners, are some of the best fasteners. However, it must be remembered that an adhesive is not a cure-all and that for it to provide strength it must be used as directed, with attention to mixture (when the adhesive is two-part), temperature and working time, clamping pressure, and curing period.

Until World War II there were only *water-resistant* adhesives rather than *waterproof* ones. This fact notwithstanding, thousands of hollow masts and booms were glued up with it, being protected from moisture by varnish or paint. Water-resistant glue still has a place in boat construction for interior joinerwork that is not subject to wetting and that is protected with finish coating. The modern counterpart is marketed by Weldwood as Plastic Resin Glue. This urea resin glue, which consists of a powder that is mixed with water, is less expensive than the waterproof types, has good working time, and provides a joint that is colorless when properly fitted.

Another rather new glue is a one-part aliphatic resin marketed as Weldwood Carpenter's Glue. Another brand is Titebond. These cream-colored glues are rated water-resistant but it took only a couple of weeks for the joint of a sample I made and immersed in water to fail easily. There was no protective coating on the surfaces of my sample. These glues are fast-setting and are useful for interior joinerwork.

The breakthrough from water-resistant to waterproof adhesives came with the development of a resorcinol resin glue, which is also marketed by Weldwood for small consumers as Resorcinol Waterproof Glue. It is packaged in two parts, a dark purple resin and a light-colored powder, and is best mixed by weight as instructed. It will produce a joint stronger than the surrounding wood, but the joints should be well fitted and pressure must be applied until curing has taken place. Resorcinol glue sets up quickly in hot climates, so the instructions should be studied carefully to avoid excess cost brought on by mixing too much glue for use during the time available. Resorcinol glue is often used to secure planking of cold-molded hulls.

Described as a urea-formaldehyde resin, Aerolite Glue is another waterproof glue of great benefit to boatbuilders and to builders of wooden aircraft. Aerolite is a two-part adhesive, very easy to mix and apply. One part is a powder that is mixed with water to the consistency of an easy spreading paste. The powder has a shelf life of two years; the paste's shelf life is one to three months. The second part is a water-like liquid catalyst, which has an unlimited shelf life. The paste is spread on one surface, and then the other surface is wetted with the catalyst. The two surfaces are then mated. This adhesive is strong, even without heavy clamping, it is gap-filling, and it can be used in temperatures down to 60°F. without heat.

Some of the epoxy resins are among the best adhesives for use in building wooden boats and parts. They can even be used for joining wood and polyester fiberglass parts to polyester fiberglass. Epoxy is extremely strong, it does not require pressure to achieve a good bond, and it is gap-filling if used thick enough so that it does not run out of the joints. Not needing pressure to ensure a strong joint, epoxy is easier to use than resorcinol for laminations and hulls with multiple planking layers. There are various additives such as microballoons and microspheres that can be used to thicken epoxy to proper viscosity to prevent it from running; there are also epoxies available that are thick enough for use as is.

Arcon E-152 and Arcon E-154 are spreadable pastes suited for strip or diagonally planked hulls or any other use. Chem Tech T-88 epoxy adhesive is a 1:1 ratio mixture of resin-to-hardener that could not be simpler to put together and that can be used in temperatures down to 35°F.

The strength of epoxy when used as an adhesive, plus the advantage of not requiring high pressure on the mating surfaces, really makes it an ideal material for boatbuilding. Remember, though, that mixing epoxy with the *hardener* is not at all similar to adding the *catalyst* to polyester resin. The amount of the catalyst determines the speed at which polyester resin will set up at various temperatures, whereas an *exact* amount of epoxy hardener regulates the chemical reaction that results in the cured material performing as expected. Do not tamper with the epoxy manufacturer's stated proportions for this expensive material. If the instructions specify a 1:1 mixture of resin and hardener by *volume* simply mix them this way. On the other hand, if the quality of the cured epoxy requires mixing the proportions by *weight* take the trouble to do it right. Some makers of epoxy resins have devices such as pumps to help you mix the components so the finished product will have the strength expected.

Caution to Epoxy Users

So much is written about epoxy resins and the material is so valuable to boatbuilders, principally as an adhesive, that it would be remiss not to warn that epoxy resins, especially hardeners, must be used with caution. Avoid contact with unprotected skin and breathing the fumes released by epoxies as they cure. These words are to reinforce manufacturers' directions that are often taken lightly. I have never had a problem, but I have seen others who were unhappy, so beware!

Sources for Adhesives

Most general and marine hardware stores carry Weldwood's Plastic Resin and Resorcinol Waterproof glues as well as the various brands of contact cement for sticking Formica-type plastic laminates to wood and metal. The Weldwood glues in quantities larger than quarts are handled by most marine distributors and some large lumberyards.

Aerolite is a Ciba-Geigy product distributed in the U.S. by Aircraft Spruce and Specialty Co., P.O. Box 424, Fullerton, CA 92632. It is also available from Wicks Aircraft Supply, 410 Pine Street, Highland, IL 62249.

Following are the names and addresses of firms producing epoxy adhesives:

> Arcon E-152 and Arcon E-154, Allied Resin Corp., Weymouth Industrial Park, East Weymouth, MA 02189.
>
> Chem-Tech T-88, Chem-Tech Inc., 4669 Lander Road, Chagrin Falls, OH 44022.
>
> West 105 adhesive, Gougeon Brothers, Inc., 706 Martin Street, Bay City, MI 48706.
>
> Systems Three, Systems Three Resins, 5965 Fourth Ave. South, Seattle, WA 98108. (Product tolerates low temperature and high humidity.)
>
> Poxy-Grip, Glen-L Marine Designs, Box 756, Bellflower, CA 90706.
>
> G2 and Cold Cure, Industrial Formulators of Canada, Ltd., 3824 William Street, Burnaby, B.C., Canada.
>
> Spabond, Jamestown Distributors, 28 Narragansett Avenue, Jamestown, RI 02835.

Chapter 7

LINES AND LAYING DOWN

To properly build a boat from plans, the hull lines and part of the construction plan must be drawn full size. This fact has been repeated to the point of monotony in countless "how to build" articles, but the job is so important to the successful completion of a boat that instructions in boatbuilding would be incomplete without a description of the work involved.

A few firms offer full-size patterns for hull parts or completely dimensioned drawings so the shape of the parts can be drawn directly on the material. The purpose of this is to eliminate the work described in this chapter, but these services may not have a design to suit you in their selection.

The job of drawing full size is distasteful to some, even among professional boatbuilders, but others find it to be fascinating work. Either way, it is true that once the plans are on hand one becomes impatient, but be assured that no matter how many hours are used to properly prepare for the actual building it is time well spent and will never be regretted. The full-size drawings from which molds and templates are made are especially valuable when more than one boat is to be built from the same plans, or for the construction of a one-design class boat where the hull must conform to reasonably close dimensional tolerances.

One must trace the history of shipbuilding to discover why the full-size hull lines are "laid down" on the "mold loft" floor. The full-size drawing board, so to speak, in a shipyard almost always consisted of a floor above a workshop of some sort, thus it was a loft. Molds or templates were taken off the full-size drawings, hence the terms "mold lofting," "laying down," and "taking off." The roof above the mold loft was preferably trussed, so there were no columns to obstruct the work, and there were windows on all sides and overhead to provide maximum light. The wooden floor was level and smooth, sufficiently sacred so some yards prohibited the wearing of hard-soled shoes. The floor was painted flat white or light gray, sometimes dull black, and on one edge of the floor there was a permanently fixed batten having an absolutely straight edge that served as a baseline.

Hull Lines

The work of enlarging the plans from the scale of the blueprints to full size is termed mold lofting, for it is from these drawings that molds are made for the shape of the hull and various other parts. It is imperative to understand the different lines drawn by the architect or designer to define the hull shape; as an aid to the beginner, Figure 7-1 has been prepared. Some of the lines are obvious, because from reading the design sections of yachting magazines and from prowling around hulls under construction or stored in boatyards most of you are familiar with the first three lines drawn by the designer that really characterize a hull. These are the sheerline or edge of deck as seen from the side, the profile (the outline of the bottom and ends above the waterline as seen from the side at the same time the sheerline is viewed), and the deck line, a gull's eye view of the outline of the hull as seen from above. Although these lines are important, they do not provide sufficient information from which to build a hull. Also needed is the shape of the boat between the three lines. To provide points to define the hull shape between these lines, the designer cuts the hull, so to speak, into pieces on planes that conveniently establish points for dimensions. These planes are called waterlines, buttocks, and diagonals.

If a hull could be lifted straight up out of the water without the resulting hole filling in with water, the shape of the edge of the hole would be the same as the shape of the boat at the surface of the water. On the boat, this line is called the load waterline and it is one of the most important lines drawn by the designer. For further subdivision the designer then divides the depth of the hull above and below the load waterline into convenient spaces, and draws the edges of additional horizontal planes which, for the want of something better, are also called waterlines because they are parallel to the load waterline. Then there are vertical planes called buttocks, located parallel to the centerline of the boat and conveniently spaced outboard to each side of the centerline. Finally, the edges of inclined planes are drawn and these are called diagonals, because they are drawn diagonal to the horizontal and vertical planes. These planes, like the others, are located to provide as many significant dimensioned points for the boatbuilder as is possible.

All of the aforesaid lines are fore-and-aft lines running the length of the hull, and although it has been mentioned above that these lines are drawn for the purpose of having points on the surface of the hull, actually no usable points are established until vertical planes *across* the hull have been drawn to intersect the fore-and-aft lines. The outlines or shapes formed by vertical transverse planes intersecting the horizontal, vertical, and diagonal fore-and-aft planes are called *sections*. A point on the hull is established wherever a section intersects one of the fore-and-aft lines, and by means of the many points of intersection it is possible for the builder to make molds for the exact shape of the hull as designed.

Sections may be compared to slices of bread. Just as is the case with the sections on a shapely boat, the slices through an old-fashioned rye loaf are all different, for the shape is ever-changing from end to end. A vessel's shape, then, can be transmitted into three-dimensional form by making full-size templates of the sections. When these are set up at each section's respective station the same as called for in the lines drawing, a vessel's shape in skeletal form has been established. The vessel's shape is represented in this manner just as a loaf of bread would be if every other slice was removed, while keeping the spacing of the remaining slices the same.

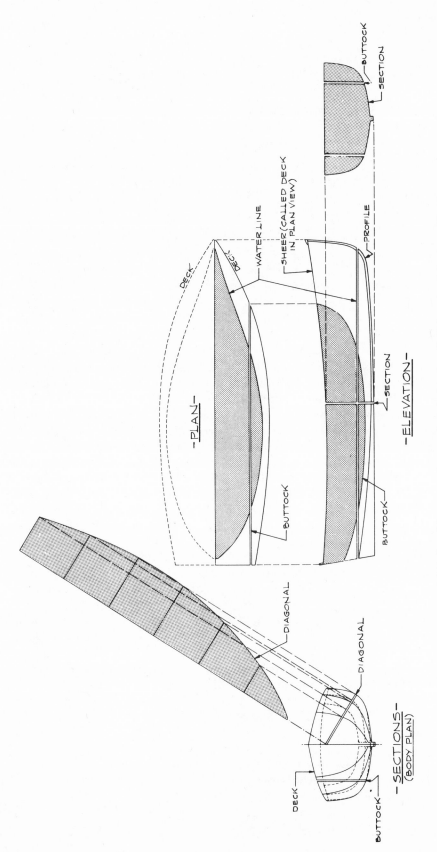

Figure 7-1. *A solid block model sawn on planes to show the location of hull lines drawn by the architect to depict the shape of the boat.*

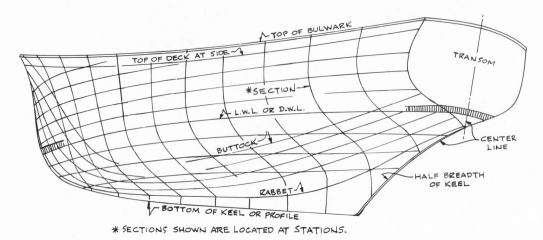

Figure 7-2.

Figure 7-1 has been included to pictorially show waterline, buttock, diagonal, and sectional planes as though a solid block half model of a hull were sawn into pieces on the various planes. The shapes of the planes are shown by the shaded areas, and on the body plan it may be seen how a point on the hull is created wherever a buttock, diagonal, or waterline is intersected by an athwartship sectional plane.

Figure 7-2 illustrates the various definitive lines in perspective.

Figure 7-3 is the scaled lines plan (that is, the designer's drawing) for the same hull shown in Figure 7-1, and on this plan are shown all the lines mentioned in the foregoing together with the necessary dimensions to reproduce them. (Incidentally, do not attempt to build a boat from these lines, as they are purely for illustration and have not been worked out for any specific purpose.) Note that spacing of waterlines, buttocks, and stations are indicated, as well as offsets for the profile of the stem, dimensions for the profile angle of the stern board (usually called a *transom* although stern board is technically a more accurate description), and a table of dimensions for laying out all the fore-and-aft curved lines. Because of the nature of diagonals, their location can only be indicated in section, that is, on the body plan.

Sometimes it is possible to define the shape of a hull without the use of diagonals, such as in Figure 1-7. In the case of a really simple hull with straight-line sections (see Figure 7-4), the sheer, deck line, chine, and/or profile provide a sufficient number of points from which to make the frames or molds. This eliminates the need for waterlines, buttocks, and diagonals, as will be explained a little further on.

Abbreviations

Before we go any further, it should be pointed out that many sets of lines plans for hulls have abbreviations for words used thus far in this chapter, and it is a help for the reader to be familiar with them.

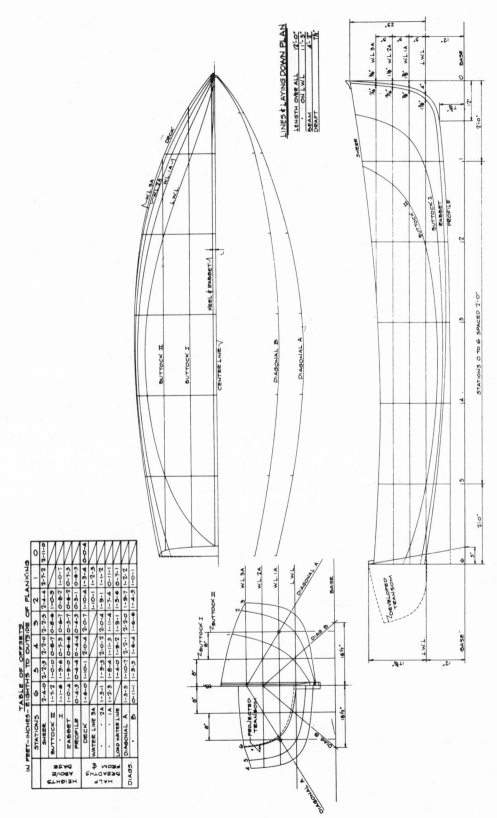

Figure 7-3. A typical lines plan and table of offsets for a round-bottomed boat.

Centerline	C.L.
Waterline	W.L.
Load Waterline	L.W.L.
Designed Waterline	D.W.L.
Buttock	Butt. or butt'k
Diagonal	Diag.
Baseline	B.L.
Station	Sta.
Frame	Fr.
Deck	Dk.
Length over all	L.O.A.
Section	Sect.
Displacement	Displ.
Salt water	S.W.
Fresh water	F.W.
Pounds	#
Longitudinal center of buoyancy	C.B. or L.C.B.
Center of gravity	C.G.

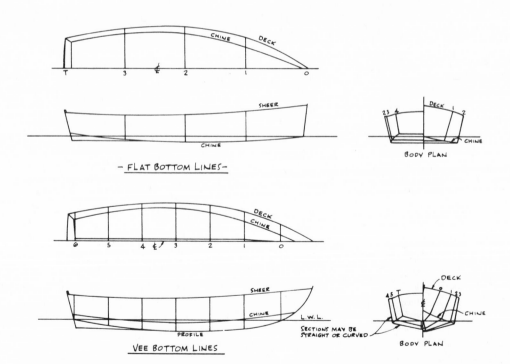

Figure 7–4. *Straight-sectioned boats have simple lines.*

Offsets

An offset is simply another name for a dimension, and is always taken from a straight line of reference such as a baseline for the elevation drawing or the centerline in the case of the plan view of the lines. In other words, it is a dimension for a point that is *offset* from a straight line, the baseline or the centerline. Dimensions are tabulated, except for some very simple hulls. This convention was made standard in shipbuilding because it is obviously impossible to write out all the dimensions on a lines plan and not have them become confused.

To eliminate a multitude of fractional dimensions, it is customary to write offsets in feet-inches-eighths of inches. For example, 2-5-3 means two feet, five and three-eighths inches. (You will find that you will read them automatically once you have tried a few.) Some designers pride themselves on the accuracy of their lines and offsets and read some dimensions to one-sixteenth of an inch; this is shown in the offset table by a plus sign or ½ after the "eighth" numeral, thus we get 2-5-3+ or 2-5-3½. One of these days metric offset tables will make life a lot simpler than struggling with feet, inches, and all those 64 fractions of an inch.

The use of the offset table will be explained further along, but at this time it would be well to note that the lines for a vessel's hull are almost always drawn to the *outside* surface of the hull. Consequently when molds are made, the thickness of the wood or fiberglass skin or the aluminum or steel plating must be deducted from the molds' lofted edges. The lines for metal ships or large wooden vessels with built-up sawn frames are often drawn to the *inside* of the plating or planking in order to save the mold loftsman from deducting the thickness from the full-size drawing of every frame, all of which must be drawn when sawn or metal frames are employed, for each frame is individually shaped before installation.

The hull lines discussed above are for a round-bottomed boat, the number of waterlines, buttocks, and diagonals involved depending upon the size of the boat. Other hull types have fewer lines. Figure 7-4 shows an ordinary, flat-bottomed rowboat having but four fore-and-aft lines, namely, the deck and sheer, and two views of the chine, which is the corner at the intersection of the side and bottom. Also shown are the lines for a v-bottomed boat having lines similar to a flattie except for the addition of a bottom profile. The sections of this particular boat consist of straight lines. If they were curved, other points would be needed to draw the sections, and these would be established by waterlines, buttocks, and diagonals.

There are also multi-chine hulls. A few traditional small craft built of wood were so shaped. Some steel hulls, generally workboats, may be multi-chine designs in order to dispense with the laborious shaping of hull plates. Figure 7-5 is the body plan for a multi-chine workboat hull.

The Mold Loft

Although we have said that the builder's first step is lofting the hull, in reality the first thing is to find a place to do the job. At a minimum, the space should be at least four or more feet longer than the boat in one direction, while in the other it must be equal to

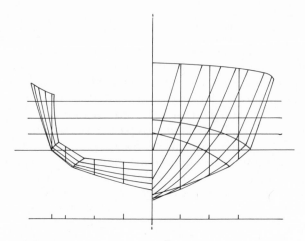

Figure 7-5.

the distance from the baseline to the highest point of the sheer, or to the top of the cabin if its shape requires lofting, plus some space on all sides for working around the drawing. Well-equipped boatyards use a level wooden floor maintained for just this purpose that is sanded smooth and coated with flat light gray or white paint. It is too much to ask that an amateur have such facilities at his disposal, so the next best alternative would be a level space, such as a floor or platform, where paper or plywood may be used to lay down the lines.

A few years ago while visiting boatyards I noticed lofting being done on a very heavy, light beige paper that was also being used for patterns for one-off parts. This material was 200-pound "Alexandrite" template paper, 12 square feet per pound. In each case it was purchased from a paper goods supply house in a nearby city. The information about the paper is given here, but the amateur builder will probably not be able to cope with the cost of this 72″ wide material. Each roll is said to weigh between 500 and 600 pounds—a lifetime supply indeed.

If you can find it in a drafting room supply shop, the old-style buff detail paper (made up to 54″ in width and in rolls 10, 20, and 50 yards long) is satisfactory for lofting small craft and is reasonably priced. Some of the paper-faced building panels are also all right, and so is plywood, as mentioned above, in standard-size panels that may be arranged edge to edge to make any size desired. Whatever the material, if several pieces are used to make up the required size, the pieces must be secured against movement.

Lofting Tools

The tools for lofting are few and simple. To draw sharp lines, flat carpenter's pencils are used, sharpened to a chisel point so a thin line may be drawn for a long distance. Resharpen any kind of pencil in midstream to ensure fine lines. Colored pencils may also be used to advantage to make it easier to distinguish between different types of lines. For measuring, a steel or fiberglass tape longer than the boat is ideal, but an ordinary folding six-foot rule will do, and the rule can also be used to lay off many short dimensions. A large carpenter's square, either as manufactured or homemade out of ⅜" or ½" wood, is needed for drawing lines perpendicular to other lines, such as for station lines in relation to the base and waterlines. You may also erect perpendiculars with a regular or improvised beam compass, as will be shown later. The adjustable bevel shown in Figure 3-1 is a must; also needed is a straightedge six or eight feet long, which you can make yourself from a piece of thin wood. For marking the really long, straight base and waterlines, you should use either a mason's chalk line, penciling the line on the floor before the chalk rubs off, or a length of light, strong fishing line stretched tightly between two nails, marking in points directly under the cord at intervals of about three feet, to be connected later with a straightedge.

Battens

Curves are said to be *fair* when they have no humps or bumps and are pleasing to the eye. To draw them, you must have a set of battens, which are nothing more than straight, square-edged pieces of clear white pine, basswood, mahogany, or other straight-grained wood. These should be at least two feet longer at each end than the line to be drawn. When the available stock isn't long enough for the job, battens can be made up of two pieces connected in the middle, where the curve is least, by making a long tapered glue splice of about 18" to 2' in length (a short splice will result in an unfair batten and therefore unfair curves). Or the line itself may be pieced if you make sure there is a fair overlap over the length of a couple of stations. For best results, you should use as stiff a batten as will go through all the points on the curve, for a stiff batten will tend to fair itself unless unduly forced, whereas a supple batten can be passed through all the points and not lie fair. It is difficult to say just what size battens should be used, as the correct size depends so much on the length of the line and the character of the curve.

A batten ½" to ¼" thick by 1½" to 2" wide, used on the flat, is suggested for relatively easy curves like the sheerline. For certain curves it may be necessary to taper the battens at the ends somewhat, with all the taper cut on one edge. For curves in the plan view, also known as the half-breadth plan, something like ½" x 1" or ½" x 1½" used on the flat, possibly tapered at the ends, or ¼" square and untapered might be tried. Like a lot of boatbuilding operations, accumulated experience will aid in the selection of batten sizes. If you have a table saw, start by making the battens on the heavy side until you get the hang of it, ripping the strips narrower as needed. Curves such as sections, the stem profile, and similar shapes will be drawn with shorter battens, probably ⅜" and ½" square, and inasmuch as these curves sometimes have harder bends in the middle than at the ends, such as around the turn of the bilge, they may have to be tapered in the middle in order to make a fair curve that touches all the points. These battens *must* be straight-grained material.

A batten is held in place with finishing nails driven on both sides of it, not through it. Not necessary by any means, but very desirable from the standpoint of readily sighting the shape of a batten when sprung to a curve, is a coat of flat black paint. The contrast of the dark batten against the light-colored floor or paper will help detect a line that is not fair.

The Grid

By examining the table of offsets, Figure 7-3, it will be seen that dimensions for the waterlines, buttocks, diagonals, sheer, and profile curves are laid out on the station lines and are measured above the baseline and out from the centerline. Therefore, it is the straight lines that must be laid down in the beginning. This group of lines, called the grid, is shown in Figure 7-6. You will note in Figure 7-7 that the grid is set up in a condensed form relative to the paper plans: the half-breadth plan is superimposed over the profile drawing to save space and to minimize the distances one must crawl on hands and knees when laying the lines down. (Some professionals save themselves from crawling around the loft floor by building a dolly of padded plywood mounted on low swivel casters.) Thus the grid is started by drawing a straight line that doubles both as the baseline for the profile view and the centerline for the half-breadth plan. The spacing of the stations is laid off along this line and the stations are drawn in perpendicular to it.

The perpendiculars may be drawn either with a set of trammel points, a regular beam compass, or an improvised one, and is done as follows. Mark a point A (Station 2 has been used as a practical example in Figure 7-6); then using the compass with A as a center, strike an arc B equidistant to each side of point A. Lengthen the arm of the compass and, using each of the points B as a center, strike two intersecting arcs above the baseline. From the intersection C draw a straight line through A on the base. The line CA is perpendicular to the base. This method can be used at each station, or it can be used at only one, with the resulting right angle used to build a large square for drawing in the remainder of the stations perpendicular to the base. This is also shown in Figure 7-6.

The spacing of the waterline planes in profile relative to the baseline and that of the buttock planes in the half-breadth plan relative to the hull centerline are taken from the designer's lines plan.

As mentioned above, the offsets for the curves are dimensioned as heights above the baseline or distances out from the centerline as the case may be. Some of the dimensions will be long enough that you will not be able to tell readily whether the end of your rule is exactly on the line or not. To be sure of this and to save time, it makes sense to nail a batten against the under side of the baseline as shown in Figure 7-6. The end of the rule can then be butted against it when making measurements. Instead of a batten, a nail may be driven at each intersection of a station with the base. You will find either way to be very helpful and certainly easier on the knees. Using the rule can also then remain a one-man job.

Sheerline and Deck Line

Either the sheerline or the deck line will be the first curved line to be drawn and faired. For the sake of argument we will select the sheerline, which the table of offsets, Figure

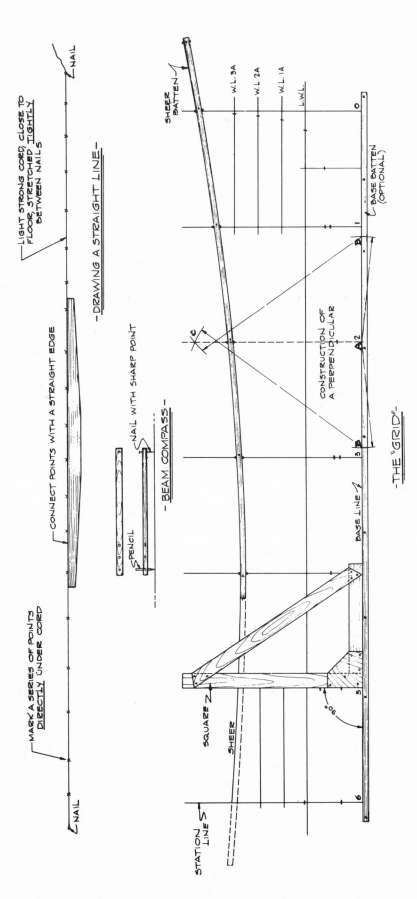

- NAIL

LIGHT STRONG CORD, CLOSE TO FLOOR, STRETCHED TIGHTLY BETWEEN NAILS

- DRAWING A STRAIGHT LINE -

MARK A SERIES OF POINTS DIRECTLY UNDER CORD

- NAIL

CONNECT POINTS WITH A STRAIGHT EDGE

NAIL WITH SHARP POINT

PENCIL

- BEAM COMPASS -

SHEER BATTEN

W.L. 3A
W.L. 2A
W.L. 1A
L.W.L.

O

BASE BATTEN (OPTIONAL)

CONSTRUCTION OF A PERPENDICULAR

- THE "GRID" -

BASE LINE

STATION LINE

SQUARE

SHEER

90°

Figure 7-6. *The grid for full-sized hull lines is comprised of straight lines and is laid out on a suitable floor.*

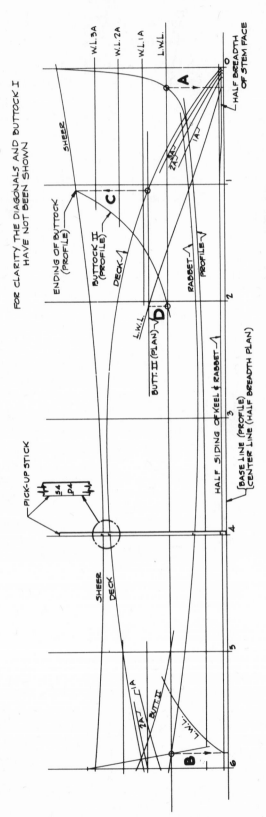

Figure 7-7. *The lofted hull lines are arranged differently from those on a designer's plan in order to save space on the mold loft floor.*

7-3, shows is dimensioned above the baseline. Starting at the bow, Station 0, the table reads 2-11-0 for the height of the sheer; so with the rule against the nail or batten measure up two feet, eleven inches above the base on Station 0 and make a mark. Move the rule over to Station 1, read 2-7-2 from the table and make a mark 2' 7¼" above the base. The process is repeated similarly at all of the stations.

With all the points marked, it is time to select a batten with which to draw the sheerline, placing it so that it extends beyond the length of the boat at each end. With one edge of the batten against the sheer point on a station amidships, Station 3 of the boat we are using as an example, drive a pair of finishing nails to hold the batten in place. Now fasten the batten at Station 2, then at Station 4, alternating towards the ends of the boat until the batten is sprung to and fastened at all the points. The batten's ends, which project beyond the boat, should be sprung to extend the curve fairly and then secured.

After the batten is secured for the entire length, sight along it to see whether there are any unfair or lumpy spots in the curve. If so, pull the nails at the stations adjacent to the unfairness and note the result. If the batten moves very far from one of the points and still does not appear to be fair, pull other nails and make adjustments, giving here and taking there until the resulting line is pleasing to the eye. You may expect points to be out of line occasionally because the designer has drawn the lines to a small scale compared to the full-size job; thus errors are bound to creep into the work. However, it must be remembered that the batten should be shifted as little as possible to obtain a sweet and true curve without hard spots.

The deck line is faired in the same manner after it has been laid down from offsets measured out from the centerline.

Profile and Rabbet

After the deck line has been drawn in and faired, you can continue working on the profile plan, drawing and fairing the profile (bottom of keel), the stem, and the rabbet. The rabbet line is normally found in traditional wooden construction, although it may or may not exist in other types of wooden hull construction, or in fiberglass or metal hulls. For these latter hulls, a similar line may be referred to by some other name. In any case, the lines plan will make all this clear.

The profile and rabbet must be faired in so that they will meet the relatively quick curves of the stem and stem rabbet. With these bow curves not yet drawn in, the best way to ensure that the two sets of curves will meet fairly is to extend the rabbet and profile forward beyond the point of tangency with the stem and its rabbet. You will note that this has been done in Figure 7-7.

The stem profile and the stem rabbet are drawn with a thin batten, as mentioned previously. When points for the stem curves have been marked in from the dimensions on the lines plan, a nail is driven at each spot, the batten is bent against the nails, and other nails are driven on the opposite side of the batten to hold it in place.

If your particular plans give a half-siding for the rabbet, this should be drawn in next before going on to the body plan.

Body Plan Sections

It is strongly recommended that the body plan be drawn on a separate portable board called a *scrive* (pronounced screeve) *board*. Such a board is easy to move around to suit making molds, and it avoids confusion of lines on the floor. Referring to the body plan for the lines in Figure 7-3, you can see that the board or paper used for the sections must be somewhat wider than the boat and at least as high as the distance from the baseline to the sheer at Station 0, the bow. Begin by drawing the baseline; then draw the centerline perpendicular to the base. The waterlines are drawn in parallel to the base, the buttocks parallel to the centerline, and the diagonals exactly as dimensioned on the lines plan. Trouble will result if the waterlines and the buttocks of the body plan are not spaced *exactly* the same as they were laid out on the half-breadth and profile plans.

Cut a few ¼″ x ¼″ wood strips and square the ends. The size of the hull being lofted dictates the length of the sticks, but generally the greatest length needed is the distance from the baseline to the highest point of the sheerline. These measuring sticks, useful on all four sides when made square instead of flat, are variously called "pick-up sticks" or "pick-up battens," or sometimes "story poles," and eliminate the necessity of accurately reading and recording numerous measurements from a rule. A stick in the pick-up position is shown at Station 4 in Figure 7-7.

To start the full-size body plan, the half-breadths of the deck line and the height of the sheer and rabbet are picked up and transferred to the scrive board (Figure 7-8). Align the end of a stick against the baseline and mark the half-breadths and heights on a stick with a sharp pencil, being careful to identify each mark with a symbol and station number.

With the end of the pick-up stick at the baseline of your body plan, mark the heights of the sheer and rabbet on the centerline. Draw short horizontal lines at each rabbet point and draw in the width of the rabbet. Draw horizontal lines at each sheer

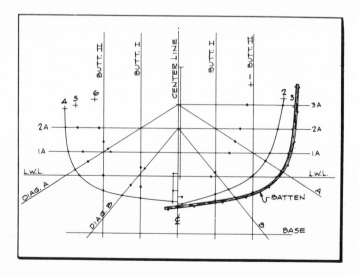

Figure 7–8. *The body plan is best drawn on a portable surface called a scrive board.*

height and with the pick-up stick against the centerline of the body plan, mark the deck width corresponding to each station. At each intersection of sheer and deck draw a small cross and label it with the station number. Each section now has two definite points: the sheer height/deck width intersection, and the intersection of the rabbet height and width.

Now to fill in some of the points in between. Nail a batten against one side of the centerline on the body plan and with the rule laid on a waterline with its end against the centerline batten, mark points for all the waterline half-breadths from the offset table and label each one. For instance, lay the rule on waterline 2A to the right of the centerline and from the offset table under Station 1 mark off 1-1-2, put a little circle around it with a 1 next to it to show it is a point on the section at Station 1; then mark 1-9-1 for Station 2, and so on. Do the same with the offsets for the other waterlines. With the waterlines done, go on to the buttocks. Place the rule on Buttock I with the end of the rule at the base and mark all the heights for Buttock I from the offset table. Follow with Buttock II. Then lay the rule along the diagonal with the end of the rule again at the centerline and lay off all the diagonal offsets along the diagonal lines. Move the batten to the left side of the centerline and lay out all the waterline, buttock, and diagonal offsets for the sections in the stern half of the boat. All the layout and transfer of measurements should be done with utmost care and accuracy. In the end, the time spent to this end will speed the job to completion faster than if the work is done in a slipshod manner.

Body Plan Battens

Nails are driven at all the reference marks on each section. Then a batten is bent around the nails of each section, using a batten long enough to extend 6″ or so above the sheer point and beyond the rabbet at the centerline, as shown in Figure 7-8. Holding the sheer and rabbet points as definitely fixed by the previous fairing of these lines, examine the batten carefully and shift it, if necessary, to get a smooth, true curve. Before doing any shifting, remember that points established by lines crossing other lines at right angles, or nearly so, are more accurate than those established by crossings at acute angles. When two lines intersect at an acute angle it is difficult to tell precisely at which spot on a line the crossing occurs; consequently it is possible for the designer, working from his small-scale drawing, to misread offsets taken from such intersections. (See Figure 7-9.) With this fact in mind, it is readily seen that for the flat

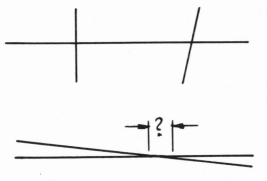

Figure 7–9.

part of the bottom sections, the best points are given by the buttocks. The waterlines give the most unreliable points for the same parts of the sections, but on the other hand, they are the best for the topside sections. Points may also be out due to mistakes in the designer's scaling technique. As a result, all the points on one line, such as a diagonal, may appear to be out by the same amount. In such a situation these points may be ignored, the other points being held if they give a fair section or line.

Fairing Diagonals

Fair the diagonals first, because they are laid out to cross the majority of the sections at a good angle. Lay a pick-up batten along a diagonal in the body plan, mark and identify all the points where it crosses the sections; then move the batten to the half-breadth plan and mark each diagonal half-breadth on its proper station. The diagonal is then faired, again proceeding as described for the sheerline. If the batten will not go through all the points and at the same time produce a fair line, the usual adjustments must be made. Bearing in mind not to make more changes than are necessary, the sections on the body plan are then corrected accordingly.

Long Line Endings

When fairing the long fore-and-aft lines, it is necessary to terminate them correctly. The location of waterline endings is fairly simple. Considering the bow in Figure 7-7, the profile of the stem has been faired and drawn permanently. Each intersection of the stem profile with one of the waterlines is a definite point in the profile plan, and the corresponding point in the half-breadth plan is found simply by projecting the intersection in the profile down to the line representing the half siding of the stem face in the half-breadth plan as shown in A in Figure 7-7. The aft endings are done exactly the same way, as indicated at B in the stern end of the same figure. It is obvious that in this particular design only the L.W.L. ends within the boat at the stern, because the other waterlines cross the section at Station 6.

Buttock endings are also quite simple. A short length of a buttock is drawn in plan to cross the deck line, and then the point of crossing is projected to the sheer. The intersection with the sheer is the ending of the buttock in the profile view as shown at C in Figure 7-7. When drawing the waterlines and buttocks, fairing points in addition to those on stations are established wherever a waterline and a buttock cross. D in Figure 7-7 illustrates how the crossing of the L.W.L. and Buttock II in profile projected to Buttock II in plan gives another point on the L.W.L. in plan.

The determination of a diagonal ending at the stem is somewhat more difficult to understand; therefore the steps taken are shown in Figure 7-10, which should be self-explanatory.

The preceding explanation of lofting a round-bottomed boat is modified for other types such as v- and arc-bottomed hulls; generally speaking, the latter types are easier to loft. However, all boats except double-enders have one additional lofting problem in common, and that is the development of the transom or stern board (unless it is flat across and vertically plumb).

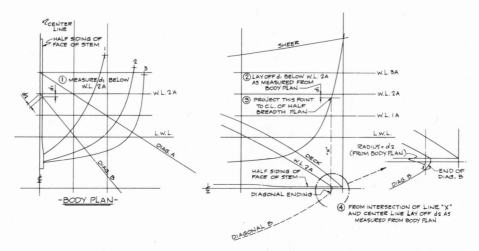

Figure 7-10. *Four steps in finding the correct ending of a diagonal that crosses the face of the stem.*

Projected Transom

After the sections have been faired satisfactorily, it is time to consider the development of the true shape of the transom or stern board of the boat. Sometimes, the transom is plumb vertical, in which case the section drawn at the transom station is actually the shape of the transom. More often, the transom is raked, with the result that its true shape does not appear in the body plan. This view is meaningless to the builder and need not be reproduced full size on the mold loft floor. The same is true of the plan view of the transom, although it may be useful for obtaining transom bevels.

The only way that a true view, and thus a pattern, of a raked transom can be gotten is if its shape is projected square off its centerline in the profile view.

Flat Transom Development

Development of the shape of the transom is sometimes puzzling to the builder, but there is nothing really mysterious about the work. The 12′ rowboat has a flat transom of the simplest type, and its transom shape development is shown in Figure 7-11. The rake of the transom in profile has, of course, been previously drawn from dimensions given on the architect's lines plan. For ease of illustration, the centerline for the developed transom has been drawn at the stern end of the lines in Figure 7-11, but this is not necessary and it may be located on a separate board or piece of paper.

The transom is just the same as any section, except that it is located at an angle with the baseline instead of perpendicular to it. Points on the transom are taken from the waterlines and buttocks the same as ordinary sections: it is merely a matter of picking up the waterline half-breadths and buttock heights at the right places and transferring them to the development drawing.

If you have space for the transom drawing at the end of your lines, as shown in

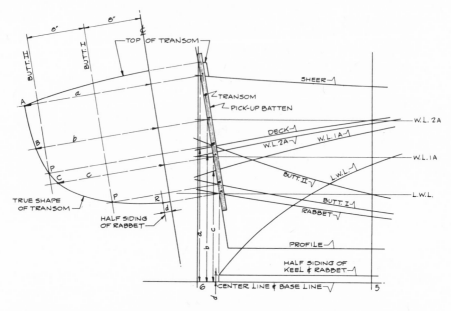

Figure 7-11. *Development of a flat transom.*

Figure 7-11, the development is exactly as indicated in the diagram. However, if you must locate the grid for the transom plan elsewhere, there is one important point to remember throughout the development, or you may end up with a stern board that will not fit as it should. On the profile drawing of the lines the waterlines are spaced 5″ apart above the L.W.L., but due to the profile angle of the transom, the distance between the waterlines drawn across the transom grid is obviously greater than 5″. Therefore, when laying out the grid, the spacing must be carefully measured *along the centerline* of the transom.

In Figure 7-11 the centerline for the transom grid has been drawn parallel to the rake of the transom, and then the intersections of waterlines and the sheer with the transom in profile are projected across the centerline together with projections of the buttock and rabbet intersections with the transom's face. With a flat transom, as in the design for this rowboat, you can lay off the spacing of the buttocks the same as they are on the body and the half-breadth plans, and draw them in the grid parallel to the transom centerline. Two points, P, are established on the transom development where the buttocks thus drawn cross the lines projected from the buttocks in profile. Lay off d, the width of the rabbet, to locate another point, R.

Now project the intersections of the waterlines and buttocks with the transom profile down to the centerline of the half-breadth plan. The waterline half-breadths a, b, and c are picked up with a batten and laid off as points A, B, and C on the corresponding lines in the grid. With all the points spotted, draw in the transom with a batten the same as you did the regular sections.

If you must draw the transom on a separate sheet, very carefully pick up the spacing of the intersections along the profile of the transom on a batten, as shown in Figure 7-11, and complete location of points as described above.

The shape thus developed describes the transom's outside face, and for a metal transom this is all that has to be done. In a wooden hull, however, the transom consists of the planking and the frame, and professionals add the thickness of the parts together and develop another shape the resulting distance forward of the first. This gives the shape of the forward face of the transom frame and, consequently, the bevels. This will become clear when we discuss hull construction.

Curved Transom Development

A curved transom on either a sailboat or powerboat is very handsome, and although the development is more involved than for the flat type, the extra work is worthwhile when the transom's finished appearance is considered. From the aesthetic viewpoint, a curved transom is not generally necessary on small craft up to 20 or 25 feet overall, but above this range the curved transom becomes a necessity, and for good looks it is an absolute must on a hull with an overhanging counter stern. This type is the most difficult to develop, due to the combination of the radius to which it is built and the angle of the transom in profile. The planks forming such a transom are bent to the arc of a circle with a radius perpendicular to the after side of the transom as seen in profile. A pattern for the shape must be made, and this is accomplished as though a cylinder were cut and rolled out flat.

A transom proportioned as shown in Figure 7-12 is developed principally with buttocks, because they cross the edges of the transom more nearly at right angles than do the waterlines, and thus are the most accurate. By this time you are familiar with buttocks and must realize that those on the architect's lines plan are not the only ones it is possible to have on a hull. There are an infinite number, and they may be spaced as closely as needed to help you make proper templates for parts. The stern in Figure 7-12 has been purposely drawn with enough buttocks to develop the transom accurately, but ordinarily, extra buttocks for development of the transom must be added between those shown on the lines plan.

Before the transom is attempted, the hull lines have been completely faired full size, usually to a station beyond the transom. To be sure of the shape of his hull, the architect designs to a vertical station at the extreme stern and then cuts it off at the desired angle in profile and in a radius in the plan view as mentioned above.

There are undoubtedly many methods of transom development in use and sworn to by their advocates. However, the system illustrated here will at least help the reader understand the principle. To avoid confusion, the profile and half-breadth plans of the stern in Figure 7-12 have been drawn separated and the transom radius made smaller than usual to clarify the drawing. Dashed lines show the projection of one view to another. After following the development of the flat transom in Figure 7-11, the use of the buttocks in Figure 7-12 is obvious, with the exception of their spacing in the grid for the expansion.

Extend the after side of the transom in profile up clear of other drawings, Figure 7-12A, and draw a centerline perpendicular to it. Tangent to the intersection, swing an arc of radius as shown on the plans. This is the curve to which the transom planking will be bent when it is built. Draw the buttocks parallel to the centerline, spaced the same as in the half-breadth plan. Project the intersections of the buttocks with the arc down to cross the corresponding buttocks in the profile view. Now prepare the grid for the expanded transom, Figure 7-12B, spacing the buttocks out from the centerline as measured *around the arc* instead of as laid out in the half-breadth plan. These

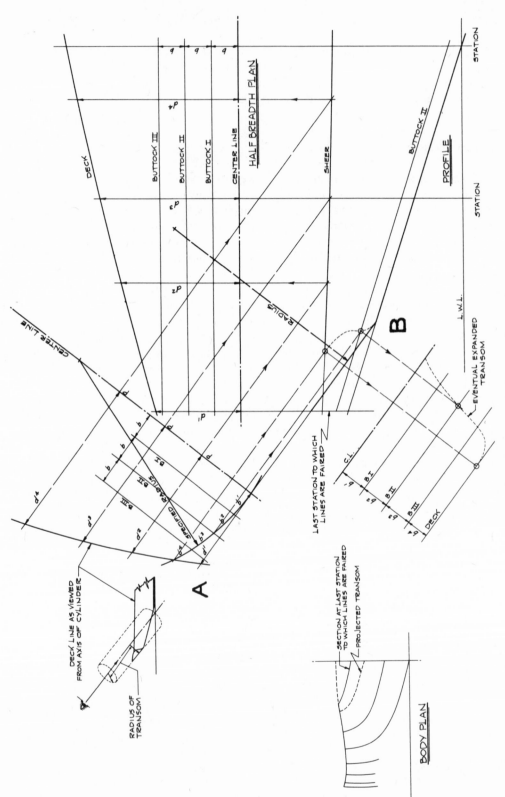

Figure 7-12. *Steps in the development of a curved transom.*

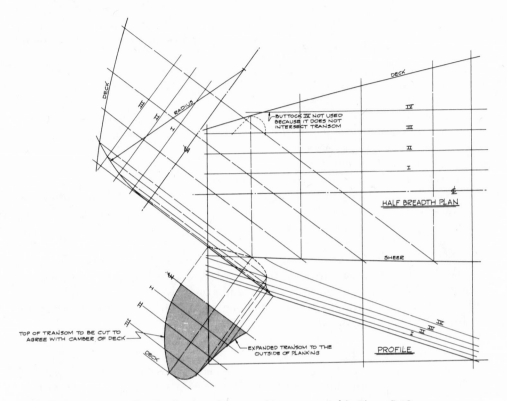

Figure 7–13. *The complete development of the curved transom started in Figure 7-12.*

measurements give the true distances between the buttocks when the cylindrical transom is rolled out flat. Project the buttocks in profile to the grid to obtain points on the edge of the transom as was done in the flat transom, Figure 7-11. For clarity only one buttock, Buttock II, has been used as an example in Figure 7-12.

In order to find the point where the transom terminates at the sheerline, the deck line is drawn in the auxiliary projection shown in Figure 7-12A. To draw the deck line in this view, select convenient points (P) along the projection's centerline; square them above the centerline and also down to cross the sheer on the profile; and then square the points of intersection with the sheer parallel to the stations to cross the deck line in the half-breadth plan. The widths of the deck at these points are lifted, transferred to the auxiliary projection, and a batten is run through them. The corner of the transom at the deck is located where the deck line intersects the arc of the transom. The half-breadth of the point is measured from the centerline around the arc and duly transferred to the grid.

Elliptical Transom Development

Curved transoms on "traditional" hull designs such as Grand Banks schooners and many yachts patterned after the type do not have a sharp corner at the intersection of deck and transom; the resulting shape is then elliptical when viewed from astern. This shape really blends well with a saucy sheerline and a spoon bow or a clipper bow. To prove that the development of an elliptical transom is not a recent problem, reproduced here is a development method drawn by naval architect R.B. Cook in 1913.

Mr. Cook's method has been redrawn in order to reproduce properly; the original hand-written instructions are best understood in print as follows:

1.   Fair out lines completely before attempting development of transom.

2.   Draw top of deck at centerline in profile, crossing transom face at A. Project this intersection to A′ and A″ as shown.

3.   From A′ sweep desired arc representing deck ending, A′B. Project B′ and B″. B′ is the first point in the profile of the transom.

4.   Using point B″ as a guide, sketch transom in body plan to conform in general to last station. Cross with closely spaced waterlines 1, 2, 3, etc., and project them to the sheer plan; project intersections with the transom face to half-breadth plan.

5.   From B′ draw a line *parallel to waterline*, intersecting transom face at D. Project to centerline of half-breadth plan, point D′. Sweep arc D′B. With same radius sweep arcs from 1, 2, 3, etc., pick up half-breadths on body plan of 1, 2, 3, etc., and lay off on half-breadth plan as *chords to arcs*, resulting in points 1′, 2′, 3′ etc., giving shape of half-breadth projection of transom face.

6.   Project points 1′, 2′, 3′, etc. to the profile to intersect the waterlines projected from the body plan, then draw the edge of the transom in profile.

Note: The arcs 1-1′, 2-2′, 3-3′, etc. are sections through the transom face parallel to the waterline. The true amount of curvature is measured perpendicular to the face of the transom, as at E-F.

Although Mr. Cook showed on his drawing how buttocks can be used to generate additional points on the transom edge, he did not mention this in his instructions. Nevertheless, that procedure is presented (and repeated) elsewhere in this chapter.

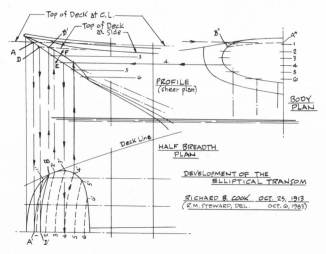

Figure 7-14.

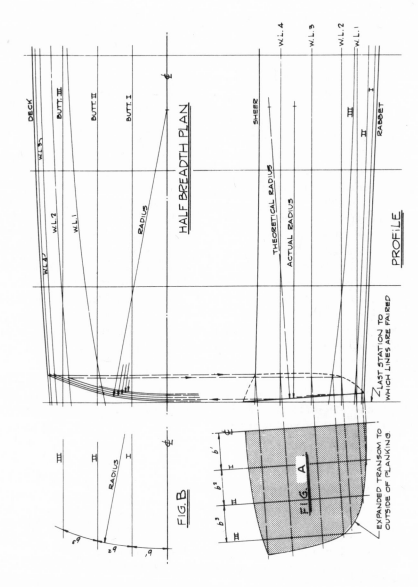

Figure 7–15. *The development of a curved transom having little rake.*

Powerboat Transoms

Sailboat transoms often have considerable rake, as shown in Figures 7-12 and 7-13, but there is usually little angle to those on modern power cruisers. A small amount of rake may be neglected in the development of the transom, and the radius can be drawn directly on the half-breadth plan, as will be explained.

Many powerboat transoms have "tumblehome"—that is, the deck half-breadth at the transom is less than the half-breadths of some of the waterlines between the L.W.L. and the deck. The transom in Figure 7-14 has tumblehome even though it is not a powerboat. Regardless of the type of hull, tumblehome causes waterlines to pile up on each other in the half-breadth plan, which can become very confusing. This is a good reason to use colored pencils to distinguish one waterline from another.

Draw the profile angle of the transom and project every intersection of it with the profile view of a waterline or buttock up to the centerline in the half-breadth plan. Holding the specified radius constant throughout, swing an arc from each of the projected points on the centerline (using the C.L. as center for the radius) until the arc crosses the line on the half-breadth plan corresponding to the line in profile. Project the half-breadth intersections with the arcs back down to the corresponding lines in profile and then across to the grid, Figure 7-15A. Of course it is important that the buttocks on the grid are spaced as measured around the arc, Figure 7-15B.

The development is the shape of the outside edge of the transom planking, but allowance must be made for the bevel on the edges, which causes the transom to be larger on the inside than on the outside face. When making the transom frame, the planking thickness must be deducted before the allowance for beveling can be made.

Computer-Aided Lines Fairing

The purpose of much of the work described in this chapter is to correct errors in the designer's or architect's lines drawing. Errors creep in due to the necessity of making a small-scale drawing, due to mistakes made in reading the offsets, and due sometimes to sloppy draftsmanship. It may not pay an amateur to depart from the time-tested methods of lofting and mold-making, but the professional should certainly investigate services that fair hull lines by computer. Such computers fair the lines from the table of offsets, resulting in corrected offsets reading to one-sixteenth of an inch or one hundredth of a foot. (It is easy to lay out offsets in feet and decimals with an ordinary surveyor's six-foot folding rule.) A logical extension of computer-aided lines fairing is the full size drawing of the body plan, and this is discussed in the next chapter.

I have used firms supplying computer-guided lofting for hulls up to 78 feet in length. Such lofting is available from Justin E. Kerwin, 25 Hallett Hill Road, Weston, MA 02193; Bristolcomp, c/o Halsey C. Herreshoff, Inc., 18 Burnside Street, Bristol, RI 02809; and Hullforms, Inc., 3667 Woodland Drive, RD #3, Baldwinsville, NY 13027.

Chapter 8

MOLDS, TEMPLATES, AND THE BACKBONE

Upon completion of the full size drawings of the lines for the hull, the builder is at last ready to start cutting wood, be it for frames for a sawn-frame boat or for molds for a round-bottomed hull or a male plug for a fiberglass or cold-molded wooden hull.

Molds are made from the body plan, and because they are only temporary, they are made from lower grade lumber than that used for the boat parts. Any lumber except hardwood is suitable, the thickness of the molds varying with the size of the boat. A rough guide is ¾" for boats to 16', ⅞" for 16 to 24', and 1" or 1⅛" for 30-footers. As you will see further along, the molds are set up on the backbone or keel of the boat, and strips of wood called ribbands are bent around the molds similar to planking, except that ribbands have spaces between them. The frames for a round-bottomed boat are bent to shape against the ribbands. There are two schools of thought as to whether the frames should be bent inside or outside of the ribbands, but it will be observed as experience is gained that setting up the frame for the boat is simplified when the frames are bent inside the ribbands. When a number of boats are to be built alike it is advantageous to make a permanent mold, in which case the frames are bent outside and the mold is removed for further use when the hull has been planked. Also, when a round-bottomed hull is built upside down the frames are bent on the outside.

The lines for the 12-footer in Figure 7-3, like those for all small boats, are drawn to the outside of planking, and the full-size lines are lofted accordingly. For setups where the frames are bent *inside* the ribbands, the molds for the sections are made only after the thickness of the planking has been deducted. Similarly, frames for conventional v-bottomed boats are made only after the thickness of planking has been deducted.

It should be obvious after you have studied construction that to make a mold for a round-bottomed boat with the frames bent on the *outside* of the ribbands, the combined thickness of planking, framing, and ribbands must be deducted from the sections that are drawn to the outside of the planking.

101

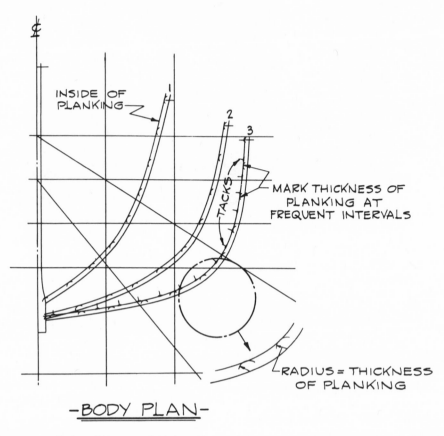

Figure 8–1. *Planking thickness can be deducted by simply drawing a parallel section inside the true sections by the amount of planking thickness. However, this is not the most accurate method.*

For methods other than conventional wooden construction, the ways of getting the deductions depend upon the peculiarities of each construction type. To make a male plug that will be used to form a female mold for a fiberglass hull, only the thickness of the plug planking or covering need be deducted. To make a male mold (or plug or jig—call it what you will) for a so-called one-off fiberglass sandwich hull as described in the chapter on Fiberglass and Other Hull Materials, the deduction must be equal to the *outer* fiberglass skin thickness plus the core material thickness plus the ribband thickness. To make a male mold for a cold-molded hull, the deduction must be equal to the total thickness of the hull planking plus the thickness of the mold planking or ribbands.

Countless boats have been built from molds where planking thickness was deducted by simply drawing lines inside the sections by the amount of the planking thickness. *However, this method is only acceptable when the planking is thin.* Let me try to simplify this. If a hole was drilled through the planking, and the thickness of the planking was measured in the hole, the planking would measure correctly *only if the hole were at right angles (normal) to the surface of the hull.* (*See* Figure 8-2.) By the same token, such a hole would only represent a truly accurate deduction when *the hole itself* lies in

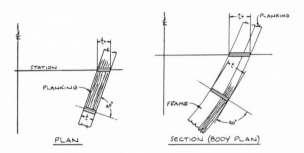

Figure 8-2.

the same athwartships plane as the stations. Thus, in a shapely hull, the deductions would be fairly accurate amidships, where the plan view waterlines run approximately parallel to the hull's centerline, but as the waterlines break away sharply toward the centerline as one progresses to the ends of the hull, the deductions would become increasingly inaccurate.

Unless the planking is thin, it is best to take a little more time and make an effort to deduct planking thickness more accurately. To make the thickness deduction almost absolutely correct, it should be done on the diagonals, even to the extent of adding diagonals in addition to those shown on the lines plan, but this chore is not necessary in most cases. Rather than use this procedure, at each station lay off the planking thickness parallel to the waterlines in the plan view of the lines, then pick up this thickness along the station line and transfer it to the body plan, laying it off normal to the section. (*See* Figure 8-3.) When this has been done at each waterline, take a batten and draw through all the points to get the inside of planking. Once you have done this for a few points the work will go quite rapidly.

When all the sections have been redrawn to the inside of planking, the molds for a round-bottomed boat can be made (unless additional deductions are required, depending on construction alternatives, as explained earlier in this chapter). Figure 8-4 shows typical mold construction and Figure 8-1 shows how the shape of the section is transferred to the mold stock by pressing the lumber down against closely spaced tacks with their heads laid on the line to be reproduced. Turn the wood over, use a batten to connect the marks made by the tack heads, then work the board to the line. Do this for each station.

It is not practical to use boards wide enough to get out an entire half mold all in one piece. Therefore, the mold is made in as many parts as necessary, and laid out in any convenient manner to suit the lumber stock. Just remember that the mold must not be too flimsy. Normally the mold should be extended a half foot or so above the sheerline, but if it is planned to build the boat upside down—a logical method for some small craft—the molds should be extended to a straight baseline above the sheer that represents the building floor. (*See* Figure 9-1.) Depending on the size of the boat, the inverted baseline is made parallel to the waterlines, and at a height enabling the greater part of the hull to be planked from a normal standing position.

Lay the mold parts on the sections of the body plan while carefully fastening them together with screws and butt blocks. Before the half mold is lifted from the plan,

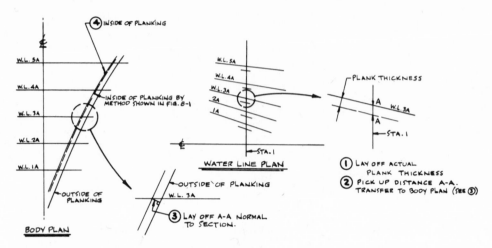

Figure 8-3. *This method of deducting planking thickness is more accurate than that shown in Figure 8-1.*

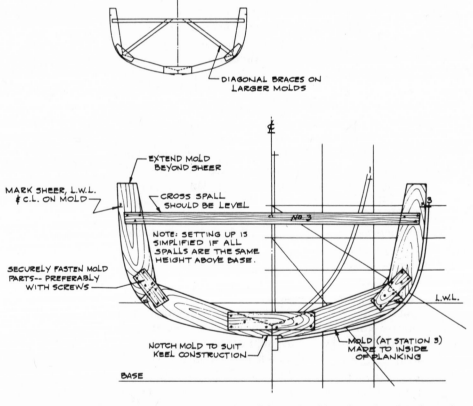

Figure 8-4. *Typical mold construction. Molds must be well fastened and braced to retain their shape when set up.*

mark it at the deck line and L.W.L. for reference while setting up and building. Turn the first half of the mold over so that the butt blocks are down and make a second half to match it. When the mold is assembled, the butt blocks will then all be on the same side. Connect the two halves at the bottom with a block, which should be notched if required by the keel construction, and fasten a crosspiece, called a spall, at or near the deck line. Spalls on all molds should be level, and if they all are located at the same height above the waterline or base, the molds will be easier to align when set up on the keel or floor.

Stem and Rabbet

The stem assembly is drawn on the full-size lines, either as dimensioned on the construction plan or, lacking dimensions, from widths scaled from the construction plan. In boatbuilding language the widths of the stem are the molded dimensions, whereas the thickness of the material for the stem is the sided dimension. Ideally, a stem for a small craft like a dinghy should be made from a natural hackmatack or oak crook as they were some years ago. This is still possible in New England. A template of the stem would be taken to the dealer in this material to select a crook with a shape similar to the stem. But it seems very few people bother with this method any more.

Most often the stem is too large to get out of a natural crook, so an assembly of wood will be made up as illustrated in Figure 8-5 or the stem assembly will be laminated. For the amateur, who does not usually count labor, a lamination is often the best way. When an assembly of parts is used, templates of the parts are made, the lines being transferred with tacks as explained for the molds in Figure 8-1. Templates are made of easily worked softwood ⅛″ to ⅜″ thick; ⅛″ or ¼″ plywood; ⅛″ hardboard such as Masonite; or lofting paper (*see* The Mold Loft, Chapter 7). Besides representing the shapes of the parts, the templates must also provide guidelines for rabbeting the stem assembly to receive the planking.

The profile of the rabbet line may or may not be dimensioned on the lines or construction plan, and even though it is shown, it should be checked full size for accuracy and fairness. The width or half-breadth of the rabbet line is generally the same as the siding of the stem and either retains a constant width throughout the length of the boat or swells in width toward amidships and then narrows again toward the stern.

It was mentioned before that countless boats have been built from molds made by deducting the thickness of planking by a less-than-precise method, and so it is with the stem rabbet. I will discuss this first and then explain how to lay out the rabbet by a more precise method that consumes but little more time.

Note in Figure 8-5 that the half-breadth of the stem (the "half siding" or one-half the thickness) has been drawn as well as the half siding of the face of the stem, and on each waterline half-breadth the thickness of planking has been drawn to get the back rabbet and bearding lines to which the material must be cut. The nomenclature is shown on the section through the stem drawn on waterline 4A in the profile, Figure 8-5. Points to plot these lines on the profile are projected from the waterlines in the half-breadth plan to the waterlines in profile and connected with a batten. The lines for the

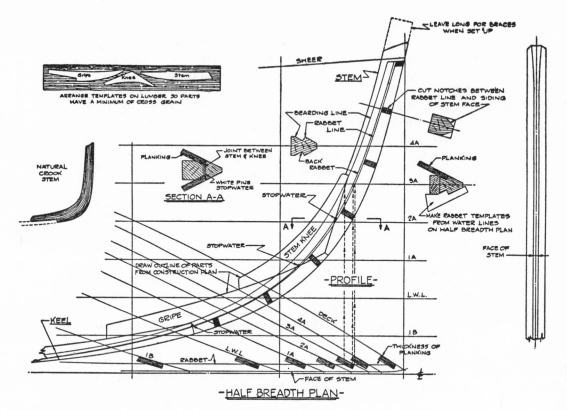

Figure 8–5.

rabbet and the outline of stem parts are all transferred to the template material at the same time.

The templates are laid out on the stem material and arranged so that there will be a minimum of cross grain in the finished part. Cut and plane the parts to shape (if too heavy for your equipment have a mill do this for you) and lay them out on the full-size lines to check the alignment of the joints in the assembled position. Mark the sheerline, all the waterlines, and the centerlines of the bolts; then bore the bolt holes and put the stem assembly together with a good bedding compound—for example, Dolfinite 2005N, 3M 5200, Boatlife caulk, or thick white lead (if available)—generously applied between the faying surfaces of the joints. (Faying surfaces are those in contact with each other.) Whether or not the bolt heads are countersunk and plugged, you should take an extra precaution to make the bolt holes watertight by using a grommet. This is a piece of cotton wicking caulking long enough to go around the bolt a couple of times. In some locales you may hunt in vain for the proper cotton wicking, which is not at all like kerosene lamp wicking; it is available from Jamestown Distributors (*see* Chapter 6). Apply bedding generously to the wicking and wind it around the bolt beneath the head just before the bolt is driven all the way home. After assembly of the stem, mark the centerline of the boat on the stem and the width of the stem face on each side of the centerline.

Referring to the half-breadth plan in the figure, make a template of stiff cardboard or thin wood for the rabbet at each waterline. Use the templates to cut a short length of the rabbet at the waterlines, and then complete the rabbet by working away the material between the templated cuts on the waterline. The rabbet may be cut with confidence if the full-size drawing is *accurate* and complete. However, even some professionals leave the rabbet just a little shallow and complete it when fitting ribbands at the time the boat is set up. In many cases this is because they have learned from experience that their rabbet is not as accurate as it might be. Here is how you can make it more accurate.

In the beginning of Chapter 7 it was stated that vertical sections are drawn at intervals throughout the length of the boat to define the shape of the hull, but it should be realized that sections can be drawn through the hull at any angle, not only at the vertical planes of the stations and buttocks, the horizontal planes of the waterlines, or the diagonal planes. The designer often does this while drawing the construction plan to get the true, accurate sizes of parts such as the stem assembly; only when a section is drawn normal to the part is full accuracy assured. Since the waterlines and buttocks are the most out-of-normal to the hull surface at the bow (and at the stern of double-ended hulls), it certainly pays to draw auxiliary sections at right angles through the stem of the boat in order to more accurately cut the rabbet.

It is well to note here that for the same reasons of accuracy, bevels should be taken off lines that are normal to the hull surface, or nearly so.

Figure 8-6 has been prepared to show how easy it is to draw sections through the stem (or the sternpost of a double-ender). The sections should be spaced at intervals close enough so that there is no question about having enough of the plotted points

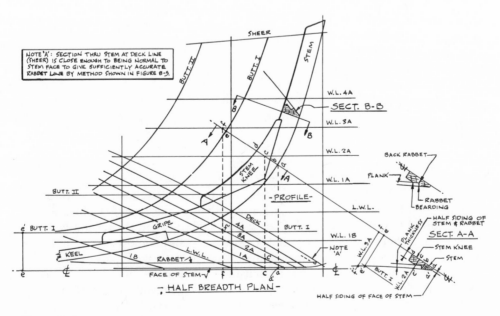

Figure 8-6.

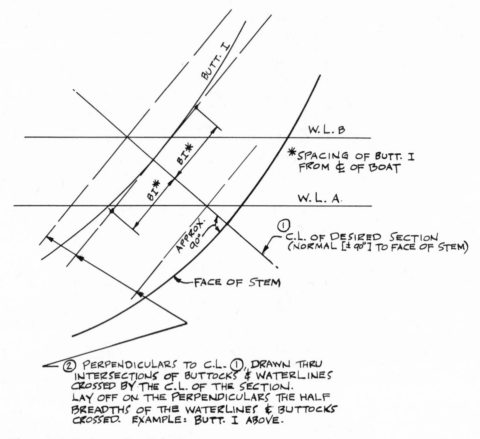

Figure 8–7. *Setting up the grid for drawing stem sections in place on the profile.*

for the rabbet, back rabbet, and bearding lines (*see* Figure 8-5) to ensure a fair line. To save time and effort, the sections should be drawn right on the lines profile, as in Section B-B of Figure 8-6, rather than apart as was done for clarity in Section A-A.

First a centerline is drawn normal to the face of the stem, long enough to cross enough buttocks and waterlines to give a number of points so a batten can be set up to draw a fair section. For instance, the centerline for Section A-A intersects two waterlines and a buttock. Then perpendiculars to this centerline are drawn at the waterline and buttock intersections and at the joints in the stem assembly. (For an illustration of how these perpendiculars can be laid off when the section is drawn directly on the lines profile, *see* Figure 8-7.) Next the half-breadths at these points of intersection are picked up as in the plan view and laid off on the perpendiculars to establish the points for the section to the outside of planking (Section A-A of Figure 8-6). After the section line has been drawn, the thickness of planking is set off, and this sets up the points for the rabbet, back rabbet, and the bearding line.

Instead of making templates for the rabbet from the half-breadth plan in the

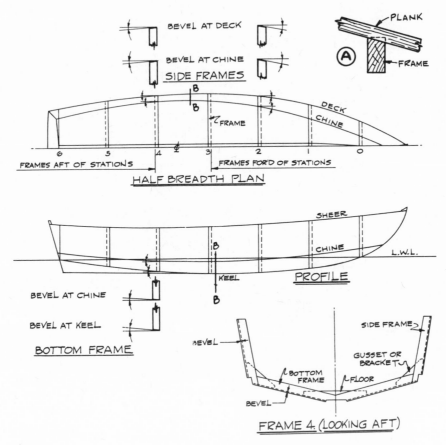

Figure 8–8

method shown by Figure 8-5, make them from the more accurate sections drawn on the profile as illustrated by Figure 8-6.

Stopwaters

Softwood dowels called stopwaters are fitted in joints in the backbone to prevent water from leaking into the hull along the joints. The locations of stopwaters is important for full effectiveness; it is imperative that they be placed wherever the rabbet crosses a joint in the backbone. Any durable softwood such as white pine or cedar will do, and there are so few of them that they can be whittled out of scrap, but they must be as round as the bored hole and a snug fit. Stopwaters are indicated in Figure 8-5 and in larger detail in Figure 8-9. It is tricky to start a drill in the right direction on the surface of the rabbet, so try tacking a piece of softwood on the side of the joint to provide a flat surface (*see* A, Figure 8-9).

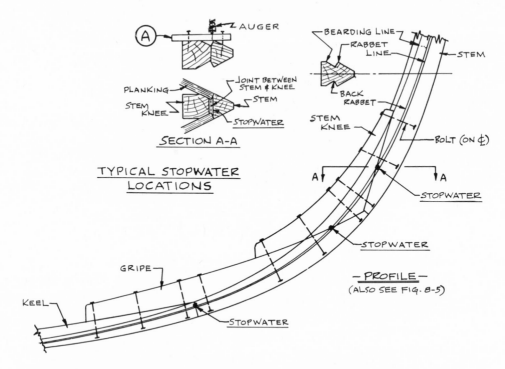

Figure 8–9. *Stopwaters are extremely important to prevent a leak into the hull wherever a joint in the stern, keel, etc. crosses the plank rabbet line.*

V-Bottomed Hull Frames

Temporary molds are not necessary for the construction of v-bottomed and arc-bottomed hulls. Instead, the body plan is used to make frames that become a permanent part of the structure. Typical v- and arc-bottomed hull frames are shown in Figures 1-3 and 1-4 in Chapter 1, but these sectional views do not reveal that the bottom and side pieces are beveled so the planking will bear against the entire siding of the frames. (*See* A of Figure 8-8 and Figure 8-10.) Note that the bevel—with rare exceptions—is *not* the same at the sheer as it is at the chine. This makes for more work, but this is the nature of boat hulls. The character, or curvature, of the deck line and chine, etc., determines the amount of bevel. At Section B-B in Figure 8-8, where the deck line and chine are approximately parallel to the centerline, it can be seen that there is practically no bevel needed. However, as the deck and chine curve in toward the centerline, forward and aft of B-B, the frames must be beveled.

For a simple boat with straight sections like that shown in Figure 8-8, the bevels can be measured as indicated—the side frame bevels at deck and chine in the half-breadth plan and those for the bottom frames at chine and keel in the profile. The bevels are cut in a straight line between deck and chine and between chine and keel respectively. If the frames have some curve, the bevels at major points as described above are just the same, but those for the side frames at points between the deck and chine are taken

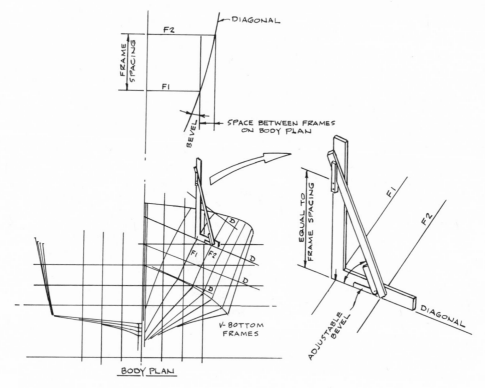

Figure 8–10.

from the waterlines in the half-breadth plan; those for the bottom frames at points between the chine and the keel are taken from the buttocks in the profile. Bevels for the notches in which the keel, chines, and clamps are fitted are taken off similarly or cut later when the boat is set up. At that time, battens for fairing the frames are run in and bevel adjustments are made by planing the frames.

To determine bevels with more accuracy, however (and this is very important to time saving in the larger hulls with a good number of frames), the bevels should be measured *normal* to the surface, much like the deduction for planking thickness previously discussed. This can be done by the method shown in Figure 8-10. The square can be made up by the builder and applied as shown to measure the bevels. Once gotten, the bevels should be marked right on the body plan in degrees for reference and then marked on the actual frame material so that it can be sawn to shape with the proper bevel. The bevels should be taken along diagonals laid out to be as close to normal as possible to all the frames crossed.

Bevel Board

Instead of using a protractor to measure a bevel each time you take one off, make yourself a simple bevel board as shown in Figure 8-11. Use a piece of plywood about

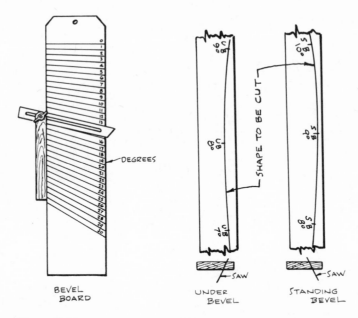

Figure 8-11.

3½″ wide and mark off angles from zero to about 30 degrees. Slide the adjustable bevel along the left edge of the bevel board until it lines up with one of the angles and read it off.

When a bevel is marked on a piece of stock to be sawn, it must be designated as either *under* or *standing*, marking the piece UB or SB. This is most important, and after you have ruined a few pieces, you will understand the principle.

Lofting by Computer

Fairing hull lines with the aid of a computer was mentioned in the previous chapter, which dealt with enlarging to full size the designer's scale drawing of the set of lines defining the shape of the outside of the hull, whether it be wood, metal, fiberglass, or otherwise. Earlier in this chapter it was explained that for round-bottomed hulls molds are needed to make a male framework on which to shape the frames and that for v-bottomed hulls frames are needed on which to build the boat. Here is where fairing by computer pays off if your project justifies the expense. A computer-guided plotter can draw full-size sections through the hull (spaced either equally or unequally) at any location desired, complete with deductions from the outside of the hull.

If lofting by computer is used, most of the lofting in the yard is avoided, but the bevels for the edges of the molds or frames will not be available to you. Therefore, you must order bevels from the computer people. Be certain that you understand how the bevels given by the computer should be applied to the section drawings. An explanation will be furnished, along with probably two or three times as many bevels as you really need. There's just no stopping that computer, but better too many bevels than too few!

The mold spacing for round-bottomed hulls and the frame spacing for v-bottomed hulls is usually at uniform intervals. Sometimes the location of joiner bulkheads, those partitions dividing the cabin accommodations, etc., are not located in the same place as molds or frames. If full-size bulkhead drawings are desired, these, too, can be supplied by the computer service, and once again you should ask for the edge bevels.

Many of the larger boats are built of welded steel or aluminum alloy framing, with a skin or shell plating of the same material. For this type of construction the computer service can supply full-size drawings from which to cut the frames to shape from flat material, so the drawings should be ordered with the deduction for the thickness of the shell plating.

Transom and Transom Bevels

As will be seen later, the station molds, the stem, and the transom are needed before the boat can be set up. The molds and the stem have been explained and the development of the transom shape has been illustrated. You also need the bevels on the transom edges. Remember that the developed shape of the transom is to the outside of the planking, and depending upon the type of construction, it may or may not represent the actual size of the finished transom. The simplest method is to let the side planking overlap the transom and to then cut it flush with the after side. In this case the plank thickness is subtracted from the edges of the transom. The best practice, however, is to make the transom to the outside of the planking and rabbet the edge for the planking. Both methods are shown in Figure 8-12.

Figure 8-12A shows that the inside of the transom is larger than the outside, except at the top edge where the shape depends upon the construction details, because the boat narrows from amidships to the transom. Consequently, like the frames of a v-bottomed boat, the edges of the transom must be beveled to allow the planks to lie flat. The bevels are taken from the full-size lines as shown—those for the sides from the waterlines in the half-breadth plan and those for the bottom from the buttocks in the profile drawing. But once again it should be remembered that this is not the most accurate way to take the bevels off, because it has not been done normal to the surface of the hull by the method shown in Figure 8-10.

Small boat transoms are generally made of wide boards whose edges are splined or doweled and waterproof glued. The boards should be sufficiently thick so that the hull planks can be properly fastened to the edge. Such transoms can also be made of marine plywood, with cheek pieces around the edges to take the plank fastenings. Larger transoms, like that shown in Figure 8-12C, are made the same thickness as the hull planking or thicker and have a frame or cheek pieces on the inside edges to take a share of the plank fastenings. There is usually a vertical member on the centerline, where a wood or metal knee connects the transom to the keel or horn timber. For the sake of appearance, the seams of transom planks are not caulked. If single planked, the seams of the larger transoms are usually backed with battens. Wide transoms also

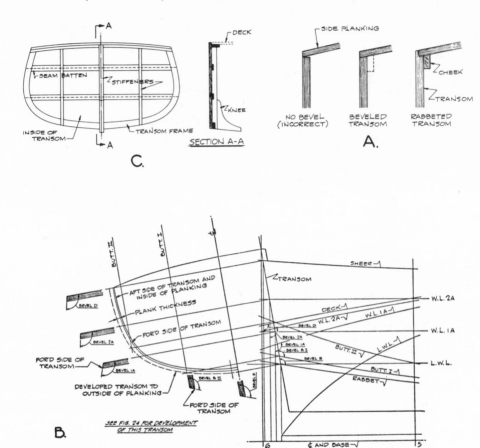

Figure 8–12.

have a series of vertical stiffeners outboard of the centerline. In a powerboat hull these are frequently spaced to bolt to the ends of full-length engine stringers.

Most transoms do not have enough radius to prevent the planks from being bent cold. In transoms that do have a lot of radius, the planks can be soaked with hot, wet rags or steamed so they will bend to the transom frame.

Keel and Deadwood

There are quite a number of keel construction methods, varying with the type of boat, the preference of the designer, and sometimes with the custom of a particular locality. The types most likely to be encountered are illustrated in Figures 8-13 and 8-14. Needless to say, for longevity, only sound timber should go into the backbone members. White oak is the usual material for keel and other backbone members. Wood from the very heart of a tree and sapwood should not be used. Other species of wood can be used as guided by local experience.

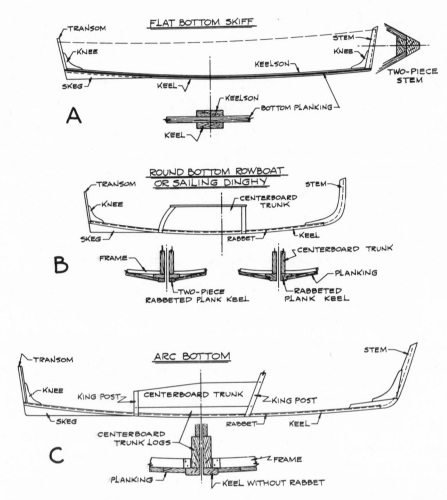

Figure 8-13. *Typical small boat keels.*

The flat-bottomed skiff construction shown in Figure 8-13A is very common. When building the boat upside down, the forms are notched for the keelson; then the bottom is cross planked and the keel fitted on top of the planking. Sometimes twin keelsons are used, one on each side instead of a single one on the centerline. Before fastening the keel, cut a slot for the skeg on the centerline aft. Straight stems are frequently made up of two pieces, as shown, to avoid rabbeting. The side planks are cut off flush with the inner stem, and then the outer stem is fastened to the inner, with sealant between the two.

The rabbeted keel in Figure 8-13B is typical construction for a great many boats. As was done for the stem in Figure 8-5, the rabbet should be cut at each station from templates and then cut away between the stations to make a continuous fair rabbet for the planking. The amateur will find it easier to make the two-piece keel if he fastens the pieces together over the molds after first beveling them to form the rabbet.

A generous amount of bedding compound should be applied to all backbone joints, as described earlier in the details of a stem assembly. Regardless of the type of backbone structure, this application is important in order to exclude any water between the joined pieces.

A few of the one-design sailboats use a keel without a rabbet, like that shown in Figure 8-13C. This is all right, but because the garboard plank (the one next to the keel on each side) is not fastened to the keel, care should be taken to attach the frames strongly to the keel. If the frames butt at the centerline, the floor timbers connecting the frame halves must be well fastened to the frames and keel. In way of the centerboard slot in the keel, the bed logs should be thick to make for good fastening through the keel.

Powerboat Keels

The keel structure shown in Figure 8-14A is typical of many modern powerboats. The keel is usually the same thickness throughout and is cut to shape from a template made from the full-size profile. A batten bent into place on top forms a back rabbet for the planking. The rabbet is cut the same as for the little boat in Figure 8-13B. The horn timber aft is rabbeted. A bronze shaft log with packing gland is installed for watertightness where the shaft leaves the hull. The bottom of the keel may be cut away or continued aft and fitted with a skeg to support the bottom of the rudder.

Note the two-piece wooden shaft log for a single-engine boat shown in Figure 8-14B. This is easier to make than a log in a single piece, because the shaft hole in each half can be worked out and grooves for splines can be cut on a table saw or with a plow plane. The purpose of the splines is to swell and prevent leaks in the same manner that stopwaters do, and they are made of softwood such as white pine. It is all right to cut through the splines with bolts so long as the bolt holes are tight. The splines swell against the bolts and function just as well as when not cut.

The semicircular grooves that form the shaft hole in a two-piece log can be made on a table saw or even with a portable circular saw by running a series of cuts of varying depths, then cleaning out with a plow plane or "worrying" with gouges. Most professionals prefer two-piece construction to the struggle of boring out a one-piece shaft log. I strongly recommend a two-piece unit.

It is very important that the shaft hole be lined with a light copper tube or lead pipe to exclude water from the wood around the hole. The ends of the tube are flanged under the bases of the stern bearing and stuffing box. Marine hardware makers such as Columbian Bronze offer an alternative method: stern bearing and stuffing box castings that are threaded to connect with a length of pipe, which serves as a shaft hole liner.

Fin-Keel Sailboats

Fin-keel sailboats up to about 30 feet may have bent keels like that shown in Figure 8-14C. Indeed even larger boats have had this type of construction, with keels thick enough to need steaming to bend the keel to shape. Probably the easiest way to build a

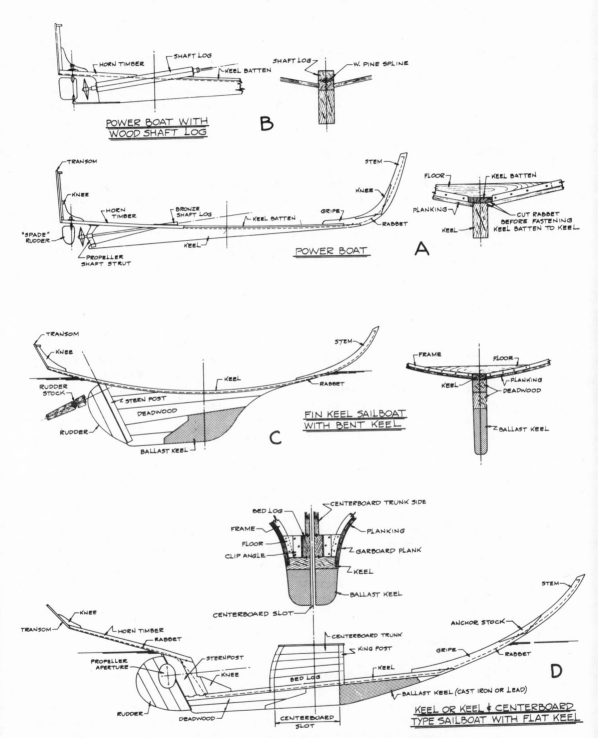

Figure 8-14. *A few of the many possible backbone structures for powerboats and sailboats.*

boat of this type is upside down, the keel being bent down over the molds and the fin keel added after the hull is turned over.

Attention must be given to the sequence of the bolting in order to properly fasten the fin. The ballast keel bolts usually extend from the casting through the deadwood, keel, and floors, although sometimes they terminate between frames. The deadwood is carefully shaped as called for by the lines. Although it requires hard work if done by hand (another very good reason to acquire a portable electric plane), a lot of effort should be put into the deadwood to make it smooth and fair, not only for the sake of appearance but also to offer a minimum of resistance as the boat moves through the water. The aft edge of the sternpost is gouged out to take the rudder stock and the rounded forward edge of the rudder. While the forward edge of the rudder can be painted by alternately swinging it hard over to each side, it is impossible to paint the concave edge of the sternpost. To prevent accumulation of marine growth, the after side of the sternpost is sheathed with light copper sheet brought around on the sides just enough for it to be fastened with tacks, or the groove can be fiberglassed. Either method is acceptable.

Large Sailboat Keels

The backbone in Figure 8-14D is typical of most keel sailboats or combination keel and centerboard sailboats upwards of 20 feet on the waterline. The keel in such boats is a thick plank of the same thickness from end to end, but varying in width throughout the length. It is rabbeted for the planking as shown in the section. The vertical position of the keel in the hull structure is drawn in on the full-size profile; then the heights of the keel at the stations it crosses are transferred to the corresponding sections in the body plan to obtain the half-widths of the keel at the stations. A centerline is drawn on the piece of lumber to be used for the keel, the station spacing is picked up and laid off from the full-size profile (the station spacing along the keel is greater than the spacing along the baseline because the keel is at an angle with the base), and the half-breadths of the top of the keel are picked up from the sections and laid off on the keel stock. Draw the outline of the keel with a batten. After the keel is sawn to the shape of the top edge, draw a centerline on the underside of the keel, making sure it aligns with the one on top, and similarly lay off the half-breadths of the keel bottom. The outline of the bottom will give the constantly changing bevel to which to cut the sides of the keel. The rabbet at each section is then templated as a guide for cutting, as mentioned before.

Gripe and Horn Timber

The gripe is the piece that connects the keel to the stem, and the horn timber connects the keel or sternpost to the transom in some types of power and sailboats. Both the gripe and horn timber are very similar to a stem. The rabbet for the comparatively horizontal horn timber is taken from the sections in the body plan. Knees are used to fasten the various backbone members to each other. Much of the backbone construction work is made clear by construction sections on the designer's plans.

Sternpost

The structure between the horn timber and the keel in Figure 8-14D and Figure 10-13, when designed as shown, can be bolted up without fouling the hole for the propeller shaft, but in this arrangement boring a hole for the shaft cannot be avoided. Normally a barefoot auger would be used, with an extension welded to the shank if necessary, and guides devised to keep the hole on course. One source for this auger is W.L. Fuller Inc., whose address is given at the end of Chapter 3. They will on request cut off the standard square end, leaving a round shank that is best powered by nothing less than a ½″ electric drill.

Backbone Bolting

After all the backbone members are shaped, but prior to fastening them together, it is recommended that they be given two coats of a wood preservative. These preparations are inexpensive and well worth the investment for their rot preventive qualities. The liquid should also be poured down the bolt holes before the fastenings are driven. Through-bolts and drift bolts, described at length in Chapter 6, are made and fitted as shown on the construction plan for the boat, and the fastenings must be studied for sequence so the assembly will go together properly. It will be seen as you go along that some of the bolts cannot be driven at this time because they pass through floor timbers (Figures 8-14A, C) that are not made and fitted in the structure until later. Once again it must be emphasized that all joints have bedding so that no crevices are left for water to seep through or to collect in and possibly start to rot the timbers. Under the washers of through and drift bolts it is advisable to wind a few turns of cotton wicking soaked in paint before the bolts are finally driven home. Very often this treatment will prevent leaks that otherwise would be troublesome or at least annoying. Wicking, and a source for it, were discussed earlier in this chapter under "Stem and Rabbet." The stopwaters mentioned earlier are fitted after the parts have been bolted.

Scarphs

It is not always possible to obtain pieces of wood long enough for the keel, deadwood, bilge stringers, clamps, and shelves. Fortunately, sufficient lengths may be found for keels more often than for the other parts, even though an extensive search is required. The backbone requires enough work of the builder without his having to splice the keel, particularly the type shown in Figure 8-14D. When it cannot be avoided, the long members are pieced out by means of through-bolted joints called scarphs. Nowadays these joints in wood are often waterproof-glued for good measure. If not glued, the joints must be bedded. Bolts are staggered when thickness of lumber permits.

   Figure 8-15 illustrates three types of scarphs commonly in use, and it should be noted that all have nibs to prevent one part from slipping by the other when under strain. The joint shown in A is the very common plain scarph that is extensively used for stringers and clamps. The hooked scarph, B, is sometimes employed in backbone

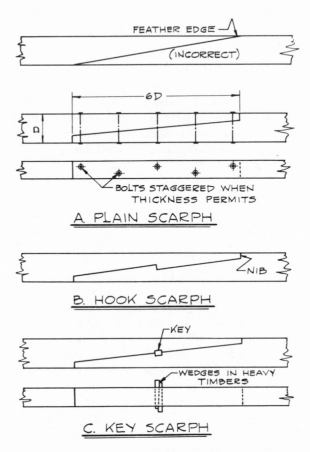

Figure 8-15. *Common scarphs for joining long members such as keels, clamps, and stringers.*

members. Just as effective, and easier to make, is the key scarph shown in C. This is simply a plain scarph mortised to take a tightly fitted rectangular key, preferably of durable wood like white oak. In large timbers the key is sometimes made of two wedges driven from both sides at the same time and cut off flush with the sides of the timbers. Such wedges are made with a taper of about one-half inch to the foot.

The scarph with feather edges at the top of Figure 8-15 is marked "incorrect," but if such a joint is properly fitted, adequately clamped (to prevent skidding out of alignment when pressure is applied), and glued with a waterproof adhesive, then this joint is satisfactory. As an adhesive I would use epoxy, thickened to avoid starving the joint. This material is gap-filling and does not require as much pressure as a resorcinol glue.

The scarphed joints and their fastenings may not be shown on the boat plans or specifications. A rough rule for the scarph length is six times the depth of the timber, while the keys and nibs are made up to one-fourth of the depth. If the inexperienced builder should not be able to locate a piece of wood large enough for the keel, the designer or a competent boatbuilder should be consulted for the layout of scarphs most suitable for use with the available material.

Tenons

The mortise-and-tenon joint is sometimes called upon to lock adjoining members having grain perpendicular to each other. The joints between the vertical sternposts and the keel in Figure 8-14D are typical. When the wood is not too thin, the tenon is made blind, that is, only part way across the pieces, and therefore it is not visible when the parts are fitted together. Whatever the case, the joint must be made as snug as possible and put together with bedding on the mating parts.

Chapter 9

SETTING UP

At this point it must be mentioned that the type of hull planking intended for a given boat will determine the setup needed to build that hull. *If you are not familiar with the various planking possibilities, refer to Chapter 11, Planking, before returning to the discussion below.*

With the backbone and molds made, the builder is ready to set up the boat preparatory to framing the hull. Just as much care and accuracy should go into the work of setting up as went into the mold loft work and construction of the backbone. Continued attention to detail at this stage will pay dividends in time saved later. The method of setting up depends upon the size, type, and construction of the hull, but in general, most small craft are best built upside down, a method that has much merit.

Regardless of the size or type of boat you are building, remember to take great care with your setup so that both sides of the hull will be *exactly* the same.

Upside Down or Right Side Up?

There was no question in the minds of the builders of the sailboats shown in Figures 9-5, 9-6, and 9-7 about how to set up; note that the ballast keels and deadwood for these boats are already in place.

On the other hand, the hull in Figure 9-9 is one of hundreds like it built upside down by this company, and for good reason: the hull shown will be planked double-diagonally. A fast and efficient method for overturning these hulls was devised early in their development.

With regard to wooden hulls, as well as wooden plugs for molded boats, size alone may not dictate whether to build right side up or upside down. As stated earlier, most small hulls—both sail and power—are best built upside down. This includes flat-, v-, and arc-bottomed hulls, because it is easier to fasten the bottom planks with the hull inverted. It also includes small round-bilged lapstrake hulls that are planked over molds; in this case the fitting of the lapped plank seams is generally simplified with the boat upside down. Cold molded hulls, too, are better planked upside down.

Strip-planked hulls, however, should be built right side up, because it is easier to nail the strips downhand, working from the keel to the sheer. Similarly, many builders of round-bottomed lapstrake hulls plank them right side up and then bend in the frames after the planking is completed.

If it has been decided to frame a round-bottomed boat by working on the inside of the ribbands as mentioned under Molds in Chapter 8, then the boat should be built right side up to facilitate bending the frames. Any other method would be impractical. In instances where the finished hull will be too heavy or bulky for the lone builder or amateur to turn over, the boat should be built upright.

Building Under Cover

Considering that weather can be a drawback if it should be cold and windy, or rainy, or very hot—then your hull should be built under cover if possible. A building also permits work to be done evenings under lights and provides convenient means of overhead bracing of molds and backbone to the roof rafters. A good solid floor is ideal, whether or not it is level and smooth. However, an outdoor construction site can be made to serve well, as many amateur builders have found from experience, although the task of bracing the frame is somewhat more difficult and weather can bring work to a halt for weeks at a time.

Building Upside Down

When building upside down, a grid must be established and the framework positioned on top of it accordingly. The following is a description of how the 12-foot skiff shown in Figure 9-1 might be set up in such a manner. A centerline is first drawn

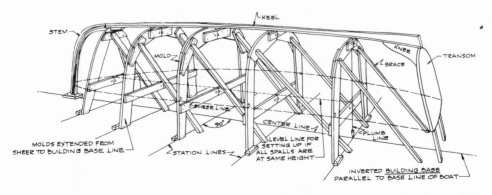

Figure 9-1. *The typical setup for building a small hull upside down, shown before the installation of the ribbands.*

in on the floor, the station spacing laid off along the centerline, and the station lines squared off from the centerline. As previously described, the molds for upside down building are extended beyond the sheer to an arbitrary inverted baseline parallel to the baseline of the boat and located above the highest point of the sheer by an amount calculated for convenient working height. The molds forward of amidships are set up on the aft side of the station lines, and those aft of amidships on the forward side of the station lines. The reason for this system will be obvious when the ribbands are applied. If the molds are set on the wrong sides of the station lines, the ribbands will be forced out of their proper position due to the shape of the hull, as shown in the sketch, Figure 9-2.

Use a plumb line to align the centerline of a mold with the boat centerline on the floor, and also use the plumb line or a level to align the upper part of a mold in a fore-and-aft direction. Fasten the molds to the floor with blocks and brace them securely against fore-and-aft movement. You will remember that it was pointed out in Chapter 8 that it would be helpful if the mold cross spalls were fitted at the same level on all molds; it is now that this fact is realized. If the building floor is not perfectly level, the line of the spalls can be used to determine where shims must be fitted between the floor and the ends of the molds to bring them to the proper height.

It must be emphasized that the utmost care should be taken to align the backbone and molds properly. An extra hour or two spent on this job will be appreciated when ribbands are fitted, frames are bent, and planking is shaped and fastened. The boat will not be the same on both sides if the setting up is not done accurately. The centerline and baseline, waterlines and station lines are all straight lines, and as such, enable the builder to erect the backbone and molds with the use of vertical and horizontal lines just as the designer laid out his lines plan and construction drawings. Shores and braces of sufficient number must be fitted to prevent movement of the structure in any direction. *Take your time here and be accurate.*

To continue setting up: drop the keel—with stem, transom, and knee attached—into position over the molds and screw the assembly to blocks on each mold. Secure the head of the stem to the building floor with blocks to hold it in position. Brace the transom after making sure it is raked to the correct angle and square across the boat. If everything has been done accurately, the station lines marked on the keel should coincide with the molds. If not, the frame is not properly aligned and must be

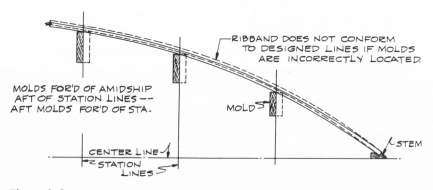

Figure 9-2.

corrected. One test of fairness is to bend a long batten, with its forward end laid in the stem rabbet, around the molds. The batten should test fair when tried anywhere from keel to the sheer. If not, test and adjust until the batten touches all the molds without forcing. The ribbands should not be installed until the molds have been aligned to your complete satisfaction.

Building Outdoors

When building boats outdoors, there are many arrangements that are workable, but probably the most satisfactory for upside down building is to use as a base a pair of substantial timbers longer than the boat. These should be secured to the ground on both sides of the centerline and made level. The cross spalls on the molds are fastened to the parallel timbers. Crosspieces are fastened between the timbers to take the stem head and the transom braces. For building right side up outdoors, timbers are placed on the ground athwartships at stations and staked solidly against movement. Keel supports are built up with blocks to the proper height, and shores are used to brace the mold laterally. (*See* Figure 9-3.) Once again, *take all the time you need to be accurate.*

Building Right Side Up

In the same manner as described for building upside down, a centerline and station lines are drawn for boats that are to be built right side up. Relatively narrow keels, like

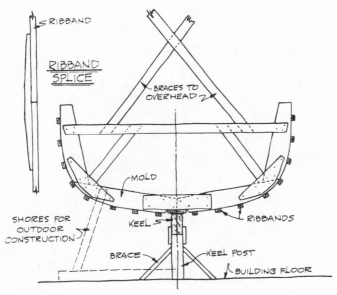

Figure 9-3.

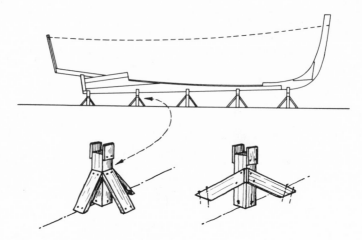

Figure 9–4. *Common forms of keel posts.*

those for motorboats, are set on posts erected at each station. The posts must be securely nailed to the floor and braced against movement, as shown in Figures 9-3 and 9-4. The heights of the posts are carefully measured from the full-size profile and checked with the keel template. Quite frequently, keels are held down on such posts by turnbuckles set up between eye bolts in the keel and floor near each end of the keel.

Figure 9–5. *The backbone of a Rhodes-designed ketch. Note the husky blocks under the deadwood, the shores to prevent side movement of the backbone, and the transom bracing to overhead.*

Figure 9-6. *The view from the stern quarter of a double-ended auxiliary after frames have been bent inside the ribbands. Note the excellent bracing of molds and sternpost. The appearance of the ribbands is pleasing as well as practical.* (Rosenfeld)

Such fastening prevents the hull from being raised off the posts when planking is forced into place with shores and wedges, as this action tends to both lift the hull upward and tilt it to one side.

Posts are also used in sailboat construction, but only to shore the stems. Sailboats are often built on their flat keels, with the ballast keel casting and deadwood added after the hull is planked up. Or the complete backbone may be finished before setting up, as in the auxiliary in Figure 9-5, which shows husky keel blocks being used to prevent shifting of the structure. Such keel blocks must be large enough to take substantial fastenings to the floor and to take the considerable weight of a boat of this type.

Ribbands

After the backbone and all molds have been set up *accurately* and properly braced, the ribbands are applied to hold the parts rigidly in position. Ribbands were briefly mentioned under Molds in Chapter 8, where it was pointed out that they are long

Figure 9-7. *The men at right are fitting ribbands prior to framing a racing sloop. Note mold braces to the rafters of the building and the strongback on top of the mold cross spalls on the centerline of the boat.* (Rosenfeld)

Figure 9-8. *This mold is being set up and carefully checked for alignment. Other molds are stacked in the background.*

Figure 9–9. *A v-bottomed hull completely set up with sawn frames and ready for double-diagonal planking.* (Courtesy of Huckins Yacht Corp.)

strips of wood bent around the molds in order to provide a form against which to bend the frames to shape between the molds. The function of molds and ribbands should be made perfectly clear by the photograph, Figure 9-6, which is a rare treat because it is not cluttered up with scaffolding. As considerable pressure is needed to clamp the frames to the ribbands, it is best that they be of moderately hard and strong wood, such as fir or yellow pine. Boats vary to such an extent that there is no general rule for size of the ribbands. They must be stiff to retain the hull shape when the frames are bent against them, but not so heavy that they are hard to bend and hold in place or that they force the molds out of alignment. As a safeguard against distorting the shape of the hull, the ribbands are applied alternately port and starboard. Ribbands are generally bent on the flat from stock such as 1¼" x 1½", and spaced about 10" apart, or 1½" x 2" spaced about a foot apart. A sample should definitely be tried around the molds before getting out the stock for all the ribbands.

The differences in ribband sizes between various hull types can be seen in Figures 9-6 and 9-7. Figure 9-6 shows the hull for a moderately heavy cruising auxiliary that has already been framed; Figure 9-7 shows the setup for a racing sloop. A comparison of the ribband sizes for the boats in the two pictures indicates that the racing sloop will have relatively light frames. The ribbands should be in single lengths if possible; otherwise they should be spliced as shown in Figure 9-3. This type of splice tends to eliminate unfair flat spots in the ribbands, but as a further precaution against hard spots, the splices should be located where bends in the ribbands are easiest.

Husky ribbands and close spacing will contribute toward a fair boat. Put them on by fastening the middle first and, working toward the ends, securing the ribbands to each mold with screws having washers under their heads. Screws will permit the ribbands to be removed easily as the planking is fitted. The top ribbands should go on first, fitted parallel to the sheer and a few inches above it. The rest of them should be run in fair lines similar to strakes of planking and as illustrated in Figure 9-6. The ribbands are spaced closer where the frames will be bent to the sharpest curves than where the frames will be fairly flat.

Careful mold loft work and setting up will make running ribbands an easy job and will eliminate the task of trimming and shimming molds to get the ribbands to touch all molds and still remain fair. If considerable trouble is encountered fairing the ribbands, it will pay to check the sections by bending a batten into position like a frame on the inside of the ribbands to see if it touches all of them while bent in a fair curve. Running the ribbands is the last job before framing is started, and the hull in this condition usually is the cause of excited anticipation on the part of the builder, for now the shape of the hull may be appreciated.

V-Bottomed Hulls

It should be understood without mention that hulls other than the round-bottomed type must be set up, aligned, and made rigid with the same care. There is no point in doing an accurate job of laying down and mold making unless the setup and the work that follows meet the same standard.

Chapter 10

FRAMING

There are two basic systems for framing a hull: transverse and longitudinal. Transverse framing is the most common, and being oriented athwartships, such frames are often called *ribs*. Transverse frames for round-bottomed wooden hulls are either bent from one piece, as in Figures 1-4 and 1-5, laminated from two or more pieces bent on top of each other, sawn from natural crooks of wood, or "double sawn" from boards and made up of two layers with staggered joints. Small to moderate hulls usually have the bent frames, although in places where material for bent frames is non-existent, such as islands in the Bahamas, the frames are sawn from crooks or double sawn according to both the size of the boat and the supply of crooks. (*See* Figure 10-1.) Sawn frames for v-bottomed and arc-bottomed hulls are shown in Figures 1-3 and 1-4. Some designers and builders have used a combination of sawn and bent frames for their v-bottomed hulls.

For the longitudinal framing system in general, transverse frames are used to shape the hull, but are spaced farther apart than in the transverse system. Fore-and-aft longitudinals are used to build up the necessary framing strength. This system can get quite complicated for construction in wood, but is well suited for metal boats of welded construction.

In this book, discussion is limited to the two types of framing suitable for the size of craft likely to be built by the amateur—bent frames and sawn v-bottom frames. Before undertaking a craft with other kinds of more complex framing, the builder should be certain before starting that he is aware of what is involved.

V-Bottom Frames

The lofting and construction of frames for a v-bottomed boat will be better understood by referring to Figures 1-3 and 1-7 and the explanation in Chapter 8. The frames are made from the full-size sections and must be beveled on the edges so the

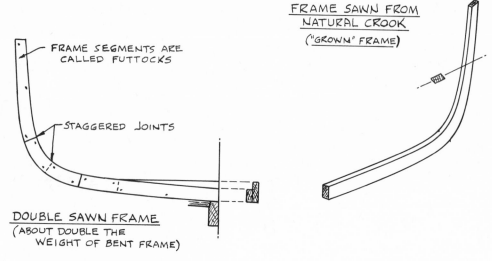

Figure 10–1. *Sawn and double-sawn frames.*

planking will bear properly. The process of picking up bevels is explained in preceding chapters.

Bent Frames

The bending of frames for a round-bottomed boat seems to disturb the amateur's peace of mind as he contemplates the construction of such a hull, but a trial should dispel this fear. For this reason, it is recommended that the novice start with a fairly small boat having light frames in order to gain experience and overcome the mental block that is the principal obstacle to frame bending. We all know that any piece of dry wood may be picked from the lumber pile and sprung to a curve of large radius, but for bending the tight curves found in frames, the wood must be both wet and hot. The material most commonly used for bent frames in the United States is white oak, because of its durability and strength, while elm is used extensively in Canada, the British Isles, and Europe. Although responsible agencies have proven that oak with a moisture content as low as 12 percent is suitable for bending if handled properly, it is recommended that the builder use unseasoned wood, because it is usually free from surface checks, heats rapidly, and needs only heat to bend rather than the addition of moisture required by dry wood.

The frame stock should be as straight-grained as possible and this is sometimes achieved by splitting a plank with the grain and then sawing out the frames parallel to the split edges. The stock should be about a foot or so longer than the finished length of the frame. It is best to bend the framing stock on the flat of the grain (Figures 6-4 and 10-2), for not only will it bend more easily this way but the wood's tendency to split when plank fastenings are driven through it is then minimized. Specifications for some boats call for a flat frame size such as 1″ x 1⅜″ bent on the flat. However, from the standpoint of theory, a frame is a transverse strength member and thus does its job

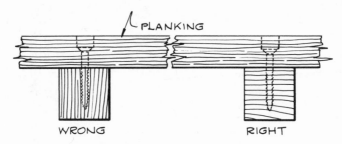

Figure 10-2. *Frames should be bent on the flat of the grain.*

best when its athwartships dimension is relatively great. If this were carried too far it would be impossible to bend the frame, so a good compromise is to make the frame square. Then it is just as strong crossways as it is fore and aft, and in practice it may be quickly turned on its other edge if it does not readily bend in the direction first attempted.

Sawn Frames for Round-Bottomed Hulls

Rare these days but still in use for large wooden vessels (such as a 90-plus-foot dragger I saw under construction in 1984) are double-sawn frames, Figure 10-1. The frame segments, called futtocks, are customarily riveted or bolted together, depending upon size. (Today they might even be joined with a suitable adhesive, provided the futtocks are carefully fitted.) The same figure shows a frame sawn from a natural crook. The famous Abaco dinghies are still built (1985) in the Bahamas with this type of framing.

Steaming Arrangements

You may have seen the steam box at a local boatyard in action. However, the source of steam does not have to be elaborate when only one boat is to be built. It may be generated in an old hot water boiler from a house, a large kettle, or any similar device rigged so a wood fire may be built under it and the steam piped to the box. The supply of water must be ample for the period of time you plan to work. Watch this point, for the water goes fast.

The steam box is wooden, made as steam tight as possible by caulking with cotton if necessary, and large enough for a half dozen frames and some room to spare. It is possible that the garboard and one or two other planks will need steaming to bend them in place, so make the box large enough for this job. There must be a door at one end, opposite to the end with the steam supply pipe, and the cracks are packed with rags to prevent steam from leaking out. The box should be located close to the boat, because bending calls for fast work before the frames become too cool. Handle the frames with cotton work gloves. A rough rule for steaming is one hour per inch of frame thickness. A few trials will have to be made to get the hang of it.

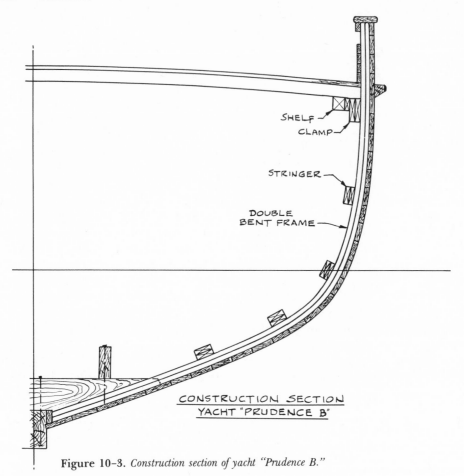

SHELF

CLAMP

STRINGER

DOUBLE
BENT FRAME

CONSTRUCTION SECTION
YACHT "PRUDENCE B"

Figure 10-3. *Construction section of yacht "Prudence B."*

Light frames are sometimes made supple in boiling water by placing them in a length of pipe set at an angle with the ground, with a fire built under the pipe's lower end. This scheme works well because, with water in the pipe, there is little danger of unduly drying the frames. Strings should be tied to the frames for pulling them out, and the upper end of the pipe should be stuffed with rags to retain the steam. Typical steaming arrangements are shown in Figure 10-4. Others on the same order may be improvised by the builder.

My good friend Pembroke Huckins once built a large hull I designed for him that called for oak frames made of two layers, each 1½" x 3¼", bent one on top of the other. He decided to make the oak supple by boiling it—the first time he had tried this—and was delighted that only a handful of the approximately 280 pieces broke during placement. Figure 10-3 is a midships construction section of Huckins' 73-footer showing the double-bent frames. Note that the clamps, shelves, and stringers have not been shaded on this drawing, which means these members were made of "nominal" lumber like 2 x 4s, 2 x 6s, etc., all readily available in the building area. In addition to the logistical advantage this offered, the lighter material was easier to fit into position.

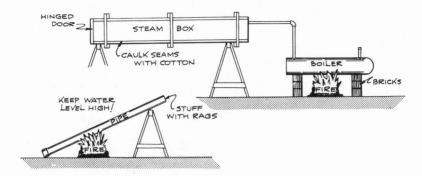

Figure 10–4. *Steaming arrangements.*

Bending the Frames

Frames may either be bent to shape in the boat against the ribbands or bent on forms and then fitted to the boat cold. The former is by far the easier method, and unless the frames for your boat are relatively heavy or the hull is extremely shapely, this system should be followed. Guided by the frame layout on the construction plan, first mark the frame positions on all the ribbands and at the keel, marking both edges with a thin batten the same width as a frame and making sure the marks are made at right angles to the centerline. Start framing amidships where the bends are less severe. This allows your experience to accumulate as the work progresses toward the ends, where sharp bends are likely to be encountered.

The actual bending procedure goes as follows. Take a frame out of the steam box and as rapidly as possible cut the heel of the frame to fit the keel and nail it in place. Then start the bending by pulling inboard on the head of the frame as you progressively force the frame against the ribbands with hands or feet, all the while twisting the frame to lie flat against the ribbands. By pulling the head inboard, the frame will bend more than enough, and it then can be flattened and forced into position against the ribbands. A gadget like that shown in Figure 10-5A may be employed to aid in twisting in the bevel should it be troublesome.

If plenty of hands are available, the frame can be clamped to the ribbands as you bend it; otherwise clamp it at the topmost ribband, give it a downward wallop on the head to make sure that it touches all the ribbands, and then temporarily toenail it to the ribbands so that your clamps will be ready for further duty on the next frame. You will soon learn that the bending must be done quickly once the frame has been removed from the steam box. If possible, two men should work on the bending while a third tends the box. When the boat is designed with frames in one piece from sheer to sheer, there must absolutely be two men bending, one on a side, each working from the keel toward the sheer, in order that the frame can be completely bent before it cools.

In many boats all the frames may be bent as described above. However, the frames in full-bowed hulls and those along the horn timber aft of the waterline in hulls like sketch D of Figure 8-14 are often troublesome due to the necessity of twisting in a bevel in a short length. Because of this, it is permissible to depart from bending at

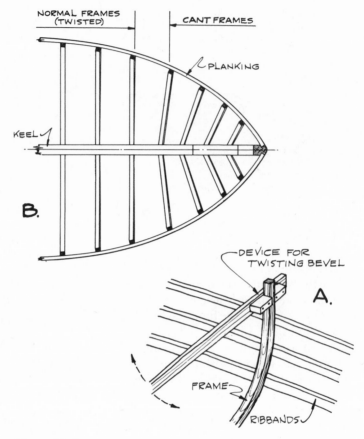

Figure 10–5.

right angles to the centerline in the extreme bow and to allow the frames to lie naturally against the planking so they slope forward from keel to sheer. These are called cant frames and are shown in Figure 10-5B. The same is true of stern frames in a double-ender.

Cold-Fitted Frames

Framing the counter stern, as the type of stern in Figure 8-14D is called, should be done very carefully if bumps and hollows are to be avoided. In the interest of fair lines, the frames for such sterns are either bent over a mold outside of the boat, as described later, or oversized frame stock is overbent on the ribbands, after which it is removed, straightened to the proper curve, and then beveled to lie against the ribbands. The inner edge is finally beveled to correspond to that on the outside of the frame so that stringers and clamps to be installed later will fit properly. These cold-fitted, beveled frames are similar in cross-section to the double-sawn frame illustrated

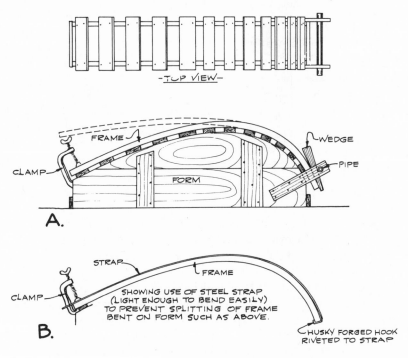

-TOP VIEW-

A.

FRAME
WEDGE
CLAMP
PIPE
FORM

B.

STRAP
FRAME
CLAMP
SHOWING USE OF STEEL STRAP
(LIGHT ENOUGH TO BEND EASILY)
TO PREVENT SPLITTING OF FRAME
BENT ON FORM SUCH AS ABOVE.
HUSKY FORGED HOOK
RIVETED TO STRAP

Figure 10-6.

in Figure 10-1. The excess curvature first bent into the frame is accomplished by padding the ribbands with short lengths of wood in way of the frame location. Curvature can be taken out of a frame after it has cooled and set, but none may be added.

If the use of cold-fitted frames cannot be avoided, you must make one or two forms similar to Figure 10-6A over which to bend the frames. To get an idea of the curves required for the forms, bend a piece of soft iron rod or lead wire against the ribbands and use it as a guide to build a form. The frames must always be bent to more curve than necessary, and the form can be padded to vary the shape. When ready to bend, the end of the frame is slipped under the pipe shown in the figure and wedged; then the bending is done with a steady pressure. Leave the frames on the form at least overnight so they will cool and set properly and not lose too much shape when removed. When there is too much curve, the frames can be straightened with a device like that shown in Figure 10-7 on a bench or a corner of the shop building. Reverse curves can be made on the form by bending one curve at a time, allowing the first bend to set well, and then nailing braces across the curve to hold the shape while the reverse is being bent.

Due to tensile stress, the outer fibers of a frame will tend to split when the curve is sharp, but someone found long ago that a metal strap bent along the outside of the frame is a very successful way to combat this breakage. The strap shown in Figure 10-6B is typical of the simple scheme involved and is very handy. The tendency to split is also present when bending sharp curves against ribbands. If you find some bad

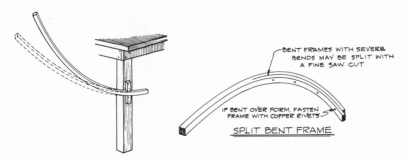

BENT FRAMES WITH SEVERE
BENDS MAY BE SPLIT WITH
A FINE SAW CUT

IF BENT OVER FORM, FASTEN
FRAME WITH COPPER RIVETS

SPLIT BENT FRAME

Figure 10-7.

curves, a strap similar to that illustrated may be devised to do the same job. In most cases the strap need only extend somewhat more than the length of the hard bend, such as around the turn of the bilge of a motorboat. After some practice you will be able to judge which bends may give trouble, like those in the S frames forward of the counter of boats like Figure 8-14D, in which case the frame stock may be split with a fine saw cut as shown in Figure 10-7 to permit the bend to be made easily. As a matter of fact this is easier than using a strap when the frames are bent in the hull inside the ribbands. When the frames are bent outside of the ribbands, a strap is not difficult to use. If splitting is resorted to, the frame should be fastened in way of the cut as soon as possible.

Floor Timbers

One of the most important members of the hull frame is the so-called floor or floor timber. These pieces of flat-grained material, usually oak, are the strength connection between the frames and backbone. Without floors, severe strains would be imposed on the garboard planks and their fastenings along the rabbet, and the hull would probably not remain tight. Floors are generally placed alongside every frame to ensure that each frame is securely fastened to the backbone, but there are certain exceptions to this rule. You will see plans for some powerboats and light centerboard sailboats with floors located only at every other frame, but in the interest of safety, most boats of the cruiser type, whether sail or power, do not omit any of them.

Floors are set on edge on top of the backbone structure and drift or through-bolted to it, depending upon their location in the boat. Fastenings to frames are either bolts or copper rivets. There are always two bolts through to the keel where the width of the backbone permits, and good practice calls for three or four fastenings to the frame on each side. Floors are shown in Figures 1-3, 1-4, 1-5, 6-1, 8-8, and 8-14D and are clearly visible in Figures 6-15, 9-5, 9-8 and 10-9. The latter picture well illustrates the bolting of frames to the floors.

It should be noted in Figure 9-8 that floors have already been fitted to the backbone, although the boat has not yet been framed. This method is common practice for the professional builder, but would be recommended to the amateur with reluctance, because the mold loft work involved might try his patience to the breaking point. With this system, each floor must be preshaped from a full-size section drawn at each frame, and correct bevels must be cut on three edges before the floor can be bolted in position. In v-bottomed hulls, floors must also be preshaped, being an essential part of each frame. However, the shape is obtained simultaneously with that of each frame being built, and there are not so many of them to make, so the lofting is not as much of a chore as it is with bent-frame hulls.

The thickness of floors should be as specified on the plans and is usually the same as the frames in v-bottomed boats. In bent-frame hulls most of the floors are the same thickness or slightly less than the thickness of the frame. Those under the mast steps and engine beds in both types of boats are made heavier to take the extra strains found in those areas and to accept the fastenings that run through the adjoining parts at these points. Floors in way of ballast keels are bored for bolts through the keel casting and are of a siding equal to the ordinary floors plus the diameter of the bolts.

Like all joints in a well-built boat, it is imperative that floors be carefully fitted. They are made to have full contact with the frames, and where the frames twist in the ends of the boat the floors are beveled off to fit tightly as shown in Section A-A in Figure 10-8. Due to the hull curving in toward the centerline forward and aft of amidships, the twist in the frames will be toward the ends; consequently the floors are placed on the forward side of the frames forward of amidships and on the aft side of the frames from amidships to the stern. An occasional floor may be located otherwise for one reason or another at the option of the designer.

The bottom edge of a floor is beveled to fit the member it rests upon, and many professionals prefer to notch them a half inch or so over the keel to aid in preventing movement of the parts when the hull is stressed. Limber holes are cut on the bottom edges of floors before installation (Figure 10-8) so rain or bilge water will drain to the low point of the bilge for removal by pumping. The outboard edges of the floors are beveled so the planking will bear against them. This bevel may be obtained from a ribband in the vicinity, or a short batten may be sprung around the adjacent frames for the same purpose.

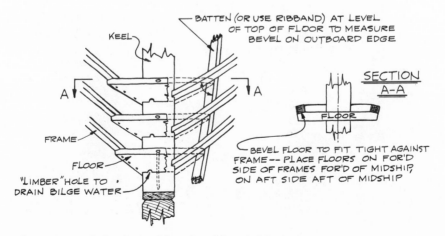

Figure 10–8. *The beveling and fastening of floors is important.*

Fitting and fastening floors is a chore indeed but very important for the longevity of a wooden hull of normal construction. I know of two sailboats that had additional floors installed after at least 25 years of service. The work required to install them was almost overwhelming, but both craft were cherished by their owners and were sailed for many years afterward.

Longitudinal Strength Members

Although fore-and-aft stringers and clamps may not be fastened in place before the hull is all or partially planked, they may be considered part of the hull framing because they are used whether or not the boat is decked. Stringers and clamps are planks on edge fitted on the inside of the frames. They strengthen the hull considerably and to be most effective they should fit snugly and be carefully fastened. They are made of hard pine or Douglas fir and sometimes oak where weight is not

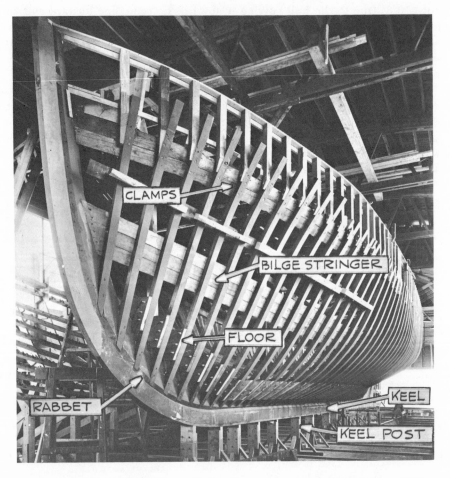

Figure 10–9. *This photograph shows why bent frames are often called "ribs."* (Rosenfeld)

objectionable. To save weight and make installation easier, the clamps and stringers, in other than the smallest hulls, are tapered in width from a maximum amidships to about one-half the width at the ends of the boat. Stringers and clamps are clearly shown in the photograph of the workboat in Figure 10-9. If material is not available to install these pieces in single lengths, they may be pieced out with scarphs as described in Chapter 8 and as shown in Figure 8-15.

Bilge stringers are used in all round-bottomed boats except the smallest ones, and in powerboats there may be several on each side of the hull. They are not found in v-bottomed boats because of the chine. Stringers give valuable support if a boat should run aground and lay over on her side. There is usually one stringer on each side made up of one or more strakes, and when multiple, the strakes are wedged tightly together. The bilge stringer is fastened to each frame with staggered flat-head wood screws, except in heavy construction, where bolts are used. In the highest quality boats the screws are counterbored and plugged where they will be visible in quarters, and the upper and lower inboard corners of the stringers are sometimes chamfered or beaded on a machine for appearance by professional builders. The stringers should be located as closely as possible to the position shown on the drawings, run as far fore and aft as is practical, and depending upon the relative thickness of the piece, sprung or shored in place for fastening.

The sheer clamp is located on the inside of the frames as shown in Figure 10-10. Figure 10-11 has been especially drawn to show that in decked boats the upper edge of the clamp is set down from the sheer line a distance equal to the thickness of decking plus the depth of the deck beams. It is important to keep this point in mind or else the sheerline will not be at the right height. The clamps are bolted to the frames for maximum strength. This means that if the amateur should go ahead and completely plank the hull before installing the clamps, the bolts would have to extend through the planking, possibly interfering with the plank fastenings.

There are two ways of getting around this, although I am a little ahead of myself, since planking will be discussed in the next chapter. One way is to fasten the upper two planks in place temporarily until planking is completed. After the molds are taken out of the hull, the two planks are taken off to enable the fitting and bolting of the clamps and then replaced and fastened for good. The other method is to transfer the sheer heights from the molds to adjacent frames, then cut away enough of the molds to install the clamps before planking. The uppermost ribbands hold the frames in

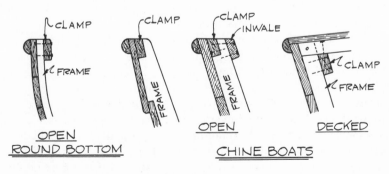

Figure 10-10. *Sections showing sheer clamps.*

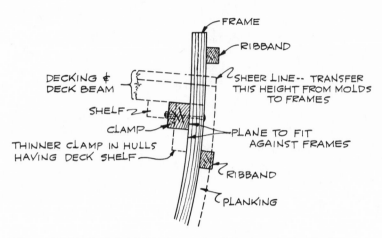

Figure 10-11. *In decked hulls, the top edge of the clamp is placed below the sheer.*

position during this work. The molds, of course, cannot be used for another boat without some rebuilding. The clamps are run from the transom to the stem and the outside faces are planed to fit snugly against the frames. Except in straight-sided boats, this is always necessary if the clamp has much depth (Figure 10-11). Like the bilge stringers, the lower inside corners are sometimes chamfered or beaded for looks.

Clamps in v-bottomed hulls are installed and fastened when the frames are set up, and with the chines, are used to hold the frames in alignment. Because of the depth of v-bottom frames, the clamps are more often screwed than bolted.

Engine Stringers

In order to distribute the weight of the engine, and also to aid in elimination of hull vibration, engine stringers are found in all properly designed motorboats. Sometimes of oak, but more often of such woods as fir or yellow pine, the stringers are run as far fore and aft as possible. To accomplish this, they are occasionally pulled toward the centerline forward to permit them to extend further and still be securely fastened on top of the floors. This applies to both stringers in a single-engine boat and to the inboard stringers in a twin-engine craft. The outboard stringers for twin-engine installations are usually too far out to catch the floors and are set on the frames. They are run straight and cannot be as long as the inner members due to the curving hull shape. It is desirable to have the stringers in single lengths, but if necessary they may be scarphed, the joints being planned to avoid conflicting fastenings.

The stringers are notched ⅜" to ½" over the floors and frames, and through or drift bolted to the floors. Outboard stringers not resting on floors are through-bolted to the frames. (*See* Figure 10-12.) The centerline of the propeller shaft is laid out from the drawings and the engine stringers spaced equally to each side, the distance being figured from the horizontal center-to-center distance of the engine holding-down bolts, with allowances made for the thickness of the engine bed material.

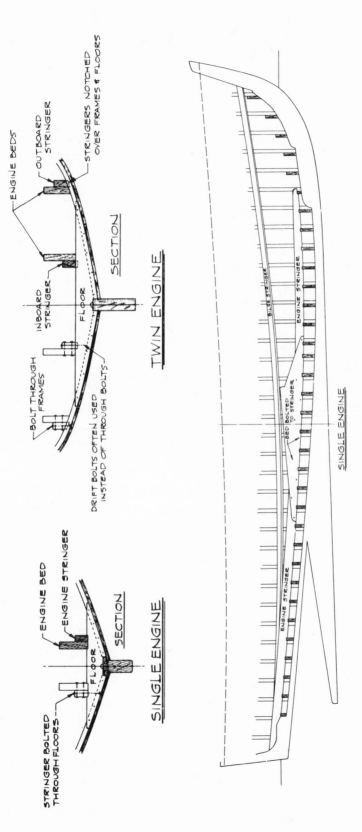

Figure 10–12. *Engine stringers and beds in a powerboat hull.*

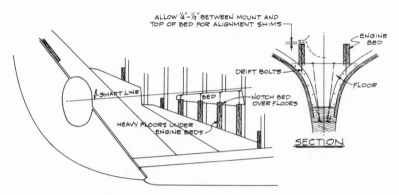

Figure 10-13. *Auxiliary sailboat engine bed installation.*

Engine Beds

In motorboats the engine beds are bolted to the engine stringers, Figure 10-12, and may or may not be notched over the floors. If enough bolts are used to transfer the engine thrust to the stringers, notches are not necessary. The present custom of having the engine in an auxiliary as far aft as possible does not lend itself to the installation of stringers, and in this case the beds are notched over the floors and drift bolted to them. (*See* Figure 10-13.) In all boats the installation diagram for the engine must be consulted to determine the vertical position of the bottom of the bolt lugs in relation to the centerline of the propeller shaft in order to determine the top edge of the beds. Anywhere from ¼″ to ½″ is allowed between the lugs and the beds for the insertion of hardwood shims when the engine is aligned with the propeller shaft, unless the engine is fitted with mounts that have a vertical adjustment.

Chapter 11

PLANKING

Planking a hull—with something other than veneers or panels—is often the most difficult part of boatbuilding for the amateur and always one of the simplest aspects for the professional. The beginner has trouble laying out the width of the planks and the run of the planking seams, while the expert does not seem to give it much thought due to accumulated experience and first-hand teaching. The stumbling of an amateur is understandable, because it is not easy to learn planking from a book or even to explain the subject in words. It is strongly suggested that he study the planking on boats in yards, especially of the type he will build. Through the ages a good many methods of planking have been devised, but only the most common ones will be discussed here.

The individual planks are called strakes, and for appearance they should be nicely proportioned, shaped so the lines of the seams are pleasing to the eye from every direction. Seams open and shut a little due to shrinking and swelling, and for well-kept appearance, especially on the topsides, the strakes should not be too wide or the seams will become unsightly as well as difficult to keep tight.

Carvel Planking

It will be well to discuss smooth planking at first (Figure 11-1), as this method is the most common, and much of what is said about carvel planking a round-bottomed boat will apply also to other methods.

Carvel planking is made with the seams tight on the inside and open on the outside to receive cotton caulking, which makes the planking watertight. The bevel on the seams is called "out-gauge" (Figure 11-1A) and should be made so the opening on the outside is about ¹⁄₁₆" per inch of plank thickness. The planking material should be ordered somewhat thicker than the specified finished dimension to allow for planing and sandpapering and for hollowing (backing out) the inside face of planks on sharp

145

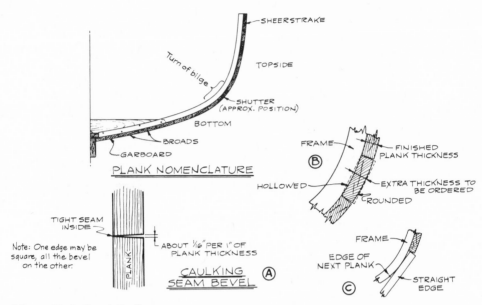

Figure 11-1. *Carvel planking.*

turns (Figure 11-1B). Most of the hull planking will not need more than an extra ⅛″ for finishing, but that on the turns may require more. A straightedge held on a frame will determine the amount (Figure 11-1C). It is not recommended that an amateur choose to build, as his first project, a boat having planking that is less than ½″ finished thickness. However, if you have the ability as well as the courage to undertake planking less than ½″ thick, then go ahead, but remember at that dimension the seams cannot be caulked and therefore must fit perfectly in order to avoid leaks. A hull with thin planking, though, can be covered with fiberglass, provided the additional weight does not destroy the reason for thin planking in the first place.

Butts in Planking

Some small-boats can be planked with full-length strakes, but inasmuch as the usual available lengths of planking material are from 12 to 16 feet in intervals of two feet, the strakes will ordinarily consist of two or three pieces butted end-to-end. (Note that stock longer than 16 feet, if obtainable, may require a special order.) From the standpoint of strength, the location of butts is important, and a plan should be laid out before the work is started, taking into consideration the material at hand. Rather than try to visualize the butts on the frame of the boat, it is much easier to make a rough diagram as a guide.

Figure 11-2 shows a satisfactory way of laying out the butts, and you will note that no two of them should be in the same frame space without three strakes between, and adjacent strakes should not have butts without three frame spaces between them.

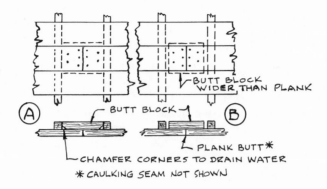

BUTT BLOCK
WIDER THAN PLANK

BUTT BLOCK

PLANK BUTT *

CHAMFER CORNERS TO DRAIN WATER

* CAULKING SEAM NOT SHOWN

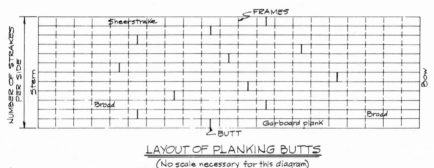

LAYOUT OF PLANKING BUTTS

(No scale necessary for this diagram)

Figure 11-2.

Butts are made midway between a pair of frames (never on a frame except in massive construction), the joint being backed by an oak or mahogany block as thick as the frame (because the fasteners are the same length as those holding the planks to the frames), and 1″ to 1½″ wider than the strake of planking. Butt blocks should be sawn to length to fit between the frames, planed on the outside to fit snugly against the planking, and should have their outboard corners generously chamfered to drain water that otherwise might be trapped on top of the block, Figure 11-2A.

There are those who advocate cutting the length of a butt block short of the space between the frames, Figure 11-2B. This is standard procedure when building a v-bottomed boat with widely spaced frames, and it does eliminate any chance of stopping drainage, as shown in Figure 11-2A. Nevertheless, when the ends of the block are properly fitted and bedded, the work goes a bit more easily, especially if the builder is working alone.

Bear in mind too that the butts in the planking must have a caulking seam, Figure 11-1A, like the edges of the fore-and-aft strakes of planking, and this must be cut before the butting plank is "hung."

Soak the butt block in a wood preservative such as Cuprinol or Woodlife and also treat the planking in way of the butt block location. Set the block in place with a bedding compound, being careful not to clog the drains. Then toenail it to the frames to hold it in place temporarily while fastening through the planking.

Planking Procedure

Let us consider carvel planking a simple round-bottomed boat like the 12-footer used to illustrate loft work in Chapter 7. The normal planking sequence for the amateur is to fashion the sheer strake first, then the garboard, the two adjoining broad strakes, and the bottom planking to the turn of the bilge, and to then alternately plank one strake under the sheer strake and one on the bottom, with the shutter, as the last plank is called, coming about midway between the bottom planking and the sheer. (*See* Figure 11-1.) Because it is difficult to clamp the shutter, it should be a plank that is fairly straight, without twist, and that does not require steaming.

The first consideration is the total number of strakes to be used, determined by the widths amidships at the longest frame. The garboard will be the widest, and the widths will decrease toward the turn of the bilge, with the topside strakes the narrowest and all about the same width. The sheer strake can be a little wider than the rest of the topside planks because of the rub rail often used.

As to exactly how wide to make the planks on a given boat, this is where your inspection of other boats can help. The following is offered as a general guide to proportion: 6″ to 8″ for the garboard, diminishing to 4½″ for the topsides and 5″ to 6″ for the sheer strake. These sizes are not hard and fast, but it should be remembered that for good appearance, the topside strakes below the sheer strake should not be over 4½″ wide amidships. Naturally, these widths apply only at amidships, as the frame girths at the ends of the boat are less, and the planks must taper in width toward the ends. Again for appearance, the taper should be uniform.

Bend a thin batten around the midship frame, mark the length from the keel rabbet to the sheer, and lay out the plank widths. Then lay off the width desired for the sheer strake on the midship frame and run a full-length batten around the frames for the purpose of obtaining the bottom edge of the plank. The plank should be tapered a little at the bow and stern and the batten must be fair. When the appearance of the line is satisfactory, mark the edge of the plank at the boat's ends and on all the frames, and remove the batten. Of course, it is understood that the top edge of the plank is the sheerline, from which the thickness of the decking, if any, must be deducted.

With the shape of the sheer strake determined and marked out on the frames, it must be transferred to a plank for cutting. This must be done accurately, so the plank will fit properly without "edgesetting" (springing edgewise into place). The procedure for doing this is known as spiling.

Spiling

The shape is obtained with the aid of a spiling batten, which is a piece of softwood somewhat longer than any individual strake, about 4″ to 6″ wide, and ³⁄₁₆″ or less in thickness. Several such battens should be on hand, because they will be mutilated with use. The batten is clamped or tacked to the frames; make sure it lies flat against the frames for its entire width and that it is not sprung edgewise. Its upper edge should be a little below the top edge of the plank to be made. This does not mean that the edge of the batten will be parallel to the plank edge. If it is, the batten has probably been sprung on edge, and the plank made from the spiling will not fit. The whole idea of the spiling batten is to place it like the plank to be made and so determine the *difference* in shape between the edge of the batten and the edge of the plank. For greater accuracy on hulls with a lot of sheer, a batten with a curved edge should be made if the batten should lie more than a couple of inches from the plank marks.

To use the spiling batten, take your carpenter's pencil compass and set the legs with a gap about ¼″ more than the greatest space between the edge of the batten and the plank marks on the frames. With one leg of the compass on the plank mark, make a point on the batten square down from the line of the top edge of the plank. (*See* Figure 11-3.) Repeat at every frame and at the ends of the plank, labeling the points with frame numbers and identifying all points for the particular plank with a numbered or lettered circle so they will not become confused with points for other planks later on. Do not change the opening of the compass while spiling the plank. Mark cuts across the batten for the butt, the stern ending, or the stem rabbet, as the case may be. Now take the batten off the boat and lay it on the board that is to be used for the plank (Figure 11-3B). Still not changing the compass opening, reverse the procedure, and this time, with one leg of the compass on a point on the batten, mark points on the board. Before making any actual marks, test with the compass and shift the batten until the points will be as close to the edge of the plank as possible in order not to waste width; then tack the batten against movement.

Mark all the points and the endings of the plank. Remove the spiling batten and run a fairing batten through all the points and draw the edge of the plank with a pencil. Do not worry if the shape of the line is peculiar. If the spiling has been done correctly, the plank will fit in place when bent around the frames. Now at each frame on the boat, pick off the width of the sheer strake that was previously laid out with a batten and marked on the frames. At the corresponding frame marks on the board, lay out the plank widths and run a batten through them to draw a line for the lower edge of the plank. If the boat is decked, allow a little extra on the upper edge for the crown of the deck, then saw out the plank.

Plane the upper edge for the crown and the lower edge square and clamp the plank

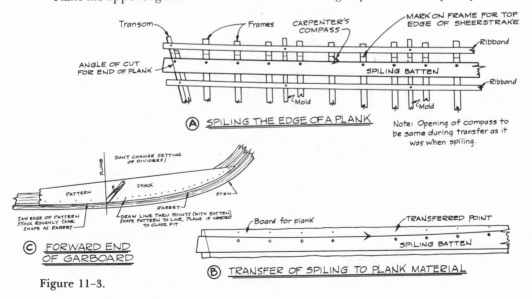

Figure 11-3.

in place. Unless there is something obviously wrong it can be used as a pattern for the same plank on the other side of the boat. After that, it can be fastened in place. Bear in mind that the butt end of a plank has to have outgauge for caulking, just as with a plank edge. Incidentally, always use a block of wood between the plank and a clamp so scarring from pressure will not occur.

Garboard Strake

The garboard plank is likely to be the most troublesome plank of all, but once it is fitted in place the remainder will seem all the easier to fit. What sets this strake apart from the rest is that its shape is determined by the contour of the rabbet and also by its role as a starting point for the rest of the planking. In order to have a nice, fair upper edge from which to start the tapering of the remaining planks, the garboard might be wider at its forward end than at amidships. This is not unusual, because the plank is twisted into place at its forward end, and if it were to be tapered narrower forward than amidships the upper edge might dip down. This is the general rule, although its application depends entirely on the hull form.

To get out the garboard, a spiling is taken for the lower edge by the method described previously, except that the spiling batten should be cut so that it comes closer to being an actual pattern for the plank, especially at the stem, where the end of the garboard will be well rounded to fit in the rabbet. The spiling marks must be close together where the curve is pronounced, and they are made plumb vertical from the rabbet line. (*See* Figure 11-3C.)

An extra step at this point, but advisable particularly for the first-time builder, would be to make an accurate pattern of the forward end of the garboard plank, using wood thin enough so it can be twisted to touch the frames without "edge-set" (bending edgewise). The spiling is done the same way as when using a spiling batten, but in this case *make the pattern actually meet the curve of the rabbet*. A good fit will result with no waste of planking material. The garboard should be the only plank requiring special pattern work.

Lay out the width of the garboard at the midship frame and, as you did for the bottom edge of the sheer strake, run a batten on the frames for the top edge of the garboard. The width at the ends of the garboard and the two broad strakes should be such that any excessive curvature is removed, so that the remainder of the strakes will be fairly straight when they are flat before being bent on. This straightening, however, should not be overdone, or there will be too much upward curve at the forward ends of the remaining strakes. As stated before, the garboard will probably be as wide (or a little wider) forward as it is amidships, but the test is to sight the batten you have placed and see that the line it makes is fair and pleasing in appearance from wherever you look at it. In the case of the 12-foot skiff, the width at the transom will be a little less than at amidships. As before, mark the edge on all the frames, remove the batten, and take a spiling of the edge. Saw out the plank, plane the top edge square, and plane the edge against the rabbet so it is open a little on the outside for the seam to receive caulking.

The forward end of the garboard will probably need steaming to get it in place; it is possible that this will be the only plank on the boat that will need such treatment.

While the plank is steaming, assemble at hand plenty of clamps, wedges, and material for shores to the floor (if the hull is being built right side up). When ready, fit the forward end of the plank in the rabbet first and clamp it, then as quickly as possible bend the plank in place while it is still limber. Get the plank flat against the frames with shores to the floor. Cut a shore a little short, toenail it to the floor, and drive a wedge between the top of the shore and the plank. If the bottom edge does not lie properly in the rabbet, clamp a piece of oak to the frames above the plank and drive wedges against a block on the plank edge to move it sideways. Never drive a wedge directly against the edge of a plank, or the edge will be crushed. Fasten the plank in place if it fits satisfactorily. If it doesn't, there is nothing to do except to let it cool, when it can be removed and the fit corrected. If you are lucky, it will not need more steaming for replacement. Don't be discouraged, for in a normal boat the garboard is the most difficult plank to fit, and it may even cost you some wasted material before you produce one that is right.

Broad Strakes

The next plank to go on is the one above the garboard, called the first broad, and a spiling is taken of the edge that will lie against the garboard. Before running a batten for the upper edge, you have to decide how to taper the plank so the remaining planks will be straight and easy to make. Start by tapering it in proportion to the space between the garboard plank and the sheer strake. This is done by counting the number of strakes shown on your midship planking layout batten, and at every third or so frame, called the spiling frames, dividing the distance between the top edge of the garboard and the bottom edge of the sheer strake by the planned number of strakes. At this time mark only the width of the first broad on the frames. Now run the batten and look at the line from all directions. It may be that the plank will want to be wider at the forward end in order to straighten it or give it a more pleasing appearance when viewed from forward. If so, make it a little wider, but don't overdo it. When the line satisfies, mark the frames, remove the batten, take a spiling for the top edge, and saw and plane the plank to shape. The next two or three planks are lined out with the same system so that when the turn of the bilge is reached, the remainder of the planks between there and the sheer strake may all be of uniform width and taper.

Width Scale for Remaining Planks

The planks between the last of the bottom planks and the sheer strake may be lined out by dividing the unplanked girth at each spiling frame into equal spaces. However, the work can be made easier if you use a planking scale made with a batten about ⅛" x 1". Mark on the batten the greatest space still to be planked, which will be near the middle of the boat, and also the shortest space, wherever it may be. Then arithmetically divide the greatest girth distance by the number of strakes still to go on. Let us say the answer is 4½"; therefore call the corresponding mark on the scale 4½". Do the same with the shortest girth and, assuming the answer is 3", call the corresponding mark on the scale 3". Now find the number of eighths of an inch there

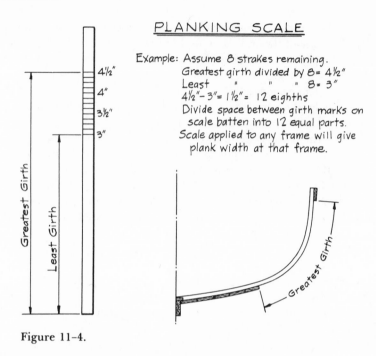

PLANKING SCALE

Example: Assume 8 strakes remaining.
          Greatest girth divided by 8= 4½"
          Least   "   "   " 8= 3"
          4½"–3"= 1½"= 12 eighths
          Divide space between girth marks on
          scale batten into 12 equal parts.
          Scale applied to any frame will give
          plank width at that frame.

Figure 11-4.

are between the two girth marks on the scale, 12 in this case. Divide the space on the scale between 3" and 4½" into 12 equal spaces and label them so each one represents ⅛". (*See* Figure 11-4.) You will see that the scale, when applied to the unplanked girth of any frame, will give the width of the strake at that frame.

It only takes a few minutes' time to make a planking scale, and with it you can go along and note the plank widths on as many of the frames as you like for reference when making the remainder of the strakes. From now on, it is unnecessary to run battens, although each plank must be spiled. However, if you find that the seams are not coming out as they should, it is best to run a batten to straighten things out and then redivide the remaining space once again.

The ribbands are only removed as they become an interference to making a plank. To keep the hull from becoming distorted, do not put more planks on one side of the boat than on the other. As you fit a plank, make a mate for the opposite side, remembering that the planks are not truly opposite. In other words, due to hollowing, for instance, the planks on opposite sides are not exact duplicates and may be compared to a pair of shoes.

Hollowing and Rounding

Hollowing of planks, Figure 11-1B, is best done with a wooden plane having a rounded bottom. Alternatively, I have heard that a plane iron ground to a curve can be made to work in a regular flat bottom plane. After a plank is hollowed to fit the curve of the frames, mark the finished thickness on the edges with a marking gauge and roughly round the face of the plank before fastening it into position. This will save work later.

Stealer Planks

The typical auxiliary sailboat hull, with the greatest girth to be planked located at a frame well aft of amidships, requires short planks known as stealers. These generally start at the rabbet in the sternpost and end at varying positions forward of the sternpost, depending upon the number of stealers and the shape of the hull. A study of such a hull will show that these short planks are necessary to straighten the remaining planks as the turn of the bilge is reached. The photograph, Figure 11-5, of a hull built over a permanent mold, in the process of being turned over, clearly shows the shape of the stealers along the keel. (Referring to remarks in preceding chapters, the deadwood and ballast keel will be fitted to the hull in Figure 11-5 after it is right side up.) Often, to avoid plank ends that are too pointed to take a fastening, stealers are nibbed into their neighbors, A in Figure 11-6. In this particular type of planking there is no garboard running for the length of the keel rabbet, but it still is possible to have one as illustrated by B of Figure 11-6. There are numerous possible variations, and it is strongly urged that before beginning the job, a study be made of the planking on a boat similar to the one being built for whatever pointers can be picked up.

Plank Fastenings

The type of fastening will be as specified on the plans or according to your own choice. Normal planking is secured with three fastenings per plank at each frame where the width of the plank will permit, such as throughout the bottom, and two at each frame in the narrow topside strakes. The fastenings are staggered to the extent allowed by the width of the frames, and planks that cross floors have an additional fastening or two driven into the floor. The butts are fastened with five in each plank end as shown

Figure 11–5. *Stealer planks are used to straighten the remaining strakes as the turn of the bilge is reached.*

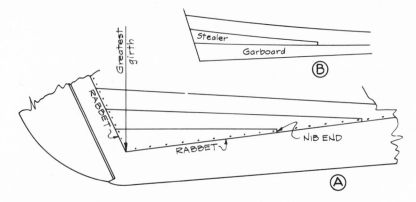

Figure 11-6. *Two methods of using stealer planks.*

in Figure 11-2. Butts in larger size auxiliaries are frequently bolted. Drilling for fastenings and plugging is discussed in Chapter 6.

After planking, the hull is ready for preliminary smoothing, done by planing with a jack plane and using long strokes to smooth off high areas. With a shorter smooth plane you are liable to plane hollow areas in the planking. Rubbing the hull up and down with palm and fingertips will reveal high spots that are not readily seen with the eye.

Caulking Carvel Planking

Before smoothing the hull further, the plank seams are caulked to make them watertight. This is a very critical step in hull building. By caulking too hard it is possible to pull the plank fastenings and force a plank away from the frames; if the caulking is too lightly driven, it will be forced out of the seam by the swelling of the planks when wet. Just the right amount of caulking adds considerable stiffness to the planking.

The entire job of correct caulking is a skilled art, and if the amateur plans to employ professional help with his boat at any stage of construction, here is a good place to do so. Don't let this discourage you from tackling the job, however.

When the plank thickness is ⅝" or under, a strand or two of cotton wicking may be rolled into the seams with a caulking wheel or driven with a thin-edged making iron. Thicker planking must have regular caulking cotton in the seams, obtainable at marine supply stores in one-pound packages made up of folds of multiple strands. On a *clean* floor or other surface 25 to 30 feet long unfold the bundle to the full length of the strands; then separate the strands. They break easily, so handle them with care. Now take two strands at a time and roll them in a ball. Also make a couple of balls from single strands for use in narrow seams and plank butts or for adding a piece to a double strand for use where the seam is wide. Keep the cotton clean, or else you will have to pick wood chips and pieces of trash off the strands as you use them.

A few caulking tools are shown in Figure 11-8. The caulking wheel is not difficult to

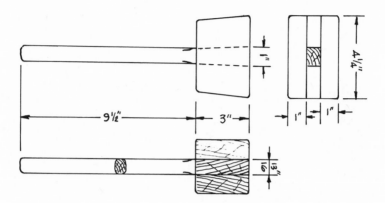

Figure 11-7. *A homemade mallet.*

make if you are unable to buy or borrow one. Mine is made from a piece of 1⅛" thick x 1⅞" x 8" long hardwood; the brass wheel is ⁵⁄₃₂" thick, 1½" in diameter, has a ⁵⁄₁₆" brass axle, and is shaped in section as shown. For regular rather than rolled caulking you can get by with just two making irons: a No. 0 with a ¹⁄₁₆" thick edge and a No. 1 with a ⅛" thick edge. A dumb iron is used to open up seams fitted too tight. For certain hulls it is easier to caulk the garboard plank seam at the keel with a making iron having a bent blade; the tool is a "bent iron."

It is said there is something special about using a caulking mallet instead of a hammer—there is a certain ring to it, and resilience. Mine was given to me by a stair builder who worked in a shipyard during World War I. The head is 10" long: the middle 3 inches are 2" in diameter and then it necks down to 1½" diameter at the ends. The 14½" long handle is ⅞" diameter at the head end, tapering to 1¼" at the heel. The steel bands are hand forged. Those at the middle of the head are ⅛" thick x ½" wide, while the 1" wide bands at the ends of the head are tapered in thickness from ³⁄₁₆" to a bit more than ¹⁄₁₆".

A mallet that has worked just as well for me as the traditional caulking tool just described is sketched in Figure 11-7. This was made of hickory scraps culled from a neighbor's kindling supply (which in turn came from scraps culled from an axe handle manufacturer). Fifteen years ago it was stuck together with epoxy resin thickened a bit with Cabosil. A mallet such as this is handy for all sorts of jobs, including caulking.

Start at one end of a seam and tuck an end of the cotton strand in the seam, leaving a little sticking out to drive into the seam at the end of the plank; then gather the cotton in a small loop with the caulking iron and drive it in the seam with a making iron. Normally the No. 0 making iron will do, changing to the No. 1 where the seams widen. Next to the first loop drive a second, and so on down the seam. The trick is to make the size of the loop just right so that the bulk of the cotton is correct for the width of the seam, and this will necessarily vary if the seams have not been made uniform. After you have driven a few feet of loops, go back to the beginning and drive the cotton in the seam far enough to make room for the seam composition that is put in later. This is being done by the caulker in Figure 11-9. If at any point the seam should not be

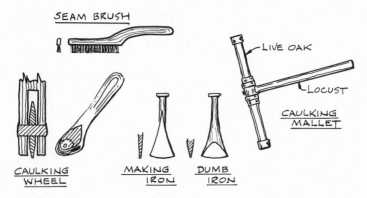

Figure 11-8. *Seam caulking tools.*

open enough to take the caulking, drive a dumb iron into the seam to spread it wider. Careful fitting of the planking will reduce the work with a dumb iron to a minimum.

The cotton should not be driven all the way to the bottom of the seam. When finished being driven, it should be in the *middle* of the seam depth, formed in a tight rope-shaped strand which should make a slight depression for itself in the plank edges. Heavier blows with the caulking mallet will be needed in hardwood planking like mahogany. Thus, good caulking calls for the right amount of cotton bulk, determined not only by the thickness of the strand but also by the size of the loops, and the right amount of mallet pressure to make the strand force a depression in the plank edges at the right depth. Don't forget to caulk the butts.

One source for caulking cotton, wicking, irons, and seam composition is Jamestown Distributors, whose address appears in Chapter 6.

Smoothing

After caulking, paint the seams with thickish paint, using a narrow seam brush made for the purpose. If you can find one, this tool is a time-saver. Be certain not to leave any cotton bare of paint. Wipe off any paint that gets on the outside of the planking while doing the seams. When the seams are dry, smooth the hull again with a plane, set for a finer cut this time to get the remainder of the high spots. All the while, rub the palm of your hand diagonally across the planking to find the bumps and hollows. If not smoothed perfectly at this time, the unfair portions will show up when paint is applied, and then the hull must be left as is or else a part of the job must be done over. Sandpaper the hull after planking, gradually using finer grit until it is as smooth as you want it. Garnet paper is better than sandpaper; although more expensive, it cuts faster and lasts longer. Carefully fill the seams with hull seam composition made for this purpose; apply ample pressure with a putty knife to fill the seam to the bottom. New boat planking will swell and push the compound outward, so use a dowel or similar tool to finish the seams a bit hollow.

More About Caulking

The caulking procedure described above is the old standby method and is as good today as it ever was, but modern materials permit the use of a different filling compound for the seams and even permit the cotton caulking to be omitted. So many old hands have sworn that the cotton caulking tightens the whole hull structure, and indeed caulked boats have been so satisfactory for so long, that, for that reason and also the matter of expense, I would stay with the method. These new compounds are expensive, and less will be needed if the seam is partly filled with cotton.

Absolutely clean bare wood in the seam is required for proper adhesion of the modern compounds. This is no problem with a new hull, but it certainly would take a lot of work to prepare the seams of an old boat. The cotton and seam sides are not painted in the old-fashioned way, but woods such as teak and Douglas fir, and perhaps yellow pine, have an oil that impairs adhesion and consequently need coating with a special primer made by the manufacturers of the polysulfide compounds. Check the makers' recommendations carefully in regard to seam priming. The polysulfide compounds may be a two-part mix; the silicones are not.

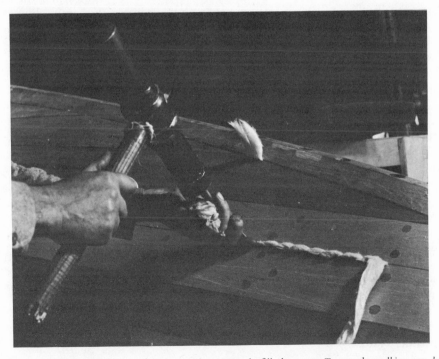

Figure 11–9. *Caulking is looped just enough to properly fill the seam. Too much caulking can harm planking.*

Hull Painting

For preservation while the boat is being finished, the outside of the hull above the waterline can be painted with an undercoater of the same brand that will be used for the finish coats. Paint the hull below the waterline with antifouling paint thinned according to instructions on the label.

A few remarks about paints are in order. Take my word that house paints will not do for boats. Good paint is cheap insurance, so use only marine paints to protect and beautify your hard work. Most of the marine paint firms have descriptive booklets that tell you how to do a good paint job from start to finish, and it is recommended that you stick to the rules. There are different systems, all of them good nowadays, and instructions should be followed carefully. The only suggestion I have that may not be found in a paint company booklet is to cover the entire inside of the framework and planking (except where visible in quarters) with two coats of a wood preservative and nothing else. If you think you might paint the inside of the hull at a later date, then use a clear preservative such as Cuprinol or Woodlife, which acts as a primer and is considered paintable after a few days of evaporation time.

Choosing an antifouling paint for the bottom of the hull can be a baffling experience. None of it is cheap. *If cost is not a factor*, then use the top grade made by a reputable marine paint manufacturer. This may remain effective as an antifoulant for two years, but if your boat is a big one, then the high cost of the paint is offset somewhat by a saving in haulout charges. If, however, the top grade is too expensive, then ask other boat owners what they use, provided your boat will be kept in the same waters. Finally, if your boat will be immersed only when in use, then antifouling paint on the bottom is not necessary. Instead, use a hard topsides paint for easy washing.

"Oil" Finishes

Small open boats in the New England area are often coated inside when new with an oil mixture, frequently made by the boatbuilder, rather than with paint or varnish. Simple to apply, an annual coat freshens appearance and helps preserve the hull. However, a first class job requires surface preparation similar to that for a good varnish finish—that is, all blemishes, pencil marks, and the like must be removed prior to finish treatment. An excellent oil mixture on the market, containing a hardener to avoid stickiness, an ultraviolet shield, and a generous proportion (60 percent) of oil, is available from Walter Simmons at Duck Trap Woodworking, whose address appears in Chapter 3. The original formula was handed down from Walt's grandfather. Be advised that Simmons cites a short shelf life for this product and cautions the buyer to carefully determine whether this or any similar mixture is compatible with sealers used in the boat's hull seams, rabbets, etc.

Lapstrake Planking

Sometimes called clinker planking, lapstrake planking is very different from carvel planking. In the first place, because of the stiffness of the planking it is possible to plank directly over the molds, the frames being bent in place when the planking is completed. Secondly, inasmuch as one plank laps over the next, the planking must start at the garboard and proceed upward to the sheer strake without any change in order. The nature of the planking prevents efficient smoothing after completion, so each plank is planed before final installation, but a light final sanding may be done after planking and before painting.

The strakes are lined out and spiled the same as for carvel planking, but the width of the laps must be taken into account when laying out the widths of the planks. Lapstrake planking is used principally for small boats where light weight is preferred. This method of planking is very stiff due to the full-length fastening of the laps along their edges, and thinner material can be used, resulting in a saving of weight.

The section in Figure 11-10 shows how the upper edge of each plank is beveled so the next one will fit tight against it for the width of the lap. The bevel varies from one end of the plank to the other due to the shape of the sections. Figure 11-10A shows how the bevel may be gauged with a rule at any frame or mold. Your plans should call for a specific width of lap, but the minimum is about ⅜″ on planking as thin as ¼″ and a little wider as the plank thickness is increased. As a guide when beveling, it is helpful to scratch the lap width on the plank with a marking gauge or mark it with a pencil. At each mold or spiling frame, the correct bevel is cut on the plank for the length of an inch or so. The job then becomes bench work to cut the bevel for the entire length of the plank, using the short cuts as guides.

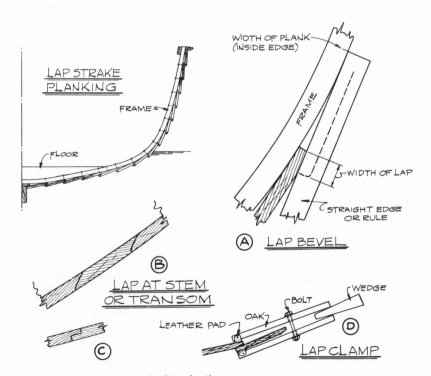

Figure 11–10. *Lapstrake planking details.*

The planks must be flush where they fit in the stem rabbet or against the transom. This is done by changing the bevel to a beveled rabbet (Figure 11-10B) in order to avoid a feather edge on the outside. Some builders prefer a tapering half-lap joint, finishing off at the very ends of the planks with an equal lap like Figure 11-10C. This can be done quickly and neatly by a Stanley rabbet plane with its gauge set for the width of the plank lap. Naturally, all beveling of laps must be carefully done or leaky seams will result, but it is surprising how rapidly this part of the work goes along once experience has been gained. Always remember that while the shape of any one plank is the same on both sides of the hull, the bevels are opposite. In other words, the planks are made right- and left-hand.

If the lapstrake boat is being planked over molds, the frame spacing is marked off on the keel and on each plank as it is fitted. The laps are copper riveted (or clench-nailed, as the case may be) between the frame positions as each plank is made and placed in position. (*See* Figure 6-8.) After completion of planking, the frames are bent, using the marks for guides. The planks are then riveted to the frames at each lap. (Rivet fasteners and clench nails for lapstrake planking are discussed in Chapter 6.) The lap rivets should be spaced about 1½″ apart in ¼-inch planks, and up to about 3″ in ¼-inch planks. At the stem and transom, screws are used to fasten the ends of the planks.

The seam between the stem rabbet and the plank ends is caulked as in a carvel-planked hull. At the transom do not caulk so hard that the planks strain the fasteners.

The shallow throat depth of an ordinary C clamp does not permit it to clamp the laps, so builders have devised the clamp shown in Figure 11-10D. A half dozen or so will be needed to hold the planks while the edges are riveted. If the boat is lapstrake planked over frames in the conventional manner, the planks are clamped to the frames just like smooth planking.

Finally, it should be noted that modern marine sealants made from polyurethane or polysulfide have effectively eliminated the need for a perfect dry fit of the planking laps—as was required of the old-timers who built by this method. A bead of 3M 5200, or Sikaflex 241, or Boatlife caulk can be neatly applied so there is a minimum of squeeze-out or excess when the laps are clamped and riveted.

Double Planking

The purpose of double planking is twofold: it insures watertightness without periodic recaulking, and a sleek finish that is relatively easy to maintain. Double planking is expensive, because the planking job is really done twice, notwithstanding that each layer of planking is thinner than normal and easier to apply. The total thickness of planking is the same as single planking, but weight can be saved over a single-planked mahogany job by planking the inner layer with a good, lightweight wood, such as white or Port Orford cedar. On the other hand, some of the weight saving is offset by the additional quantity of metal used to fasten the two layers between the frames.

The garboard plank is usually made single so that it can be readily replaced if necessary; also, it is easier to plane a proper caulking seam on a single edge. The sheer

Figure 11–11. *The Rangeley boat, a classic of fine lapstrake design.* (Dick Durrance photo)

strake and the first broad are also single thickness but are rabbeted for the outer layer as shown in Figure 11-12. The seams of the inner layer are arranged to come at the middle of the outer strakes. The planking is lined out and spiled the same as for a carvel job, for there is actually no difference except that there are two layers. Of course, the width of the outer strakes is the primary consideration. The inner strakes are fastened sufficiently with small screws, and when the outer strakes are fitted, the fastenings to the frames are long enough for the total thickness of the double layer. Before each outer strake is fastened, it is first coated on the inside with a double planking compound, such as one made by Dolphin. An alternative treatment once used by two of the best practitioners of this planking method—Nevins and Herreshoff—is a thick coating of shellac between the inner and outer layers of planking. All seams are fitted tightly together without outgauge, as no caulking is necessary.

Between frames the layers of planking are fastened together from the inside with screws along the edges of the inner strakes and also along each side of the middle of the inner strakes to fasten the edges of the outer strakes. These fastenings are round-headed screws with washers under the heads. The whole job is very strong because the two layers are so completely tied together. Naturally the outer layer must be thick enough to take the screws from the inside. An example of layer thickness proportion would be a ⅝" outer layer against ⅜" inner planking, making a finished thickness of 1".

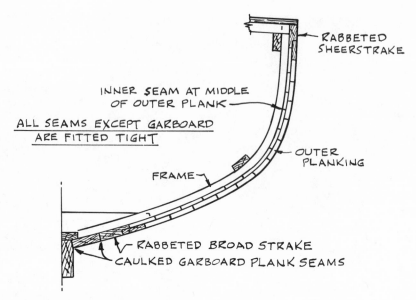

Figure 11–12. *Double planking details.*

Batten Seam Planking

This planking system is most closely associated with v-bottomed hulls, and owes its name to the fact that its seams are backed on the inside by battens to which the planks are fastened along the edges, as shown in Figure 11-13. One of this country's largest producers of v-bottomed stock cruisers used seam batten construction for many years, and it is a method being used again for building replicas of the beautiful varnished mahogany runabouts of pre-World War II. Batten seam construction has been popular with amateurs, because lining out the plank edges is fairly simple. The frames may be spaced relatively wider because the planking is stiffened by the battens. Figure 11-14 shows a well-built frame ready for planking.

A marine sealant such as Sikaflex 241 is applied to the batten in way of plank being fitted; this eliminates having to caulk the seam. However, the seam between the garboard plank and the keel is caulked in the usual manner.

To build a boat by this method, the v-bottomed hull is set up with chines and clamps fitted and fastened in place. The seam battens are then clamped to the frames, having been located by dividing each frame into a number of equal parts, the spacing depending on the width of the available planking material. The plank widths may be greater than with carvel planking, say an average of 6″ amidships. The battens are sighted for appearance, and when they have been adjusted, if necessary, so that they look fair, the top and bottom edges are marked where they cross the frames, stem, and transom frame. With the battens removed, the framework is notched so the battens will be flush with the inside of the planking when fitted. The battens are fastened in each notch with one or two flat-head screws.

A plank is clamped so it overlaps a batten, and pencil lines are drawn along the edges of the batten from the inside. Thus the shape is obtained, but remember the net

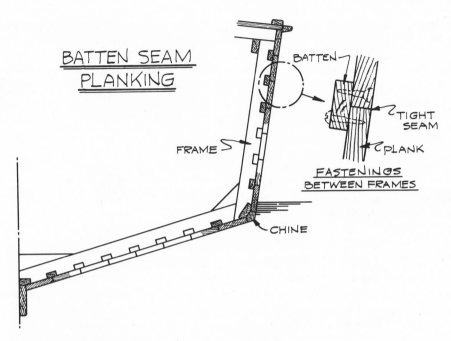

Figure 11–13. *A typical section through batten seam construction.*

Figure 11–14. *A hull framed for batten seam planking.* (Photo courtesy of William G. Hobbs Yacht Sales.)

width of the plank is to the middle of the batten, so half the batten width must be deducted from (or added to) each edge of the plank. If the frame spacing is very wide and there is no clamp against the planking at the sheer, as in the boat in Figure 11-13, the sheerline may be preserved by spiling the top edge of the sheer strake from a fairing batten sprung around the frames. Screw fasten the planking to the frames and to the battens along the edges.

Strip Planking

Strip planking—planking a hull with narrow edge-fastened strips of solid lumber— has enjoyed popularity in certain areas for many years. Currently the edge-fastening system consists of an adhesive plus nails to hold the strips together during the curing cycle of the adhesive. Strip planking was also practiced before the era of waterproof adhesives, but the fits between the strakes of planking had to be as near perfect as possible. The skin resulting from modern edge-fastening produces a dimensionally stable structure that lends itself to sheathing with fiberglass or other such synthetic materials. This planking method can be used to build either round- or v-bottomed hulls, and I have even seen strip-planked trunk cabin sides.

Strip planking is reasonably easy for the amateur, *the shape of the hull dictating just how many complications will be encountered*. Unless girths of the hull from keel to sheer are the same throughout the length of the hull (and normally they will not be by any means), there is usually more to strip planking a hull than just nailing one parallel-sided strip to another just like it. It is easy to understand that when the girths vary, something must be done to compensate for this, just as with carvel planking.

The dimensions of the strips are a matter of design, but they are usually at least ½″ thick, and anywhere from the same dimension in width up to a width of one and one-half times the thickness. There is an advantage to using square strips: it gives the builder the opportunity to select the best grain. Due to the natural expansion and contraction of wood, the strips are best laid with the grain running in the direction shown in Figure 11-15C. Thickness is governed by the shape of the hull—the strips must bend on the hull without coming close to breaking. At the other end of the scale, the strips must be stiff enough to remain fair when sprung to the shape of the hull.

Sections through strip planking are drawn in Figure 11-15. The amount of curvature regulates the amount of beveling required, as can be seen in Figure 11-15A. Note the open seams around the turn of the bilge on the unbeveled strips. The smaller the boat, the greater the relative curvature to be reckoned with. Some builders hollow one edge and round the other to eliminate beveling. (*See* Figure 11-15B.)

If the strips are not long enough, they must be scarphed. You can make a miter box of sorts for doing this by hand, or the cutting can be done on a bench saw or with a radial saw. The length of the scarph should be about five times the strip thickness. Scarphs should be glued on the workbench, not on the boat.

The length of the nails should be about two and one-quarter times the width of the strips. The choice of metal for the nails is largely a matter of economics. If cost does not matter, either Monel Anchorfast or Stronghold silicon bronze nails are the first choice. When getting down to pennies, it is all right to use hot-dipped galvanized

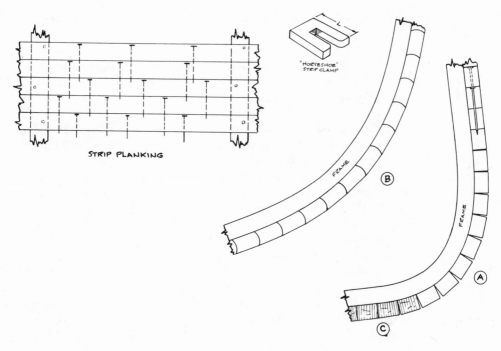

Figure 11-15. *Strip planking details.*

common wire nails, because they are buried in the wood (or should be!), not exposed to water. The spacing and number of nails should be just sufficient to clamp the strips tightly in place while the adhesive cures. Nail heads are set slightly below the surface of the wood with a nail set. Some like to drive the nails at an angle to the strip for a locking action. If the hull mold contains bulkheads or other permanent framing, every other strip or so should be fastened to such a member with a nail or screw.

Before epoxy resins became available, resorcinol glue was used between the edges of strip planking. Resorcinol is a very good adhesive; however, it needs pressure during curing time and is not noted for its ability to fill gaps. In strip planking there is sufficient pressure possible from the nail fastenings, but the fits between the adjacent strakes of planking must be pretty close or the resorcinol will run out of the seam. Now there are epoxies, which do not need much pressure, and to which a filler can be added, thickening the adhesive so it won't run out of the joint if the fit is less than perfect.

There are options when it comes to setting up a mold over which to build a hull with strip planking. The edge-fastened skin is so stiff that the number of frames that would be needed normally for the same thickness carvel planking is drastically reduced. Or the frames might be omitted altogether, with the hull planked over temporary transverse molds of suitable number to shape the hull. Bulkheads and a few frames, if needed, can be added to the structure later, or bulkheads can be part of the setup and left in the hull. The hull is best built right side up (unless it is to be quite large), and is best set up in a building with plenty of overhead clearance so that the keel can be high enough off the floor that there is a minimum of working in a stooped position.

The builder should be advised that strip planking is often a two-person job, because the wide interval of molds or bulkheads minimizes the number of places where strips can be clamped into position. However, the reduced number of molds needed for this planking method means a saving of time and material in the setup.

Some of the best strip planking workmanship ever turned out was done by Ralph Wiley in his yard on the eastern shore of Maryland. A few of his strip-planked deep-keel sailboats that I saw were planked with mahogany strips about 1¼″ square. The parallel-sided strips extended from the sheer and ran to well below the waterline, where Wiley then tapered the strakes suitably and worked the edges to bevels for perfect glue fits. The planking was, of course, started at the keel and was planned in advance to determine where the tapering would stop and the parallel-sided strips would take over. In my opinion, beveled strip planking thicker than ⅞″ is just too much of a job for the first attempt by the amateur.

Before tapering frightens unduly, let us look at a layout for strip planking hulls of simple form used by Fred Bates, designer-builder of Damariscotta, Maine, that eliminates tapering. Referring to A in Figure 11-16, planking strips are laid starting at the keel and are temporarily held in place, not permanently fastened. Then a distance equal to a number of strip widths is laid off from the sheer at each frame or mold, and a line is drawn on the strips by springing a batten through the points. The strips are carefully marked for exact location, then removed and cut to the line, and are permanently replaced with glue and fastenings. The remainder of the hull is planked with parallel-sided strips to the sheer.

Fred has a good scheme for keeping the strips of planking aligned while nailing. He makes a dozen or so of the horsehoe clamps sketched in Figure 11-15. These are cut

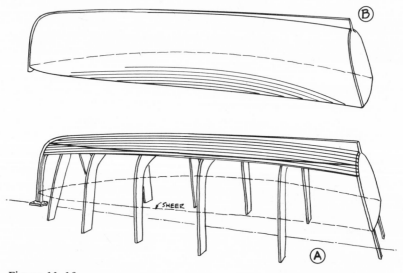

Figure 11-16.

from scrap ¼" plywood, varying the depth L, with a slot width of slightly more than the strip thickness.

A number of Rhodes-designed sailboats were built using parallel strips with rounded and hollowed edges. There was no tapering of the strips; they started at the keel and ran out at the sheer, as indicated in Figure 11-16B.

Ray Kargard of Marinette, Wisconsin, produced a Rhodes one-design sloop whose shape was particularly well-suited to strip planking. Ray planked with round- and hollow-edged strips machined on all four sides in a single pass. For production purposes, molds were erected upside down; the frames were bent over permanent ribbands. The sheerstrake was spiled and the lower edge made convex to mate with the hollow edge of the first strip. The garboard plank was also spiled. Finished widths for the sheerstrake and the garboard compensated for differences in the section girths.

Still another version of strip planking that I have seen was a method where hull strips were laid on diagonally. This strake arrangement resulted in a herringbone appearance as one looked down into the hull.

Plywood Planking

The fact that a hull is v-bottomed does not automatically mean that it can be planked with plywood: plywood can be bent without distortion in only one axis at a time and thus should only be used to plank hulls designed with its limitations in mind. The sections of vessels designed for plywood construction generally consist of developable curves—curves that consist of portions of cylinders and cones. It should not go unnoted that experienced builders have succeeded where theory dictates the impossible. However, the methods used just about defy written description. Suffice it to say then, that you should review the plans of your boat carefully before deciding to plank it with plywood panels.

Plywood is stiff material; therefore, planking thickness can be less than it would be with conventional wooden planking. Also an advantage is its ability to cover large areas quickly. Often, standard plywood panels will be too short for you to plank in one panel from bow to stern. If so, either special panels must be ordered or else the regular panels must be butted end to end. These joints, which should be detailed on the plans, are generally made with good-size butt blocks. The joints should be waterproof glued and well fastened with screws or rivets.

Note that plywood panels butted end-to-end do not want to bend in a fair curve due to increased stiffness in way of the butt block. As indicated in Chapter 4, you can scarph plywood yourself or suppliers will do it for you.

While being fitted, the plywood should be fastened with just enough screws to hold it in place. When the fit is satisfactory, remove the panel and apply marine or waterproof glue to chines, rabbet, frames, etc., and bend the plywood on again, again with just a few screws to hold it. Working as fast as possible because of the glue, drive the remaining screws, of which there are a great many. Work from the middle of the panel toward the ends, drilling for screws and countersinking the heads slightly below the surface of the panel so they can be made invisible with marine surfacing putty.

Figure 11-17. *Scarphed stock with dog leg to suit curve of plank, a saving (in this example) of 40% in width.*

Some builders use plywood instead of solid lumber for the inner layer or even both layers of a double-planked hull, even when there is considerable curvature. They apply the plywood in pieces as large as will bend on the hull and in this way save labor over the usual double-planking method.

Some builders, too, of lapstrake boats have switched from solid lumber to plywood. A shop that has tooled for a production run will typically plank a hull over a rugged jig consisting of inverted section molds and permanent ribbands. When boats are built one-off, the setup is more conventional, and the planks are cut and hung like solid stock. However, in both cases—custom and production—the plywood is generally scarphed to glue a "dog leg" as required by the shape of each plank. (*See* Figure 11-17.) At the sheer a three-piece dog leg may be required, but this procedure minimizes the amount of sheet material needed for an S-shaped plank.

A plywood plank, being a dimensionally stable laminate, lends itself to *glued* lapstrake construction, especially when the glue used is an epoxy. An increasing number of builders have been exploring this method in recent years, but a detailed discussion of the variations on this theme is beyond the scope of this book.

Cold-molding

A cold-molded hull consists of multiple layers of thin veneers (as thin as ¹⁄₁₆″ for small boats) or strips bonded to each other with a waterproof adhesive to form a stiff, strong skin. Generally, the first layer of strips is laid up diagonally at about 45 degrees to the centerline of the mold or frame, the second layer at 90 degrees to the first, the third at 90 degrees to the second, etc. Depending upon the designer's specifications, sometimes as many as five layers of thin strakes are used to build up the desired thickness. While the glue is curing, the strakes are secured with staples, nails or screws, which are usually removed after the glue sets up. As noted in the section on adhesives, the modern waterproof glues—resorcinols and epoxies—set up at room temperatures, thus the reason for the term cold-molding.

Although all cold-molded hulls are built upside down, they can be built by various methods. The method used by most amateurs is to laminate a skin over a skeletal framework, which usually consists of some sort of backbone, transverse forms (some of which are bulkheads and frames), and longitudinal stringers. Another method is to build up a hull on a male mold, which may be either a strip-planked plug or a form with closely spaced ribbands. In this case, the supporting structure does not become a part of the hull; the finished shell is lifted off the form, and structural members, such as bulkheads and transverse frames, are installed as necessary. Still another method combines these two: the first layer of planking is strip-planked over a skeletal framework and then successive layers of planking are laid on diagonally.

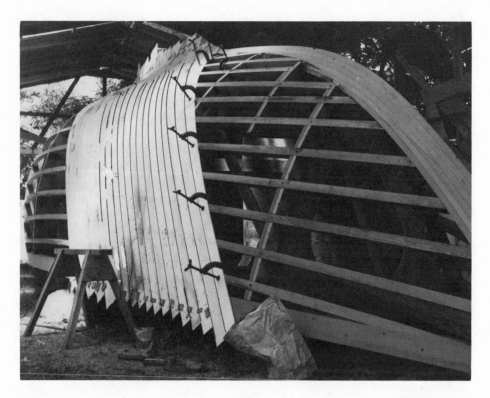

Figure 11–18. *The first skin being applied to a framework of molds, bulkheads, and stringers.* (Photo courtesy of John Guzzwell.)

Each method has definite advantages for particular applications, and there are variations within each method as to skin thickness, number of planking layers, and the number and weight of internal strengthening members. The designer draws up his construction specifications with the intended vessel's size, its shape, and its purpose in mind. In the last 15 years, the cold-molding process has been the subject of much scientific research and development. The end result has been that designers have been able to specify hull construction scantlings with strength-to-weight ratios approaching that of aluminum. The leader in this field has been the firm of Gougeon Brothers, who developed the WEST (Wood Epoxy Saturation Technique) System. Some builders emphatically disagree with the claimed amount of wood saturation, but I withhold judgment.

Whatever the method chosen, cold-molding has several attractions. A hull built with a cold-molded skin can be built very light because of the stiffness of the laminated planking, or if desired, a very stiff hull can be built by laminating the hull up to a desired thickness. Either way, the hull construction entails lighter work than that needed to construct a wooden hull by the traditional method. The interest has been heightened for many because high quality is easier to achieve when working with light materials. Tied closely to this is the availability of the superb adhesives, particularly the epoxies. To cap it all off, the dimensional stability of laminated planking means that the outside of cold-molded hulls can be fiberglassed for protection from abrasion. Thus, it is possible for the amateur to build a tough, strong, long-lived hull that might otherwise have been beyond his ability with other methods.

However, although it might seem to the amateur that laminating up a hull of thin strips is child's play compared to bending frames and spiling and cutting out planks, there is no substitute for skill and care in any facet of boatbuilding. The lines must still be accurately lofted, and a true and sturdy mold must be constructed. There is still a great amount of spiling to be done to get the joints between the planks to butt tightly against one another. Indeed, some professionals have opined that, to build a cold-molded boat, a builder must go through a complete planking routine for each layer, meaning that the hull is planked not just once, but at least three and perhaps as many as five times, depending upon the numbers of layers. In addition, some hull shapes can prove tricky to build; hulls with reverse curves seem to give a great amount of trouble, and one professional builder has stated that such hulls should not be attempted by anyone less than a really skilled, patient craftsman.

There are three excellent books listed under Recommended Reading that deal with cold-molding at considerable length. These are *Modern Wooden Yacht Construction* by John Guzzwell, *The Gougeon Brothers on Boat Construction*, and *Cold-Moulded and Strip-Planked Wood Boatbuilding* by Ian Nicolson. Much can be learned about the details of cold-molding from these books, which have been written by those with a great deal of experience with this type of construction.

Diagonal Planking

Although it predates cold-molding by quite some time, diagonal planking is very similar to cold-molding. In fact, as it is practiced now, using waterproof glue between the planking layers instead of fabric soaked in a waterproofing agent as was formerly done, it can be considered to be a form of cold-molding. What makes it a bit different is that it employs strakes that are thicker than veneers and that it often consists of only two layers of planking. Because of the greater strake thickness, this method is used mostly on v-bottomed powerboats, where the change in shape that each strake encounters is much less severe than on round-bottomed hulls. The planking is generally fastened to a framework consisting of keel, chines, clamps, and transverse frames (or in some cases, a fewer number of transverse frames or bulkheads together with longitudinals). A frame hull awaiting double diagonal planking is shown in Figure 9-9, Chapter 9.

The scheme of diagonal planking is shown in Figure 11-19, and can be seen to be similar to that of cold-molding. The planking material is made of uniform width, 2″ to 4″ wide, depending upon the size of the hull. The first layer is laid up at a 45-degree angle to the keel and is secured with glue and screws or nails to frames, chine, and keel or sheer clamp, with the edges of the strakes also being glued to one another.

Toward the bow, the planks must be tapered, as the convergence of the bottom and the topsides tends to change the angle of the planks too much out of parallel with

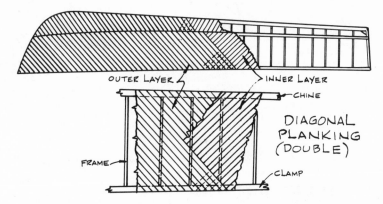

OUTER LAYER

INNER LAYER

CHINE

DIAGONAL
PLANKING
(DOUBLE)

FRAME

CLAMP

Figure 11-19.

those amidships. Tapering brings the planks back approximately into line; the angle is not critical, as long as the planks cross several frames.

The second layer is glued to the first and is also edge-glued and fastened in place with screws to the keel, chines, clamps, and frames. To provide clamping pressure between frames, the intersections of the inner and outer strakes are clout nailed. The clout nail heads are countersunk while the nails are backed up by a helper inside the hull. When planking strakes are ⅝″ thick or more, the fastenings between the framing can be wood screws driven from the inside to eliminate puttying over the heads on the outside of the hull. After the adhesive has cured, the planking is smoothed by sanding.

Chapter   12

DECK FRAMING

The decking of a boat normally is laid on transverse beams, which not only provide support for the deck but also help to hold the sides of the hull together. The latter aspect is important in all boats designed to be decked, especially in sailboats. These days, however, innovative construction methods for lightweight racing sailboats combine both transverse and longitudinal deck framing.

Clamps and Shelves

The deck beams must be of good size and strongly connected to the hull if they are to contribute the strength required of them. In small boats they are fastened to the clamp and the frame heads (Figure 12-1A and B). As hulls increase in size, an additional stiffening member called a shelf, or deck shelf, is fitted on each side of the boat. The shelf is generally of the same material as the clamp, and its position on the flat against the clamp provides a greater landing area for the beam ends, which are fastened through it instead of the clamp.

In small craft, screws are used as fastenings, but in larger vessels through-bolts are always used. Bolts have the extra advantage of being able to be tightened if necessary, whereas screws through beams are not accessible once the boat is decked. To lessen the concentration of fastenings in the vicinity of the deck beams, shelves are fastened to the clamps *between* frames. (*See* Figure 12-1.) They are sprung in place on edge in single lengths when possible, or in several pieces joined by scarphs, with the joints located toward the ends of the boat, or they can be laminated. The inner edges may be left square, but the outer edges should be planed to fit snugly against the clamps. The shelves must be fitted with a pitch corresponding to the camber of the deck beams so that the beams will bear on the shelves' entire width. The best way to get the bevel is to temporarily set a few deck beams in place so the bevels may be measured every few

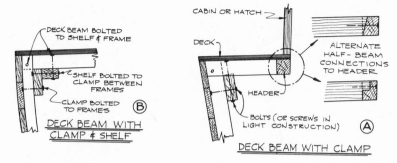

Figure 12-1.

feet, or at least at every station. The edges of the shelves can then be planed to the proper angle. (*See* Figure 12-2A.)

When the clamp and shelf are bolted together, they function as a single member, shaped like an angle-iron, that contributes strength and stiffness in two directions; for maximum benefit, *they should be connected at the ends of the hull.* At the bow this is done with a breasthook, which is a knee of sorts fitted between the shelves and bolted to them. The hook was often sawn out of a natural wood crook, either of oak or hackmatack. Just as good a connection is a piece of oak or a laminated plywood sandwich laid on top of the shelves and through-bolted (Figure 12-3A).

The shelf/clamp assemblies join one another at the stern via the transom. For a flat transom, this connection takes the form of quarter knees, which are sawn from crooks and bolted in place on top of the shelves and against the transom cross framing at the underside of the deck. With a curved transom, the connection is more difficult. In this case the knees must have the proper deck camber and fit the transom curve as well. Unless you are a skilled loftsman who can work out the intersection of the deck and transom on the floor, it is best to make these pieces by the cut-and-try method.

The plan view shape is easy to obtain, as it is shown on the deck framing plan for the boat. The shape of the top edge of the knees is best obtained on the boat. Install

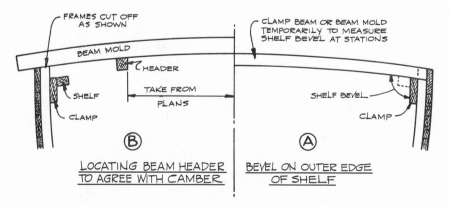

Figure 12-2.

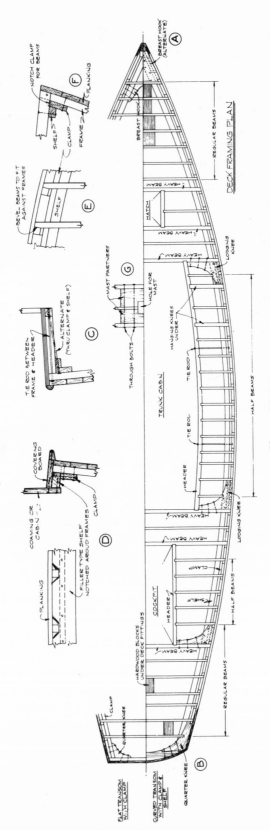

Figure 12-3.

the deck beams for the five or six feet ahead of the transom and at intervals of three or four inches on each side of the centerline, clamp a batten on top of the beams, its aft edge just touching the inside of the transom. Mark the transom at the underside of the batten each time the batten is clamped; a line through the marks will represent the underside of the decking as well as the top curve of the quarter knees. The battens can also be used to measure the bevel needed for the aft edges of the knees. Shaped as they are in every dimension, these pieces are really quite a job for the amateur, and thus a job to be proud of when completed for the first time.

Deck Beams

The deck beams should be made of oak or ash where maximum strength and durability are desired, and of spruce where lightness is a consideration. There should be a beam at each frame, and they should be cambered, both for strength and so the deck will quickly shed any water that comes aboard. Where the camber is normal the beams can be sawn to shape. Where there is high camber, such as is often found in cabin tops, it is best to laminate the beams of three or more pieces over a form, using waterproof glue. Beam construction is shown in Figure 12-4A. Most of the beams will have the same siding, but at hatches, mast partners, and the ends of cabin trunks, the beams should be heavier by about 75 percent than the regular beams. (*See* Figure 12-3).

Although it is customary to represent the beams and frames on the plans in the manner shown in Figure 12-3, Figure 12-3E shows that the beams must be beveled to fit against the frame heads. This is because the frames are twisted to lie flat against the planking, which curves toward the centerline toward the ends of the boat. Due to a combination of deck camber and flaring hull sections, the inboard corner of the clamp must sometimes be cut away so the beams will land on a flat surface instead of a point. This is sketched in Figure 12-3F. Remember that what counts is the close and careful fitting of all structural parts of the hull.

Deck Beam Camber

The amount of camber is given on the plans or in the specifications and is stated as a depth of curve of so many inches for a given length, using the length of the longest beam. To make a beam pattern, or a beam mold as it is called, the procedure in Figure 12-4B is followed, or the camber may be laid out easily with the mechanical method shown in Figure 12-4C. The method shown in Figure 12-4B is self-explanatory and is suitable when only one camber curve is needed, but C is faster and very useful should you run into a cabin top where each beam has a different camber. In this method, three nails are driven in the pattern board, one at each end of the beam length and one at the center of the beam length at the top of the arc. Then two straight-edged battens, each longer than the longest beam by at least two feet, are placed snugly against the nails as shown and tacked together rigidly enough to hold the angle between the battens. The camber curve can then be drawn by sliding the batten assembly from the

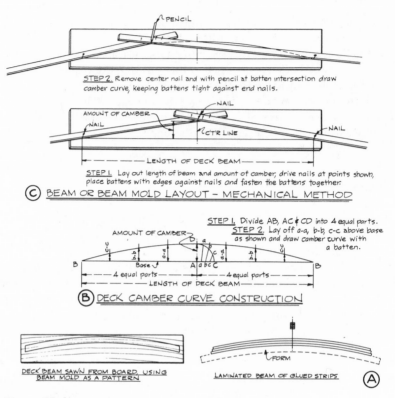

PENCIL

STEP 2. Remove center nail and with pencil at batten intersection draw camber curve, keeping battens tight against end nails.

NAIL

AMOUNT OF CAMBER

NAIL

CTR LINE

NAIL

LENGTH OF DECK BEAM

STEP 1. Lay out length of beam and amount of camber; drive nails at points shown, place battens with edges against nails and fasten the battens together.

Ⓒ BEAM OR BEAM MOLD LAYOUT – MECHANICAL METHOD

STEP 1. Divide AB, AC & CD into 4 equal parts.
STEP 2. Lay off a-a, b-b, c-c above base as shown and draw camber curve with a batten.

AMOUNT OF CAMBER

Base

4 equal parts — 4 equal parts

LENGTH OF DECK BEAM

Ⓑ DECK CAMBER CURVE CONSTRUCTION

DECK BEAM SAWN FROM BOARD, USING BEAM MOLD AS A PATTERN

FORM

LAMINATED BEAM OF GLUED STRIPS   Ⓐ

Figure 12-4.

centerline to one end of the beam and then to the other, always holding the battens in contact with the nails at the ends.

Half Beams and Headers

At the sides of deck openings the beams are short (Figure 12-3) and are termed half beams. The opening is bounded by the strong beams mentioned previously and the fore-and-aft headers into which the half beams are notched and fastened as shown in Figure 12-1A. The old-timers always dovetailed the half beams, but the connection is more often made by the easier method shown in the sketches. The headers must be elevated to coincide with the camber of the beams, and the procedure is to make a couple of beam molds, clamp them in the space between the strong beams, then pull the header up to the mold, all the while springing the header to its planned dimensions from the centerline of the boat. (*See* Figure 12-2B.)

In powerboats and small sailboats with very narrow side decks, the normal half beams are sometimes replaced by a shelf fitted on top of the clamp. The shelf in this case is simply a filler piece as thick as the deck beams, notched around the frame heads, on which is laid the decking or a covering board. This kind of shelf extends only for the length of the narrow side deck, the usual clamp being fitted from bow to stern. (*See* Figure 12-3D.)

Deck Tie Rods and Lodging Knees

When the decking consists of planks rather than large pieces of plywood, the deck framing is stiffened with tie rods running between frame heads or clamps and the headers (Figure 12-3C). These fastenings also take some of the load off the connections between header and half beams. For additional stiffening there may be "lodging" knees in the deck frame to provide strength at ends of large openings in the deck or at masts. These knees are sawn from hackmatack or oak crooks and are planed on top to conform with the deck camber. They are bolted or riveted to the beams and shelf or clamp. (*See* Figure 12-3.) Alternatively, the knees may be made from marine plywood, and further laminated to a specified thickness if necessary.

Deck Blocking

Wherever there are fittings on deck such as cleats and tackle blocks, there should be blocks fitted between the beams to take through-fastenings. The blocks provide more wood for the fastenings to bear against, and they distribute the load to the beams in the case of shearing forces, and over a greater area of decking when upward strains are encountered. The blocks can be of oak, mahogany, or plywood and should be planed on top to conform to the deck camber and sawn to a tight fit between beams. Blocks are shown in the deck framing, Figure 12-3.

Mast Partners

The deck framing plan in Figure 12-3 is for a sloop having its mast stepped through the cabin trunk, the top of which has large blocks called mast partners fitted between beams. These blocks are always as thick as the depth of the deck beams between which they are fitted, and they are made of hardwood or laminated plywood and through-bolted. The supplementary sketch, Figure 12-3G, shows a set of typical mast partners, whether located in the trunk top or the main deck.

All comparatively large deck frame surfaces, such as blocking or lodging knees, should be coated with thick bedding as the decking is laid. This serves to keep out water should there be a leak in the vicinity. Take special care to treat the raw edges of any plywood used.

Hanging Knees

The forces exerted on a boat by seas and by masts in sailboats work to collapse a hull in a manner similar to the way that a packing box from which the ends have been removed collapses when a man stands on it. These forces try to hinge the hull structure at the deck corner—this is only one of the reasons why properly sized and located fastenings are important if long hull life is to be expected. Brackets called hanging knees are fitted for resisting such sideways strains. Like lodging knees, they have been traditionally made of natural crook oak or hackmatack and always through-

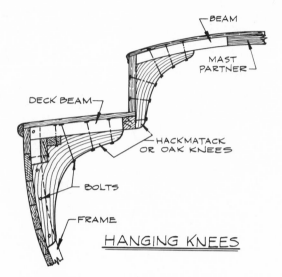

Figure 12–5.

fastened insofar as possible. Metal, in the form of flanged plates, plates and angles, or castings, is often used for knees and has the advantage of not splitting with age as wood is liable to do. Hanging knees are generally used in pairs at the masts and singly at the ends and midlength of long deck openings. Figure 12-5 shows typical wooden hanging knees at the mast partners of a sloop having its mast stepped through the cabin trunk.

Figure 12-6 shows an alternate method to natural crook or metal knees, using marine plywood instead. Thickness will depend upon the size of the boat, ranging from a single thickness ½" or ¼" to heavier if needed (built up by laminating with ½" or ¼" thick pieces); once again, through-bolts in snug holes are used insofar as possible.

Modern Construction

The quarter knees, lodging knees, and hanging knees described earlier as oak or hackmatack natural crooks are used in traditional construction. The problem with such knees is to find them and then to pay a reasonable price for them. It should be realized that there are modern materials and techniques available for small craft that can eliminate the need for traditional crook knees of oak and hackmatack. As pointed out before, knees can be laminated of wood or plywood or be made of flanged metal plates. Or, knees need not be used at all due to the enormous stiffening provided by modern materials: a well-fitted and secure plywood deck can do the work of lodging knees, and properly secured plywood interior joiner bulkheads in effective locations often take the place of hanging knees.

In any case, be guided by the plans for your boat. The designer should provide details of the structure in way of masts when panel material is used for weight and labor savings.

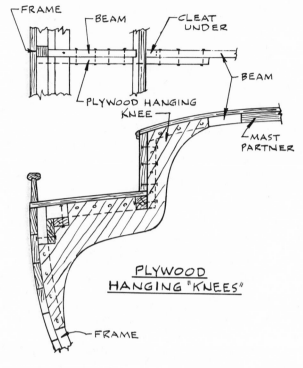

Figure 12-6.

If there are a number of bulkheads and full-height joiner partitions in a hull, as is common in many power cruisers packed full of cabins, head enclosures, etc., a deck consisting of two layers of plywood glued together can be supported by these bulkheads and partitions with a minimum of other deck framing—just a few transverse beams or longitudinals where it is necessary to reduce the span of unsupported areas.

Chapter 13

DECKING

Due to the availability of waterproof plywood and synthetic fabrics, various decking methods described when this book was first printed in 1950 are now virtually obsolete. They are of interest still to restorers and to traditionalists, but discussion here will be brief.

Tongue-and-Groove Deck

Tongue-and-groove nail-fastened boards make an inexpensive deck because the width of the material, anywhere from 4″ to 6″, permits the deck to be quickly built, with the boards parallel to the centerline of the boat as in Figure 13-1A. Very often these decks are made of non-durable material, unseasoned in the first place, and quick to rot if the deck covering leaks. The straight-run deck is not as strong as other types and the tongue-and-groove construction has the disadvantage that the thin upper edge of the groove tends to warp between the fastenings (Figure 13-1B). The only covering for a tongue-and-groove deck of wide boards that will come and go easily with the moisture in the air is old-fashioned canvas duck. The groove warping shows through the canvas as ridges and the canvas life is shortened by wearing along these ridges.

Unless the boards are laid in single lengths, there must be joints in the decking, and these should be scattered as much as possible. For strength and to prevent curling, the butt ends must be well fastened, and it is not practical to make such a butt on a deck beam. Instead, the ends are fastened between the deck beams to blocks similar to planking butt blocks.

These decks are generally fastened with common galvanized nails; with age the fasteners have a way of working upward and poking holes in the canvas, causing it to leak. Galvanized wood screws would be better, and annularly threaded bronze nails

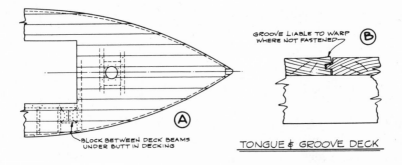

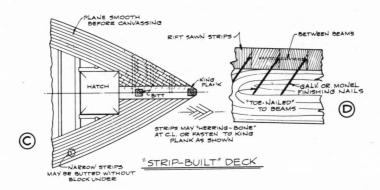

Figure 13-1.

better still; but on the whole, a tongue-and-groove deck really does not have much to recommend it except low cost, and in time even this is doubtful.

Strip-Built Deck

The strip-built type of decking shown in Figure 13-1C is strong, rather quickly laid, and suitable when the deck is ½" thick or better. The strakes are usually square, or perhaps just a little wider than their thickness, and for maximum rigidity they are sprung to the curve of the deck edge. It is best to cut any laid decking from rift-sawn boards and lay it with the edge-grain up, for this way there will be a minimum of shrinking and swelling across the width of the deck. (*See* Figure 4-3.) Galvanized finishing nails are used for fastening and are satisfactory because they are hidden and not exposed to sea water. The fastidious, of course, can substitute nonferrous Monel or bronze nails at many times the cost and eliminate all misgivings. The strakes are fastened to each other between the deck beams and toenailed to the beams as shown in D of Figure 13-1. At the deck edge, the outermost strip is fastened to the sheer strake of planking.

If a strip-built deck is built with waterproof-glued seams like a strip-planked hull (Chapter 11), it will be enormously strong if the seams are fitted reasonably tight.

After being planed smooth and sanded, such a deck can be finished bright, painted, or covered with canvas (refer to "Canvas-Covered Decks" below) or light synthetic cloth and then painted.

Plywood Deck

A main deck or cabin top of marine plywood is strong, light, and quickly laid. The arrangement of the pieces of plywood must be planned with care to provide maximum strength for the deck and for minimum waste of material, taking into consideration openings in the deck for hatches, cockpit, and cabin, together with the size of the panels available. In the previous chapter, the function in construction of lodging knees under the deck at openings and at masts to minimize horizontal racking was mentioned. Following the same reasoning, the plywood should be cut so seams do not come at the ends of large openings in the deck as shown in Figure 13-2A. The butts should overlap as shown in the sketch, and joints should be located between the beams where the panel ends can be securely screw fastened to a butt block underneath. Joint locations are not as important if the plywood is waterproof glued to the deck beams, because this adds considerably to the horizontal strength.

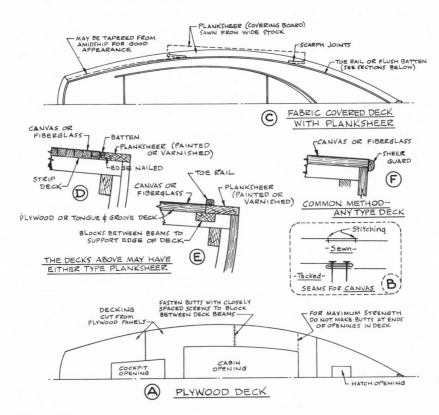

Figure 13-2.

The deck panels should be fastened around the edges and along the deck beams with closely spaced flat-head screws or annularly threaded nails. Countersink the fastening heads slightly below the surface and cover them over with a surfacing putty, non-oil base if the deck is to be covered with fiberglass cloth and resin.

A well-fitted plywood deck properly glued to the deck framing can be fastened with non-ferrous staples. Plywood up to ½" thick can be fastened with coated Monel staples driven by compressed-air-powered staplers. The coating increases the staples' holding power so it is just about impossible to withdraw these staples from white oak deck beams. (*See* Chapter 6.)

When a plywood deck is specified to be ¼" in thickness or more, the curvature due to camber and sheer might make laying the deck in a single thickness either very difficult or even impossible due to the stiffness of seven-ply panels. As soon as it is obvious that the flat panels will not conform to the surface, the job must be done by using a double thickness, such as two layers of ¼", ⅜", or ½" plywood, which should be waterproof glued together to provide the most strength.

Canvas-Covered Decks

Because boat decks—both laid and plywood—are still being covered with cotton canvas in certain areas by some builders, the method merits a brief description.

Canvas for covering should be bought wide enough to go over the entire deck in one piece if possible, allowing enough width to turn down over the edge of the deck. If a suitable width cannot be had, get a canvas worker to sew two strips together so that there will be a seam down the centerline of the boat. When unable to use sewn canvas, tack it on the centerline with a double fold. Seams are sketched in Figure 13-2B.

The weight of the canvas varies from 8-ounce for small boats to 10- and even 12-ounce for decks that are liable to get considerable wear. Although there are canvas cements on the market, it is recommended instead that the canvas be laid in *wet* marine paint (not house paint). This of course will be applied to the deck just before laying the canvas.

First stretch the canvas fore and aft along the centerline. The canvas should be stretched as tight as possible, and this is at least a two-man job. It is better accomplished by rolling the ends of the canvas around sticks so that more area can be worked on than can be handled by just your two hands. Pull the canvas down over the edges of the boat and secure it with tacks, which will be hidden by moldings. Tacks should be copper or Monel, never steel or even galvanized, and should be very closely spaced in order for them to hold the pressure.

After the ends are fastened, start working amidships, pulling from opposite sides of the boat and tacking as you go along until the canvas is completely fastened around the edges. Where the canvas covers openings for cabin and hatches, cut it about 4" inside of the openings, stretch it tightly, and temporarily tack it to headers and beams; it will be turned up inside deck structures later as they are added to the boat.

When the canvas has been completely fastened, it is a good idea to apply the deck paint undercoater. Believe it or not, one of the best methods is to wet the canvas to further shrink and stretch it just before painting. Do this with a scrubbing brush and paint the surface before the canvas is dry. At any time later, one or two more coats of flat paint can be added, then a final coat of deck paint.

Covering Surfaces with Glass Reinforced Plastic

I am going to touch only on covering the most dimensionally stable wooden structures—plywood panels, diagonally planked cold-molded hulls, or glued-seam strip-planked hulls (Chapter 11)—with fiberglass cloth, the most commonly used of the synthetic fabrics. There is often disagreement about covering these surfaces: should the cloth be laid on bare wood and then saturated with resin, or should the bare wood be coated with resin, and the glass cloth laid in the tacky resin, smoothed, and immediately saturated with another coat of resin? I don't think it makes much difference, but I have found that the "wet first" method makes an already messy job even worse.

The Glen-L Marine book, *How to Fiberglass Boats*, provides a straightforward account of fiberglassing procedures and should be read prior to a first attempt at fiberglassing. For further information about the book, refer to Recommended Reading after Chapter 17 of this text.

Polyester resin is the most widely used of the resins and should be of the "laminating" type until the last build-up coat; this coat, which will be sanded smooth, should be "finish" resin. The book mentioned above describes how to make an additive that changes the laminating resin to a finish resin, the latter giving the hard and sandable surface necessary for painting.

Stable surfaces like plywood can be covered with a single layer of cloth, while corners, such as the chines of a v-bottomed boat, are reinforced with doubling strips. The adhesion of the wood surface is improved if rough sanded.

Do not use an oil-based putty or filler in dents or over the heads of fastenings. Instead, make a putty by mixing a powder called Cabosil (or a similar product such as microballoons or microspheres) sold by resin suppliers.

Epoxy resin has a greater adhesion to wood than polyester but is significantly more expensive. However, epoxy does minimize the risk of the overlay delaminating from the wood. In addition I prefer epoxy to any other resin when covering a surface that has been previously painted.

Fiberglass decks are painted after being sanded smooth, a fiberglass primer being used as the first coat.

If the cabin sides and such items as hatch coamings are to be finished bright, the decks should be covered before the installation of the deck joinerwork. When everything is to be painted, the watertight method is to build the cabin, etc., and turn the fabric up against it for an inch or two, "feathering" the edge of the covering by tapering it with the sander so it is not visible in the finished job.

The fabrics are also available in tape form. These narrow strips are great for strengthening and making watertight exterior woodwork joints that will be painted.

Warning: Heed all safety precautions when working with resins and synthetic fabrics.

Decks with Planksheer

The completely canvas-covered deck needs a molding on the sheer strake (Figure 13-2F) in order to hide the edge of the canvas. An attractive alternative is a deck with a varnished or contrasting colored covering board at the edge of the deck (Figure 13-2C). This piece is called the *planksheer* and is sawn from wide boards. The joints between segments are scarphed rather than merely butted, and are generally screw-fastened from the top to butt blocks under the deck.

The canvas is stopped at the edge of the planksheer in either of two ways. The inner edge of the planksheer can be rabbeted (Figure 13-2D), the canvas run down into the groove and tacked, and the groove filled with a tightly fitted batten of wood to match the planksheer. Another way is to employ a toe rail set at the inner edge of the planksheer as shown in Figure 13-2E. The fabric is tacked along the edge and the toe rail is fastened over the canvas with plugged screws. This is also a suitable termination for decks where the fabric covering is fiberglass rather than canvas.

The outermost strake of a strip-built deck is edge-fastened to the planksheer for support, but the outer edge of a tongue-and-groove deck would be sprung downward if stepped on between beams where unsupported, perhaps to the extent of tearing the canvas—fiberglass covering a tongue-and-groove deck is not recommended—and splitting the edge of the decking. To prevent this, and also to support the ends of the deck planks where they run out at the edges, there must be blocks fitted between the deck beams.

Caulked Decks

There are two types of caulked decks. In larger yachts, where weight does not make too much difference, deck planking 1″ thick and upward is laid. In smaller boats, where weight is important, thinner decking is laid over a sub-deck of marine plywood.

There is no denying that the old-time caulked decks were prone to leak, usually over someone's berth, but waterproof plywood has come to the rescue. Covered with fiberglass to prevent rot, plywood becomes an ideal underlayment even for the thicker caulked decking.

A typical laid and caulked deck is drawn in Figure 13-3 for a sailboat, and the construction also applies to powerboats. The planksheer is fitted first as described before; then the narrow strakes are sprung parallel to the edge of the planksheer. The reasons for the narrow strakes are twofold: they may be sprung without too much trouble, and the narrow material will not shrink and swell much or check. The wood for a laid deck must be clear and should be in long lengths. Any joints are located so they are quite far apart in adjacent strakes. The wood must be rift sawn so the grain can be laid on edge, because flat grain will eventually lift and splinter—a condition that is both unsightly and hard on bare feet. Suitable woods are good white pine, Douglas fir, Port Orford cedar, and Burma teak. The last named is the best and, like most good things, by far the most expensive. It has a natural oil that seems to make the deck everlasting (if given reasonable care) and it does not have to be varnished or painted. Scrubbing with salt water in the sun will bleach it out to a whitish color so that, together with its long life, there is no deck quite equal to teak.

Teak decks do get dirty and do not look well if neglected, but since so much teak trim is being used on fiberglass boats to offset their otherwise antiseptic appearance, there has been a flood of teak cleaners and treatment systems put on the market. Most

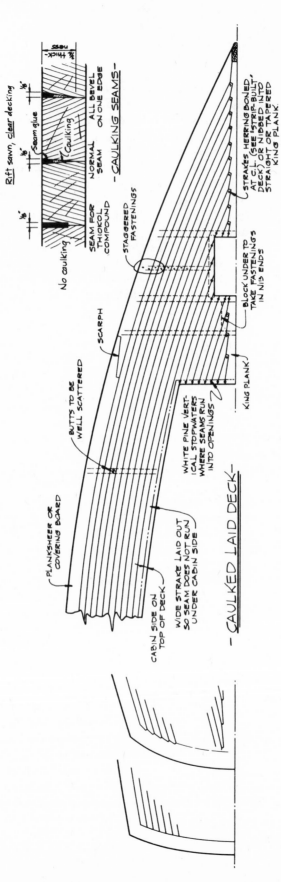

Rift sawn, clear decking

- CAULKING SEAMS -

No caulking

Seam glue

Caulking

NORMAL SEAM

ALL BEVEL ON ONE EDGE

SEAM FOR THIOKOL COMPOUND

⅜" thick-ness

STAGGERED FASTENINGS

SCARPH

BUTTS TO BE WELL SCATTERED

PLANKSHEER OR COVERING BOARD

CABIN SIDE ON TOP OF DECK

WIDE STRAKE LAID OUT SO SEAM DOES NOT RUN UNDER CABIN SIDE

WHITE PINE VERT-ICAL STOPWATERS WHERE SEAMS RUN INTO OPENINGS

KING PLANK

BLOCK UNDER TO TAKE FASTENINGS IN NIB ENDS

STRAKES HERRING BONED AT C.L. (SEE "STRIP-BUILT DECK") OR NIBBED INTO STRAIGHT OR TAPERED KING PLANK

- CAULKED LAID DECK -

Figure 13-3.

of them do a good job and are easy to use, but be certain to follow directions because adjacent painted parts can be damaged by some teak cleaners.

Until the chemists got busy making up new seam compounds, standard practice was to bevel the edges of the deck strakes for caulking to make them watertight, as shown by the enlarged sections in Figure 13-3. The seams were caulked with cotton, then filled with a heated seam glue which, in time, left much to be desired. Now available are thiokol-based sealers that can be run in simple, square seams like the one shown in the figure. After the decking is laid and secured, the open seams are masked with tape. The seam filler is then applied with a regular household-type caulking gun. Care must be taken to avoid air bubbles by keeping the tip of the cartridge at the root of the seam so it is filled from the bottom up. The seams are over-filled and the excess filler is cut off with a *very* sharp chisel after the thiokol has completely cured a few days after paying.

A 1⅛" or 1¼" thick deck will have strakes about 1¼" wide, and this proportion is about right as the thickness of the decking becomes greater in larger boats. Your plans will specify what the designer wants. It is suggested that you use flat-head screws as listed in the table, Figure 6-3. The screws will be countersunk and plugged with bungs of the same wood as the decking, and due to the size of the plug, there will be room for just one fastening at each deck beam. Note in Figure 6-3 that the screw gauge may be reduced for decking, resulting in a smaller bung at times.

It is noted in Figure 13-3 that the strakes may be herringboned at the centerline like the strip-built deck or nibbed into a king plank as drawn. Either way there must be blocks under the deck at the centerline to take fastenings. It is not desirable to let deck seams run under cabin sides, and to avoid this, the strake next to the cabin opening is made wider, as drawn in Figure 13-3. Sometimes the decking strakes are run parallel to the cabin sides, requiring the ends to be nibbed into the planksheer as well as the king plank. Quite a lot of fitting is needed, as the taper on some of the nib ends will be very long. Still another way of decking is to run the planks straight fore and aft, nibbing both into the planksheer and a margin plank around the cabin (unless the cabin sides, too, are straight) and fastening the plank ends to blocks under the deck where the lengths run out at the sides. You will find that the method used in Figure 13-3 is not only common but is pleasing to the eye. When planking is completed, the seams are caulked and payed; then the entire surface of the deck is planed and sanded smooth.

Planking a laid deck over a sub-deck of marine plywood is similar to constructing a conventional laid deck, with the exception that the strakes are not being fastened directly to deck beams. The decking should be thicker than the plywood sub-deck; as an example of proportions, a ⅜" fir plywood sub-deck would be covered with a ⅝" thick teak overlay. Plugging fastening holes can be avoided if desired by back-screwing the teak to the plywood from underneath. Pains must be taken to prevent rotting of the sub-decking should there be a leak in the seams of the teak strakes. In fact, the best builders cover the plywood with 10-ounce fiberglass cloth before laying the teak deck. As an alternative, the teak can be laid on plywood covered with thiokol compound (without allowing it to cure, of course)—a messy but effective job.

If the teak strakes are not back-screwed, the ⅝" thickness mentioned above is sufficient for counterboring and plugging screw holes in the conventional manner.

Chapter 14

DECK JOINERWORK

The amount and character of deck joinerwork will vary with the type of boat. Open boats like daysailers will have simple cockpit coamings, while larger yachts might have a deckhouse, cabin trunk, hatches, watertight cockpit, and bulwark rail. This work should be done carefully and neatly because, regardless of how well you have built your hull, the occasional visitor will make a snap appraisal of your boat based on the appearance of the deck structures. Proper maintenance, too, is necessary, for nothing looks worse than bare and stained woodwork, peeling varnish, or scarred and dirty paint. Even though it is said that a book cannot be judged by its cover, my advice is to take a great deal of care when finishing parts that meet the eye and to keep them shipshape. A discussion about finishing follows, because the builder must keep thinking about the ultimate appearance while doing every bit of the exposed deck joinerwork.

Finishing with Varnish

Traditionally, the finest yachts had vast areas of varnished deck joinerwork of teak or mahogany; indeed, the antique or classic boats and yachts that have been cared for are an unforgettable sight to behold. In current construction, for various reasons, any large areas of varnished fine woods are most likely to be faces of plywood rather than solid lumber, and if fortunate the faces are of veneers thick enough to survive a few refinishings to bare wood. Nowadays, varnished wood ("brightwork") is limited to trim moldings used to accent fore-and-aft lines such as the sheer of the hull.

Teak and mahogany are moderately hard and resistant to scarring, but either of them can be dented by abuse and suffer from neglect. Their natural appearance, though, has appeal to many, and such a finish takes work to produce initially and to maintain. These woods have an open grain that must be filled for a smooth finish. Clear, natural filler is used for teak, while paste filler stains of desired color are applied to the mahoganies. The wood must be sanded to a perfectly smooth finish before filling; then the filler, thinned to brushing consistency, is spread on and allowed to dry to a dull appearance, at which time the excess is wiped off across the grain with clear cotton waste or rags. This is easy after a little practice. After a day of drying, the first coat of varnish can be applied. When this is dry, it should be sanded with a fine-grade abrasive. Repeat for six coats or more and you will have a finish that you will be proud to show off. The work and work area must be clean and free of dust while varnishing.

The waterfront and boatyards are full of highly opinionated people who freely hand out an enormous amount of advice about what kind of varnish to use. As you become more and more experienced, you, too, may also swear by a particular brand, or a mixture of brands. But regardless of the kind of varnish used, the essentials of varnishing remain the same: cleanliness, absence of moisture, and sanding in between coats to kill the gloss.

Finishing with Paint

There is a section about painting in Chapter 16, but I merely want to point out here that, instead of varnishing, you may be painting wood deck joinerwork, such as Philippine mahogany (solid or plywood), fir or MDO plywood, or fiberglass-covered wood. For the finest appearance, and indeed an all-paint finish can be very attractive as well as easy to maintain, the wood must be just as smooth as if it were to be varnished. With a paint finish, the heads of screw fastenings need not be plugged, because countersinking below the surface and covering with a polyester putty will do as well. This is an advantage when working with material that is thin.

Bear in mind that a wooden boat with a painted superstructure can wear varied colors, thus enabling it to avoid the antiseptic appearance of a molded, mono-chromatic, fiberglass superstructure on a production-line glass hull.

Use only a good grade of marine paint. Start with an undercoater, apply glazing compound to smooth out irregularities, sand smooth, apply a second undercoater, glaze again if necessary, and sand lightly and carefully before painting the first finish coat. Sand lightly again to kill the gloss, then apply a second coat of finish.

Starting in mid-1979, the highly touted two-part polyurethane coatings used on aircraft and yachts were marketed in brushable form by several firms catering to the marine trade. For the previous 10 years or so, this high-gloss, durable coating had been available only in a sprayable form not at all adaptable for amateur application. If you are brave and reasonably affluent, use of the polyurethanes can result in a superior finish that will leave the applicator ("painter" is really not proper) truly button-bursting proud.

Cabin Trunk and Cockpit Coaming

The plans of your boat will show you the kind of cabin and coamings (along with heights and half-breadths), type of toe or bulwark rail, size and location of hatches, and other related information; the best I can do is discuss joinerwork details in

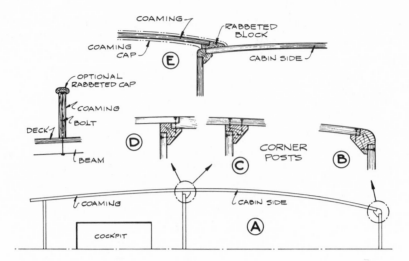

Figure 14–1.

general. The largest structure you will tackle is the cabin trunk, or deckhouse, depending upon the design. If the curve of the cockpit coaming on deck is a continuation of the cabin side, it will be best and easiest to make both coaming and cabin side out of one long piece as in Figure 14-1A. Long, wide mahogany boards are usually available for this, but if not, the width can be made up by edge joining the board with glued splines. If the cabin side is to be of plywood longer than standard panels, these can be made up in the same way.

The shape of the bottom edge of the cabin side, whether it is to rest on the deck or overlap it, is best obtained with a template of thin wood carefully held in place at the deck opening and scribed to the shape. The top edge is taken from the mold loft floor, where it was laid down from the plans. Remember to leave a little extra on the top edge so it can be planed to the camber of the trunk top.

The old-timers dovetailed the corners of the trunk—beautiful but almost unbelievably exacting and time-consuming work—while general practice nowadays is to fit the ends into suitably rabbeted corner posts and to fasten them with glue and plugged screws. (*See* Figure 14-1C.) When making corner posts, make the rabbet deeper by $\frac{1}{16}$" or so than the thickness of the cabin sides, and after assembly, work off the radius corner to a perfect fit.

The sides of the cabin, rather than being vertical, should be sloped *inboard toward the centerline* slightly to keep them from appearing to lean outboard. Sometimes for aesthetic reasons the cabin sides are sloped inboard considerably. This can be a chore for the amateur builder, but the results are often more than pleasing. It is easy to fit the cabin sides inside the deck beam headers as shown in Figure 14-3B, but such a joint is difficult to keep watertight unless the deck is fiberglassed and the fabric turned up against the cabin side for a couple of inches. If the cabin sides are to be finished bright, making turned-up fabric impractical, great care must be taken to fit and bed the cabin sides against the deck edge to ensure watertightness. Thus, it is best to set the cabin sides as shown only when the deck is canvas covered or fiberglassed. With a laid

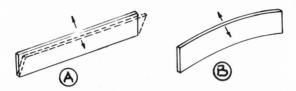

Figure 14–2.

and caulked deck the best way is to make a rabbeted sill piece as sketched in Figure 14-3C. This job is a real challenge, but it is absolutely first class.

Permit me to digress for a moment. I have noticed that a number of shippy-looking traditional-type sailboats are being designed with cabin trunk sides which, in plan view, are straight. And yet, when a mast is stepped through the trunk, there is a structural advantage in *not* having straight sides. To prove this, cut a strip of cardboard and hold it straight on a table; note how easily it hinges along the bottom edge (Figure 14-2A). Now spring the strip to a curve and note the resistance to bending when loaded sideways (B of the same figure).

When trunk sides of solid lumber are specified to be as thick as 1¼″, they should be fastened with bolts through the deck and beam header, with the bolts countersunk into the top edge. Drilling must be very carefully done so as not to ruin the lumber. When the cockpit coaming is thinner than the cabin side, make it out of a separate piece and let it into the trunk at the after end as shown in Figure 14-1D. When the cabin and the coaming are not in a continuous curve, the coaming is usually fastened to the cabin sides through a rabbeted block (Figure 14-1E).

Strangely enough, I have seen only one cabin trunk for a sailboat that had strip-built sides, nailed and glued the same as planking of this type. With the mast stepped through the trunk top, the cabin has to be strong and this is one way to do it easily, discounting amateur labor. In the one case that I saw, female forms were set up, against which the strips were clamped athwartships; the work went quickly and the trunk was very strong.

Sometimes the intersection of the cabin roof and sides is designed with considerable curve at the edges, like that shown in Figure 14-4, or even more so.

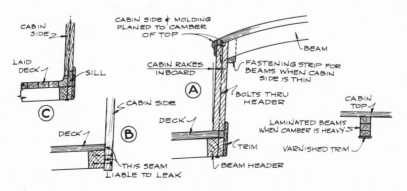

Figure 14–3.

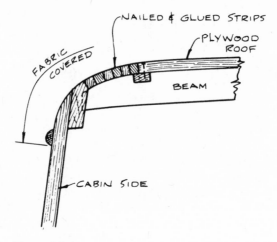

Figure 14-4.

Depending upon whether the roof is single or double planked, it might be impossible to give a quick bend to the plywood edges, especially in view of the curve in plan view. In this case a solution is to strip plank the edge as shown.

Toe Rail

Small sailboats are fitted with toe rails on deck (Figure 14-5A) that are used as a foothold when the boat is heeled, and from long use, have come to be looked on as being decorative as well as practical. The rails are either set slightly inboard of the deck edge or at the inboard edge of the covering board, as mentioned in Chapter 13, and are fastened with plugged screws. Where joints are necessary, the butting pieces are scarphed. The under edge of the rails has scuppers cut at and near the low point of the sheer so that rainwater and spray will drain overboard. The rails may be of the same thickness throughout, but more often they are tapered on the inside face. Small toe rails may be of constant height from end to end, but they look better when tapered; the heights are frequently shown on the lines plan.

Bulwark Rail

Larger boats have what is called a bulwark rail. In most large yacht designs these rails are tapered in height from bow to stern and usually tapered in thickness. Details are shown in Figure 14-5B. Bulwark rails are secured by drift bolts run about every 18″ through the deck into the sheer strake, and are topped with a neatly shaped cap, screw fastened and plugged. The cap is sometimes omitted for economy. Joints in both rail and cap are always scarphed, and the bottom of the rail is scuppered to drain water that otherwise would be trapped on deck. If no deck scuppers (pipes that drain water from the deck overboard through the hull near the waterline) are fitted, then the bottom of the rail scuppers must be at the deck level to drain rainwater. When there

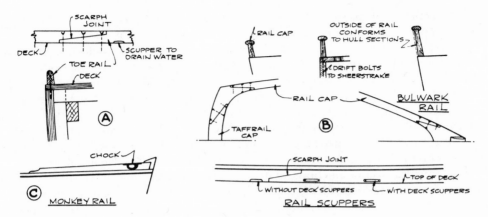

Figure 14–5.

are deck scuppers, the bottom of the cuts in the rail are placed about ½″ above the deck so that ordinary rainwater will not run through the scuppers to streak the topsides with dirt. The forward end of the rail is fitted into the stem rabbet, and the cap is shaped at the stem and across the transom as shown in Figure 14-5B.

Installation of the bulwark rail will call for some ingenuity on the part of the builder. Templates should be of thin wood, sprung in place, and the bottom edge shaped to fit the deck. Then the rail heights at the stations are laid out and a batten is run to fair the top of the rail. It will be a problem to hold the template in place, and the magnitude of the problem will vary with the type of boat. Bear in mind that the outside face of the rail conforms to the hull sections, that is, the rail is not installed vertically on a normal boat; thus the bottom edge bevel constantly changes. Jigs from the cabin sides and coamings and across the fore and after decks must be devised to hold the template in place, and then the rail while fastening. It is very likely that at least the forward section of the rail will need steaming to get it in place unless the rail is laminated. Much care must be taken to fair the rail sections into each other at the joints so they will be smooth. Laminating can eliminate some of the heavy work in larger boats, but it requires a jig.

Monkey Rail

Boats without a true bulwark rail sometimes are dressed up with a short monkey or buffalo rail (take your choice) forward, Figure 14-5C. This is handy as a foothold when handling an anchor in a heavy sea and can be fitted with chocks for anchor and dock lines.

Sliding Hatch

A sliding hatch is necessary to give headroom over companion ladders and elsewhere. The hatch must be rugged enough to take the weight of a man sitting or standing on it.

The cover may be flat across, but looks much better when cambered like the deck. It can be of plywood, either one or two layers glued together, but the classier covers are constructed of solid lumber, as shown in Figure 14-6. The cover is made on a pair of beams sawn to the camber, using material ⅞" thick and about 3" wide, with the butting edges grooved for soft white pine splines, which stiffen the hatch as well as prevent leaks. The joints are waterproof glued and the top pieces are fastened to the beams with plugged screws.

The logs may be constructed in a variety of styles as shown in Figure 14-6, some of which are easier to make than others. A common slide is shown in sketch A with brass tongues on the beam ends to slide in grooves in the logs. The edge of the cover is protected with a piece of split brass tubing, while the tops of the logs are sheathed with brass strips that interlock with the split tubing to keep spray out of the hatch opening. The arrangement in sketch B is similar in operation, having a rabbeted beam header that slides in the log groove. The top of the log may be sheathed if desired, and the molding on the edge of the cover makes it adaptable to canvas covering. The logs shown in sketches C and D do not have grooves, for the covers slide directly on the logs, making it necessary to sheathe them to prevent wear of the surface. In C the sliding friction is minimized by having an angle between the brass strips, so contact is at one edge only. In D there is a piece of brass let into the cover at the ends only, and it should project slightly, so the wooden cover will not touch the log. The arrangements shown in the sketches are typical and others can be devised. The metal parts can be stainless steel, but brass is quite easy to work.

An elevation at the centerline of a sliding hatch is illustrated by sketch E, Figure 14-6. The length of the logs as they extend beyond the companionway is determined by the distance from the aftermost hatch cover beam to the forward end of the hatch opening. Beyond the required length, the logs are finished with an ogee curve. Fasten the logs to the deck beams and headers with plugged screws. The bottom edges of the logs just forward of the apron must have scuppers cut in them to drain trapped water.

Strive to make the cover slide freely—nothing is more aggravating than one that sticks.

In the end, it can sometimes be less costly to buy aluminum alloy and Lexan sliding companionway hatches, such as those made by Bomar, Inc., Box W, Charlestown, NH 03603. The sliding hatches match in styling the deck hatches made by Bomar and others.

Companionway Closure

The simplest way of closing the opening in the aft end of the trunk is to fit drop boards that slide between guides, as shown in Figure 14-6. A slot can be cut in the top slide to take a brass padlock tongue screwed to the bottom of the hatch cover beam, or a cabinet lock may be fitted. The top slide should also have ventilation holes or louvers to circulate air through the boat when it is locked up. A shaped sill is fitted on the deck to keep water from running off the slides or main deck into the cabin. Double doors, usually panelled, are sometimes substituted for the drop boards.

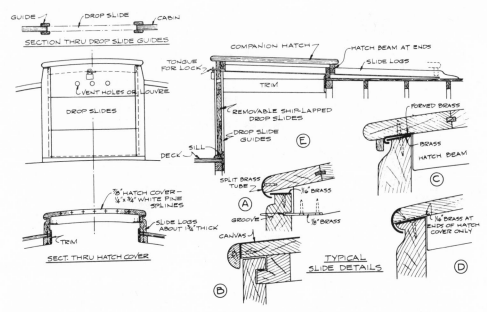

Figure 14–6.

Hatches

Openings in the deck are covered with hatches made to be watertight or reasonably so. At sea, particularly, hatches that leak are an unspeakable nuisance, making for discomfort during the watch below, so every effort should be exerted to construct them so they fit well and function satisfactorily. The pieces forming the cover are preferably splined as described for the sliding companion hatch. The frame around the cover is half lapped at the corners (here, again, the old professionals used dovetails which I consider to be too difficult for the amateur), and it is very important that the detail in sketch A of Figure 14-7 be followed. If the half lap is reversed from that shown so that the end screws in the top pieces are in the side frame that is parallel to the top pieces, the swelling of the top in width will force the corner joint apart. In other words, all screws across the width of the top must be in the same piece of frame.

The hatch coamings vary in detail according to preference or practice, but all are either through-bolted or fastened from the bottom with long, husky screws. The corners of the hatch coamings are dovetailed together or rabbeted and screw fastened as shown in Figure 14-7G, and set in marine bedding compound on the deck. In fact, bedding compound is used to keep out water under *everything* fitted on deck, whether it is woodwork or such fittings as cleats, fill plates, etc. Use either a time-tested marine bedding sealant such as 3M 5200 or a thiokol-base compound.

Sketch B illustrates a crude workboat-type hatch not very suitable for a yacht, and although frames like C are used, they are too light to be any good and should be modified into something like D, which will stay together and is fairly watertight when dogged down. The type shown in sketch E has the coaming grooved for a rubber

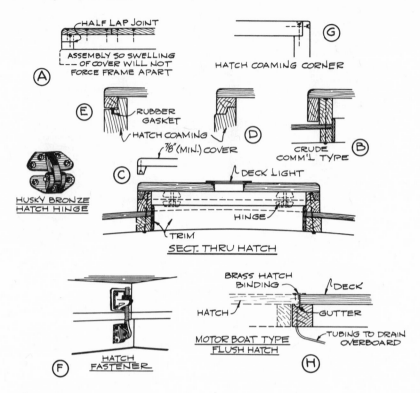

Figure 14-7.

gasket. A refinement of this is the hatch construction shown in Figure 14-8, which is the best of the lot and not too difficult to build. It is a mistake to make the parts of hatches too light. Flimsy hatches and hatch hardware just do not stand up to the abuse they must take.

The hinges shown are made by a couple of the marine hardware firms and are quite satisfactory. Through-bolt the hinges wherever possible. Note that the hatch in Figure 14-8 is shown with a plastic top. This is optional, but it admits a lot of light to spaces like the galley. Unless a strong material such as Lexan is used, it is a bit risky to use a hatch with a plastic top on the main deck of a sailboat where a crewman is liable to jump on the hatch with considerable force. If a light is wanted in a wooden main deck hatch, it is safer to use a round one with a bronze frame, like the one shown in the hatch section in Figure 14-7.

When the deck joinerwork is to be all painted, a hatch cover of marine plywood— fiberglassed if fir—is satisfactory. Some like to hinge the hatches at both forward and after sides, which is effected by fitting two sets of hinges and replacing the individual pins with a removable rod to engage both hinges on the desired side. The covers are locked from below with cast brass hooks and eyes, or dogged down tight with a bronze fastener of the type shown in sketch F (available from marine hardware concerns) located at the corners opposite the hinges. Such fasteners are especially good where a gasket must be pulled down.

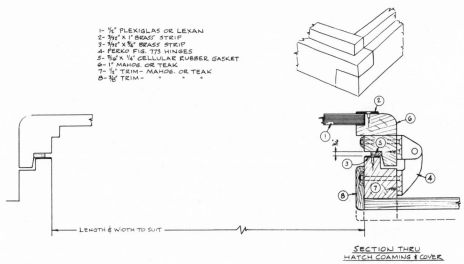

1- ½" PLEXIGLAS OR LEXAN
2- 3/32" X 1" BRASS STRIP
3- 3/32" X 3/4" BRASS STRIP
4- PERKO FIG. 773 HINGES
5- 3/16" X ¼" CELLULAR RUBBER GASKET
6- 1" MAHOG. OR TEAK
7- ½" TRIM- MAHOG. OR TEAK
8- 3/8" TRIM-   "   "   "

LENGTH & WIDTH TO SUIT

SECTION THRU
HATCH COAMING & COVER

Figure 14-8.

The builder now has the option of buying hatches instead of making them. Hatches of cast aluminum alloy frames with strong lights of polycarbonate sheet (Lexan) are also made by Bomar in a large selection of sizes. (*See* Figure 14-9.) Some of these hatches are designed with sailboats in mind and have a minimum number of

Figure 14-9. *A cast aluminum hatch by Bomar.*

protrusions so that sails can be hurriedly passed through the hatch without catching on anything.

Another source for non-wooden deck hatches is Imperial Marine Equipment, 7601 N.W. 66th Street, Miami, FL 33166.

Some complain that the plastic-topped hatches sweat, and this is also true of metal hatches. Sweating of the metal hatches can be considerably reduced or stopped entirely by applying granulated cork to the underside. Of course, it is possible to make a minimum-sweating hatch out of another material—wood!

Flush Hatches

Cockpits usually have flush hatches over engines, tanks, and storage spaces; these often are constructed as shown in sketch H, Figure 14-7, in an effort to keep rain, spray, and washdown water from running into the bilges and dripping on equipment on the way. This usual method is pretty poor because it does not take much water to overflow the shallow gutters or much dirt to clog the drain. A better method is to use a system of channel-shaped sheet stainless steel or aluminum alloy gutters attached to the hatch opening framing, wide enough to project under the opening, and having a good-sized overboard line, say ¼″ at least.

Watertight Self-Bailing Cockpit

A watertight cockpit as fitted in sailboats is simply a well sunk below main deck level with scuppers to drain water, whether it be from rain or heavy spray and seas. The sole of the cockpit can be fiberglass-covered plywood, preferably made non-skid, or bare teak.

The boat plans should provide details for the cockpit scuppers and whether or not they should be crossed in sailboats to take care of heeling—that is, whether the port scupper discharges through the hull on the starboard side and vice versa. There are various ways to fit scuppers flush with the cockpit sole; probably the easiest is to buy flush-fitting scuppers from one of the marine hardware outfits. Above all, the scuppers *must* be generously sized so that the cockpit well can drain rapidly should a sea break aboard.

The cockpit sole is laid on beams that may extend to the hull sides, or it may be supported by beam headers, which in turn are suspended from the main deck headers by long rods with threaded ends for nuts. (*See* Figure 14-10A.) Two types of water tables around the edges of the sole are shown, either of which may be used with a caulked sole. The cockpit ceiling may be permanently installed or fitted with hinged doors for access to storage spaces not occupied by fuel and water tanks, exhaust piping, etc.

Many prefer cockpit seats lowered below the main deck level (Figure 14-10B) for the feeling of security it gives. If the boat has a raised doghouse, the designer must plan the lowered seats with care in order not to restrict the visibility of the helmsman. The seats are most comfortable if sloped and fitted with a slanted lazyback. They require beams and headers for support, the latter of which are secured to blocks

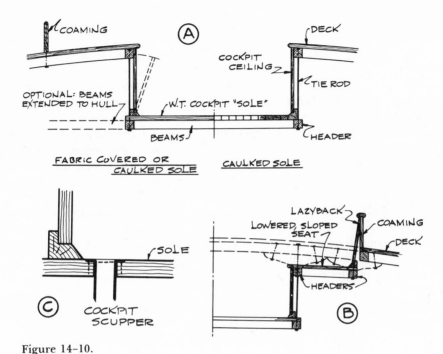

Figure 14-10.

under the main deck beams at the ends of the cockpit. (*See* dotted lines, Figure 14-10B.) Sloped seats must be scuppered with copper or other non-corrosive tubing at least ½″ in diameter (if possible) to drain water, and may be arranged with hinged sections over storage spaces.

Seats and Locker Lids

Hinged seats and locker lids on deck are prone to warp due to changes in moisture. This occurs in both solid lumber and plywood. One way to minimize this is to make a series of cuts parallel to the long direction and on the underside of the piece. This is done on a table saw or with a portable circular saw. Cleats are fitted as shown in Figure 14-11.

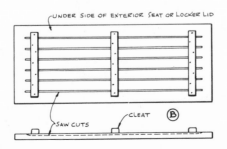

Figure 14-11.

Sheer Guards

The hull guard at the sheer, if the boat is designed for one, can vary from a simple half round or rectangle for smaller boats to a fairly heavy, built-up guard for larger hulls. The latter type can be difficult to make and install, considering the shape of the deck in plan and the changing bevel of the sections of the boat from bow to stern. The most difficult job is to install a guard at the bow of a powerboat having a full deck line forward and a lot of flare. For the larger hulls a guard must be laminated to the shape of the deck line and sawn to the bevel of the sections. The fastening of guards is very important, for they are there for the purpose of protecting the hull and must not come loose when subjected to a blow either from the side or vertically, or a combination of both.

Lower guards to protect hulls at the stern where there is tumblehome (hull wider below the sheer than at the sheer) take some hard knocks at times and also must be securely fastened. Depending upon the construction of the hull and deck at the sheer, the sheer guard sometimes needs blocking between the frames to take the fastenings, which, for heavy-duty guards, are preferably through-bolts.

Chapter 15

INTERIOR JOINERWORK

From the beginning of this manual it has been assumed that the builder is familiar and reasonably skilled with woodworking tools, having undertaken basic household projects. With this experience, the cabin joinerwork should prove to be the easiest task in the construction of the boat. Be advised though that this work may not proceed as rapidly as one might wish, because parts must be made to fit the shape of the hull in a work space that is comparatively cramped. The joints and finish can be as plain or as fancy as desired, commensurate with the ability of the builder.

Note: if we assume for the moment that the sheerline of the boat being built is an average of four feet or more above the shop floor, and that the boat is a cruiser about 30 feet long with a fair amount of interior joinerwork, then the builder should consider having power saws on deck if the arrangement of the boat permits, or a platform with power saws at approximate sheer height if the building site permits. Either setup saves hours of time spent climbing out of the boat and back in again, often to make just a cut or two. Currently on the market there is a good selection of moderately priced, downsized bench and band saws—very handy tools for on-board joinerwork, and often seen now in the boat shops.

The boat designer's drawings of sections through the interior or his specifications should show details of joinerwork construction methods, but in case these are lacking or sparse, I will show some typical structural methods. In a small craft there are not too many different details to be planned, although there might seem to be a multitude of them the first time around. Even in a hull large enough to sleep four or more persons there are only a few bulkheads and doors, the rest of the interior joinerwork consisting of berth tops and fronts, lockers, drawers, the galley work top, and the all-important icebox. Any finished carpentry in the nature of cabinetwork is enhanced by neatly fitting joints and a smooth finish, so the time spent in fitting parts and pushing sandpaper really pays off with the satisfaction of a job well done.

Waterproof plywood makes interior work much easier than in years past because this material saves labor by permitting parts to be quickly cut from large sheets rather than fabricated from boards. Bulkheads and large partitions are a good example, as these can be made of plywood in a fraction of the time formerly needed to make them either of paneling or of tongue-and-groove material.

Assuming that plywood will be used, the finish can be of any of several basic types. The most attractive of these is a real wood finish. This can be achieved by using a plywood faced with mahogany, teak, or other such veneers available in waterproof panels, stained or natural, and finished with multiple coats of varnish, each rubbed down with fine sandpaper or bronze wool between coats. Natural wood can also be finished with wax-based material, tung oil, or tung oil varnish. The tung oil liquids can be applied by hand with a soaked rag or a brush, the excess being wiped off soon afterward. The surface should be allowed to dry for a day, then buffed with bronze wool and recoated until the luster is pleasing. Moldings for trim around locker openings, etc., must be made of solid lumber. Flats such as table tops, exposed shelves, and the like are best covered with a phenolic finishing material like Formica to match the natural wood finish. In such cases, the plywood can be of less expensive fir. The natural wood decor is for the perfectionist who has the time, skill, and patience to make perfect-fitting joints throughout.

Another choice is to go with a completely painted finish or a combination of paint with natural wood trim, such as mahogany. For a painted finish, the use of faced plywood like MDO (Chapter 4) is best because it will save one or more coats of paint. Even though most of the surfaces will be painted, it is practical to cover the galley counter and other flats that receive hard wear with Formica or a Formica-type overlay.

A third choice is to cover most of the vertical surfaces with one of the tough, washable vinyl wall coverings and to paint the parts that are not practical to cover with a harmonizing color. Again, the horizontal surfaces that take wear and tear should be covered with overlay or painted. The trim can be painted to match or contrast, or it can be natural wood finish.

Still another finish is to use an overlay as much as practical on both horizontal and vertical surfaces, either in colors or wood grains. It is a little tricky to work with until you get used to it, but an attractive and unusually durable finish results. The panels are adhered to clean plywood with so-called contact cement, which is applied to both surfaces and allowed to set up dry to the touch before the surfaces are joined. Once the two cement-coated surfaces contact each other, they are stuck for good, so they must be carefully positioned. One method of preventing premature contact is to use what is known as a slip sheet, made of a piece of brown paper the same size as the Formica part to be cemented. The cement-coated surfaces are allowed to set up dry to finger touch, the slip sheet is laid on the wood while the Formica is lined up perfectly, and then while holding the parts aligned, the slip sheet is pulled out from between the surfaces so the parts can be joined.

Plywood helps reduce the weight of joinerwork; there is no sense in installing weight in the form of furniture that is needlessly over strength. The plans for the boat should specify the thickness of the plywood, but if they don't, a general guide for bulkheads is ½", ¾" in the larger hulls; dresser tops, counters, and minor partitions need not be over ½" in any boat where weight saving is desired. Shelves in lockers and elsewhere can be ⅜" or ½" depending upon the area. Be guided by common sense, because with glued and screwed parts, high strength can be achieved with plywood structures.

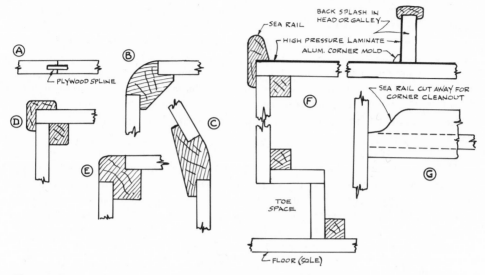

Figure 15–1.

Sometimes in sailboats the mast is stepped on deck and somehow the thrust must be carried to the hull. In some cases the bulkheads in the immediate vicinity of the mast are used for this purpose; thus they may be heavier than normal.

When bulkheads or partitions are larger than can be cut from one plywood panel, the pieces must be joined. The simplest way is to use a butt strip of plywood glued and screwed to the bulkhead pieces, but this does not look good unless it is located inside a locker or otherwise concealed from view. The neatest butt is made with a spline as shown in section A of Figure 15-1, using a glued plywood spline, but you must have the woodworking machinery to cut the rabbets accurately or have a mill do it for you. Still another way to join two plywood panels is to scarph them together, cutting the scarph with an attachment for a portable circular saw called a "Scarffer." This is shown in Figure 4-6.

Sections B through E in Figure 15-1 show different ways of building corners for bulkheads, while F is a vertical section through a galley or bathroom counter. The toe space shown at the base of the counter is well worth the trouble it takes to construct. It is a minor but important feature that permits making up berths or standing closer to counters. Dimensions for a toe space should be 3″ x 3″ (unless greater height is needed above the sole for extra thick coverings); glue and screw all faying surfaces.

Another good detail to incorporate is shown in sketch G of Figure 15-1. This shows sea rails that have been brought down to counter level at their ends to enable dirt to be cleaned out of corners. Sea rails are used to keep things from falling off counters and should be about 1″ high, or even higher when you want to retain something like a portable radio.

Where berth platforms, shelves, and the edges of bulkheads and partitions lie against the hull, their edges are curved and must be fitted by a process similar to spiling planking. This requires the use of heavy cardboard or light wood for making templates. In the case of a horizontal part, the template board must be held level athwartships for the most accurate results, while the template board for a bulkhead must be held normal to the centerline of the hull. Similarly, the points of dividers or a carpenter's compass must be held normal to the centerline when scribing points for a horizontal part, and level when scribing the shape for a bulkhead. If these procedures are not followed, the parts will not be correctly shaped, and further fitting will be required. The bevels for the parts can be taken off at intervals and marked on the template board. The template board is cut to the scribed line and used as a pattern. (*See* Figure 15-2.)

Bulkheads are often located on one side or another of a frame. Fastening a bulkhead to a frame is simple, unless the frame is not plumb vertical, which is often the case when the frames are bent rather than sawn. In such cases, the frame must be shimmed to true up the bulkhead. Thus, when framing a boat, it pays to be particularly careful to have the bulkhead frames be as true as possible. For bulkheads located between frames, a strip similar to a frame must be installed so that the bulkhead can be fastened to the hull. In v-bottomed hulls and in some round-bottomed ones, a strip can be bent cold to the inside of the planking, but where there is too much shape for this, you must either steam bend the wood, saw a frame to shape, or bend in a strip made pliable by numerous saw cuts on its inside edge. (*See* Figure 15-3A.) The spacing of the cuts is determined by trial and error, and a strip like this is best placed where it won't be visible in the cabin.

Drawers are best made of solid lumber, using ¾" for the fronts, ½" sides, and backs rabbeted for a bottom of ¼" plywood or hardboard such as tempered Masonite. They must have a device to prevent them from opening at sea. (*See* Figure 15-3B.)

Figure 15-3C shows a typical detail section through a berth.

Occasionally a product developed for residential use is made of non-corrosive material enabling it to be used as well in boats at sea. A case in point: injection-molded plastic parts manufactured for custom cabinet drawers. These parts utilize a three-point support system that may be simpler to build or install than the old method of hanging a drawer on side runners as shown in Figure 15-3.

The alternative system described here (there are others on the market) employs a mass-produced tee-shaped wooden track on the centerline of the bottom of a drawer opening, where it is secured to a short cleat. Support at the outer end of the track depends upon where it is located—for example, at a bulkhead or partition, or against the hull, etc.

A molded track holder—secured to the back side of the drawer at the bottom—engages the track, while the bottom edges of the drawer sides slide along an angle-type molded part located on each side of the drawer opening in the cabinet or berth front. (*See* Figures 15-4 and 15-5.) The molded parts are made of a slippery, low-friction material. In making a selection it is advisable that a careful detail of drawer construction be worked out and tested to satisfaction before plunging ahead with a quantity of drawers.

One manufacturer of a number of optional configurations of molded parts is Plastiglide Manufacturing Corp., 2701 El Segundo Boulevard, Hawthorne, CA 90205, or Box 1188, Waterbury, CT 06705. Ask for their catalog and design manual, which shows slide systems other than the type described here.

Another maker of similar drawer slide parts is HDI, Inc., 120 Kisco Avenue, Mt.

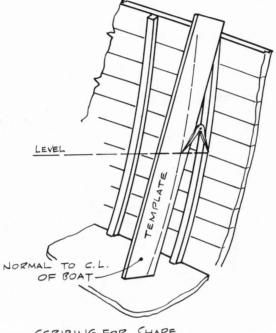

LEVEL

TEMPLATE

NORMAL TO C.L.
OF BOAT

SCRIBING FOR SHAPE
OF BULKHEAD

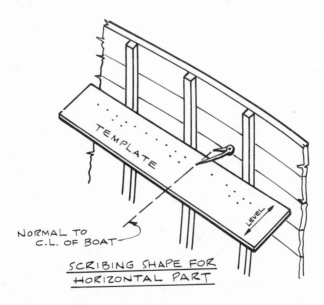

TEMPLATE

LEVEL

NORMAL TO
C.L. OF BOAT

SCRIBING SHAPE FOR
HORIZONTAL PART

Figure 15-2.

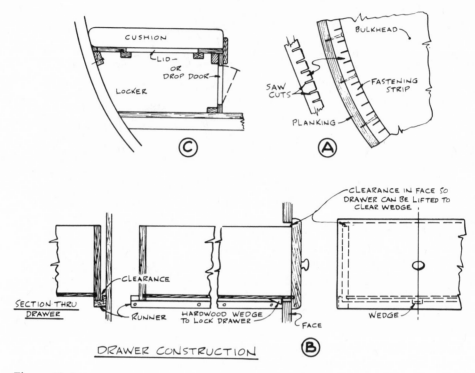

Figure 15-3.

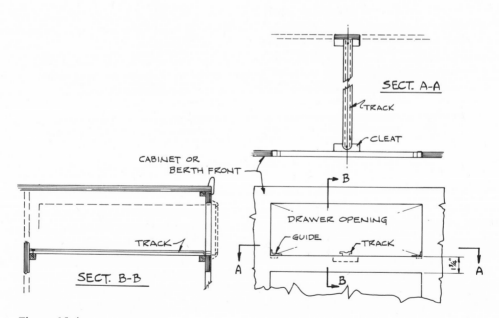

Figure 15-4.

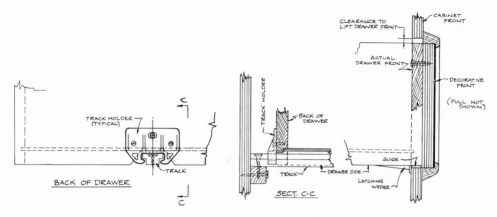

Figure 15–5.

Kisco, NY 10549. The center track of wood is made by the boatbuilder; the slide parts of nylon, purchased from the manufacturer, are the P/N 351 center guide along with the P/N 206RH and P/N 205LH located in the bottom corners of a drawer opening, as shown in the figures.

Fastenings in interior woodwork are screws for the most part. Do not use steel nails unless they are hot-dipped galvanized. In plywood joinerwork many of the fastenings can be hidden by the trim. In varnished trim, the fastening holes are counterbored and plugged or concealed by matching putty if the fastenings are nails set below the surface of the wood. Plugs in varnished work are set in either Weldwood Plastic Resin Glue or an aliphatic liquid glue such as Titebond.

Do not expect plated-steel hardware, such as hinges, drawer pulls, or lock sets, to survive for long in a boat. Although expensive, the hardware should be brass or bronze, either plain or chrome-plated, or stainless steel.

Locker Door Catch

The catch shown in Figure 15-6 was used by Nevins and other sailboat builders about forty years ago; brass elbow catches are still made in the U.S. and England. The reasoning behind this type of catch is to eliminate protrusions that are a danger and a nuisance down below when at sea in heavy weather. Nevins lined the finger hole with a brass ferrule. Nowadays there is so much teak in boat interiors that several manufacturers make hole liners of that material.

Ventilation

Proper ventilation of the hull is one of the most important items that will contribute to the long life of a wooden boat. Passage of air *must* be provided for at all times, all the while keeping fresh water from entering the boat and becoming trapped. (It must be remembered that the boat may be kept for most of its life at a mooring or a slip,

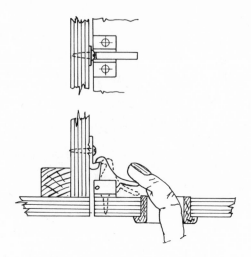

Figure 15–6. *Typical installation of elbow catch for locker door.*

unprotected by a roof.) Other than patented devices made of molded plastic, etc., the most practical ventilator developed is the cowl ventilator mounted on a box having a baffle against water, as illustrated in Chapter 16. This will bring in air from the outside, but air must be able to flow *through* the boat after it gets inside. There must be openings in ceilings (the hull lining) and lockers; where bulkheads are watertight, each compartment must be provided with a source of air for ventilation.

Doors to lockers and cupboards should have vents for passage of air at top and bottom, not only for the preservation of the hull, but also so clothes and other stowed gear will have a chance to dry out before they mildew. A few suggestions for locker door ventilation and typical door frame and stop details are shown in Figure 15-7.

Ventilation is also of importance in boats built of materials other than wood to minimize the chance of mildew and musty odors, which are sometimes extremely difficult to remove.

Ceiling

Ceiling is a lining on the inside of the hull that is used to conceal structural members, to protect stowed gear from sloshing bilge water, or to strengthen the hull. For the latter purpose, in larger yachts the ceiling is usually 40 percent of the thickness of the planking. It is spiled to shape when the hull form requires it, and the strakes are wedged tightly together before fastening. For appearance, the inner edges of the ceiling are lightly beveled so that the seams form a vee on the inside, and before fastening, the outside of each strake is painted or treated with a wood preservative. In the finest yachts the fastenings are counterbored and plugged where they would be visible in the quarters. This type of ceiling extends upward from at least the cabin sole,

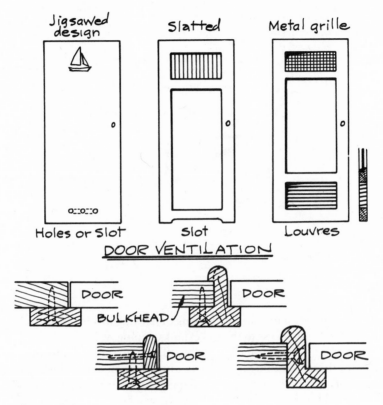

Figure 15-7.

to an inch or two below the sheer clamp, the space at the top being left for the circulation of air.

In small boats, light ceiling ¼″ to ⅜″ thick is sometimes used for the sake of appearance rather than strength and may be slatted if desired. At the outboard side of a bunk, the ceiling prevents the discomfort of frames pressing against your body, but one of the best reasons for ceiling in small boats is to protect gear stowed under berths and in the bottom of lockers from being wetted by sloshing bilge water when the boat is heeled down in a lump of a sea. For this purpose the ceiling seams must be tight, and thin tongue-and-groove can be used. Small boat ceiling should be kept light; excessive thickness is useless. White cedar or pine is suitable and may be fastened with nails or screws. Ceiling is shown in Figure 15-8.

In boats where the shape of the topsides will permit it, a sheet-type ceiling is bent into place. This can be of light plywood or hardboard, the latter being either plain or perforated with many small holes such as pegboard.

In boats where the ceiling is decorative rather than structural—particularly in motorboats—light plywood lining used to hide structures can be painted or covered with vinyl fabric or Formica-type material. The inside of fiberglass hulls, particularly forward where hull curvature is greatest, can be covered with carpeting stuck to the hull with an adhesive, or there are " hull liners" now made for this purpose. These materials are vinyl with a foam backing.

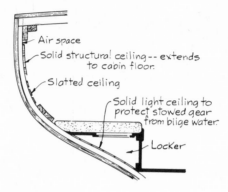

Figure 15–8.

Cabin Sole

Cabin sole is the proper name for the flooring or decking inside the hull. It must have hatches to enable ready access to the bilge, tanks, piping, valves, etc. In small boats a removable panel on the centerline is usually sufficient to serve all purposes, but make sure of this, for there is nothing more frustrating than not being able to get at, say, a sea cock; lack of access can be downright dangerous in an emergency. Plywood is an excellent material for the sole because it saves much labor and can be fitted in large pieces. The plywood can be painted for the simplest finish, or covered with vinyl flooring either in one piece or laid in squares. There are aluminum and stainless steel hatch bindings for use with the vinyl coverings. Do not make the hatches too tight, for the plywood often swells just enough to make a hatch bind.

In a sailboat it is practical to make a sole nonskid by adding a compound to the final coat of paint. It is not pretty, but it is practical. A bare teak sole is nonskid; however, it is expensive and it will hold grease stains. High quality yachts often have soles of ¼" teak laid in strakes about 2" wide with a ³⁄₁₆" thick strip of wood, light in color like holly, between each strake. The strakes are preassembled in the shop by gluing and edge-nailing the holly to each strake of teak. Plywood panels are now available faced with teak and holly to resemble the solid wood sole. See Chapter 4 for sources.

In cabins where a carpet will be used, the sole needs only one coat of paint. A carpet is warm on the feet on a chilly morning, but it requires cleaning with a vacuum to be properly shipshape, and should not be used near open hatchways. Indoor-outdoor carpet, made of synthetic fibers that will not absorb moisture, has become very popular with boatmen. It is light enough to be taken up and cleaned on the dock.

The sole is the first of the interior joinerwork to go in the hull, and it must be carefully planned ahead to establish the hatch locations. In addition, it must be adequately supported by beams and headers.

Headliners

Headlining—unheard of until people started making the insides of boats look more like homes than boats—is a covering for the underside of deck beams and cabin tops. The most popular headlining material is a vinyl fabric made just for that purpose, the best ones having an anti-mildew treatment. Other headliner materials are hardboards having decorative finishes, acoustical tileboard, and light plywood with vinyl or Formica-type covering.

Thermal Insulation

Inexpensive, lightweight fiberglass insulation on the underside of decks and cabin tops adds to comfort both summer and winter whether or not air conditioning is installed in the boat. The easiest kind to use is a type having a thin face of white plastic material on what is meant to be the down side, away from the deck above. It can be cut to fit between deck beams and stapled in place. The only way to make it look decent, though, is to cover it over with headlining.

Icebox

The icebox, which looks so simple when used, is very time consuming and difficult to construct. For this reason, if any of the ready-made boxes suit your boat, you will be much better off buying one. There are several makes on the market with a capacity of about 4.5 cubic feet, which amounts to about 50 pounds of ice. They are all plastic and have polyurethane insulation. They are built for under-counter installation, and if space permits, two of them can be placed side-by-side or stacked. These boxes are also made as electric refrigerators, but I am not going to get into the batteries, chargers, generators, and shore lines that are needed for even the smallest of refrigerators, because the service conditions can vary so widely.

When building an icebox into a wooden boat there are some important points to remember. Space should be left between the hull and the box structure for the circulation of air, and that part of the hull that will be hidden should be treated with a wood preservative or paint. Space is always limited in a boat, and to make the most of the area allotted to the icebox, the outboard side should be shaped somewhat to the hull form. The section in Figure 15-9 is typical of the situation in many boats, and here again plywood simplifies the job. Basically the box consists of an inner and outer shell, with insulation in between and a watertight liner inside.

Make the outside box first, leaving the top off, and brace it to the hull, making sure not to obstruct passage of air, as noted above. Add posts in the corners and intermediate stiffeners on bottom and sides to support the inner shell and to take its fastenings. Then coat the inside of the outer box with bitumastic paint and while it is still wet, line the box with felt paper laid with overlapping joints. This is a vapor barrier. The insulation—I suggest polyurethane foam available in planks—is then cut to fit between the corner posts and the stiffeners. Next make the inner plywood box.

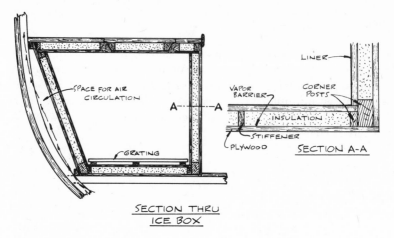

SECTION THRU
ICE BOX

Figure 15–9.

As for the drain, it must lead either overboard or, if the bottom of the box is below the waterline, to a sump tank. It is an invitation to rot to drain fresh water into the bilges of a wooden hull. The sump tank can be removable for dumping overboard or piped with a two-way valve to the bilge pump. Of course the drain should be at the low point of the bottom of the box.

Before making the box top, the liner must be fitted. A liner of stainless steel sheet with soldered, watertight joints is ideal, but the inner plywood can be fiberglassed instead, even though smoothing the corners is tedious. The final finish should be smooth to make cleaning easy.

Whenever possible, a top opening is best for the icebox, because less cold air is lost when the box is opened. Sometimes a front door is unavoidable, but the cold air will pour out quickly, and so will the contents when rolling at sea.

The finished weight of a built-in box is significant. Limit the outside of the box to ½″ thickness, the inside to ⅜″. In fact, you might omit the inside wooden box and fiberglass right on the insulation—but first make certain that the resin is not a solvent for that insulation!

Finish the box with light wooden gratings in the bottom, and fit adjustable partitions to separate food from ice.

Ready-made Woodwork

If you want to save time as your boatbuilding project nears completion, you can use ready-made parts made up by a mail order supply house. There is an outfit in California that makes, among other things, a complete line of dish, magazine, and book racks; grab rails and binocular boxes; paneled and louvered doors; and gratings and tillers. Most items are made of teak, mahogany, or oak. The name of the firm is H & L Marine Woodwork, Inc., 2965 East Harcourt Street, Compton, CA 90221. A firm in Florida that makes similar products is Atlantis Manufacturing, Inc., Building 35, Sanford Airport, Sanford, FL 32771.

Chapter 16

MISCELLANEOUS DETAILS

There seem to be many ways, some of them good and some bad, for doing every-thing. Just remember that there is no compromise in quality if one is to produce a seaworthy boat. The reader is again urged to take advantage of every opportunity to inspect boats of all types and to study the details of construction. Such observation, coupled with opinions of the experienced, will soon reveal the best way to handle any job.

Patterns for Castings

While a great many fittings for boats may be purchased from the stocks of marine hardware manufacturers, there are always a few items that are special. Here the amateur can save money by making patterns and having a foundry pour the castings. To name a few of the fittings that are usually special for the sailboat, there is the jibstay fitting, permanent backstay fitting, propeller aperture casting, rudder gudgeons and pintles, and sometimes light cast bronze floors when tanks are located under the cabin floor. Parts usually made of cast material for powerboats include propeller shaft bearing struts—it is seldom that the off-the-shelf struts fit properly—rudders, and transom platform brackets. Some of the standard fittings can be homemade, too, but this does not always pay unless you have time to burn.

Cast parts, expecially for use underwater, are usually made of manganese bronze, and there are several different alloys, ranging in tensile strength from about 40,000 pounds per square inch to upwards of 100,000 pounds per square inch. Above water, aluminum alloy castings are sometimes used where saving weight is important. Some of these alloys are not very resistant to salt water, and protective finishes for aluminum put out by some of the marine paint makers should be used. Anodizing also offers good protection if applicable to the alloy of your fittings. One of the best aluminum alloys for sand castings is Alcoa Almag 35.

The pattern-making and casting processes will be but briefly outlined, as many people with wood and metalworking experience will know all about them already. Any kind of wood may be used for patterns provided it is given a smooth finish, but soft pine is preferred because it is easy to work. The fitting is drawn on the wood, using fine lines for accuracy (pattern-makers use a knife rather than a pencil). Because the molten metal will shrink during cooling, the pattern is made oversize by the amount of shrinkage expected. The shrinkage of bronze is $\frac{3}{16}''$ per foot, and if any amount of work is to be done, a two-foot shrinkage rule should be purchased to make the layout work easier. Such rules can be obtained at good hardware stores, and are made in shrinkages of $\frac{1}{8}''$, $\frac{3}{16}''$, etc. per foot of length. A two-foot rule made for $\frac{3}{16}''$ shrinkage will actually measure $24\frac{3}{8}''$.

Inside corners on patterns have fillets to provide strength in the castings and for ease of molding. Large, thin sections at an angle to each other have proportionately larger fillets than thicker-walled sections. (*See* Figure 16-1A.) Fillets may be purchased from a pattern-maker's supply house in wax strips, which are stuck in place with a heated fillet tool as shown, or they may be made of leather and secured in place with glue. For a small job you can get along with paraffin wax. Knead the soft wax and work it into the corners, making it uniform and smooth with a fillet tool, which is simply a steel ball on a handle, or with a dowel, or with a metal rod. The pattern must have a smooth finish for release from the molding sand. Pattern-makers finish with several applications of shellac rubbed down between coats. A wooden duck decoy maker introduced me to semi-gloss Deft Clear Wood Finish, which is lacquer-based and can be applied every two hours. Rub between coats and after the final one with No. 0000 steel wool; this will produce the desired slick finish on wood that has been previously well sanded. Also, when the pattern is made, you must give the sides of the pattern a slight taper, called draft, so it may be easily removed from the mold by the molder. This is better understood by referring to Figure 16-1B.

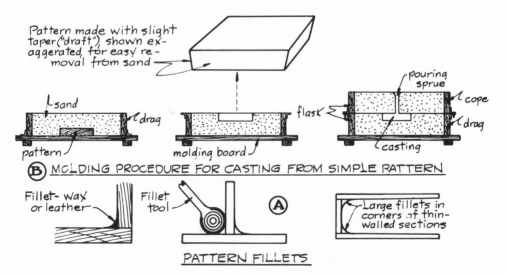

Figure 16-1.

This discussion is not to be regarded as a short course in molding, but the procedure is interesting to know. For small work, such as boat fittings, a small platform called a molding board will be used, and on it will be placed a box without ends to retain the sand used for the mold. The finished mold consists of two boxes one upon the other, called the cope and the drag, and together the assembly is called a flask. Dowel pins on the cope fit into sockets on the drag and keep the two in alignment. The pattern is placed in the drag and covered with sand of such a nature that when packed hard it will stick together; the drag is then turned over. With the pattern still in the mold, the surface of the sand is coated with a powder so that when more sand is added, the two surfaces will part. Then the cope is added, filled with sand, and rammed solid. The cope is lifted off and turned over, and the sprue, a passage for pouring the molten metal, and some small vent holes to carry off gases are cut with molder's tools. The pattern is removed from the drag, leaving a space to be filled with metal.

A flat pattern as shown in Figure 16-1 is easy to remove, but a deeper one, or one with a complicated shape, is more difficult to take out without breaking the sand unless the pattern sides have proper draft. The casting is ready to be poured when the cope is replaced on the drag. The sprue is cut off the finished casting by the foundry.

The molding procedure for the simple block pattern in Figure 16-1B is easy, but a study of the mold shown in Figure 16-2 will indicate that to produce a casting shaped like the pattern, the pattern would have to be split along the centerline. Further, if the casting is to have a hollow portion, the hollow area must be kept free of molten metal;

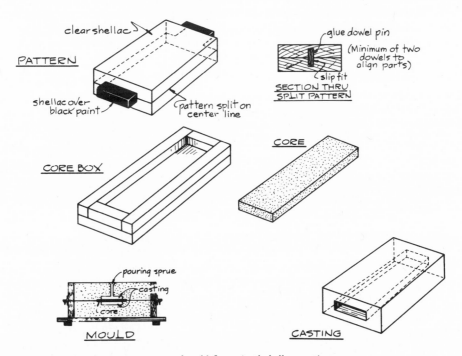

Figure 16–2. *The pattern, core, and mold for a simple hollow casting.*

this is done with a core of sand shaped like the desired hollow. A simple core as shown is made by ramming sand into an open-top box until full and then baking the sand to make it hard and strong enough to withstand the pouring of the molten metal. Cores of irregular shape are molded in a split box with dowel pins. In the pattern, the core is extended beyond the length of the casting so the imprint of the core extension in the mold will support the core. This is shown in the figure. The core print, as it is called, is painted black so the molder will understand the core. When the casting has cooled and been taken from the mold, the core is easily broken out.

Ballast Keel

The ballast keel casting for sailboats will be of cast iron or lead and will be bolted either through the keel or through both the keel and floors, as preferred by the designer. Bolts will be shown on the plans and are the largest-diameter fastenings used in the construction of the boat. They are made of rods threaded on both ends for nuts, and on the inside of the boat are set up on heavy washers under which are grommets consisting of a few turns of cotton wicking soaked with a marine sealant. Tobin bronze or Everdur bolts are used to hold lead keels, while good galvanized wrought iron or Monel bolts are used when the keel is cast iron.

Because of the weight of the metals—450 pounds per cubic foot for cast iron and 710 for lead—the size and location of the ballast must be carefully figured by the designer and just as carefully reproduced by the builder. Templates for the keel are made from the mold loft lines and, as noted earlier, the keel pattern is made with a shrinkage rule. Shrinkage of lead and iron castings is ⅛″ per foot.

The boatbuilder can make the pattern for a cast iron ballast keel, but the casting must be done by an iron foundry because of the high temperatures required. On the other hand, for a lead keel, the amateur or professional boatbuilder can make the mold *and* pour the casting.

Cast Iron Keel

When the keel is iron, the pattern is made of soft pine, and for a rectangular keel (Figure 16-3A) the job is quite simple. For a more shapely keel the pattern entails more work, and in either case the sections should be constantly checked for accuracy as the pattern nears the finished shape. The pattern for a shaped keel is made of layers of pine anywhere from 1″ to 2″ thick that are screw fastened and glued together. Those familiar with model building can see that the "bread and butter" method of construction may be used here by drawing waterlines through the keel, spaced the same as the thickness of wood used, and sawing each layer roughly to shape before fastening them together.

The holes for bolts through an iron keel are cored, and care must be taken to locate the cores in relation to the bolt spacing, always taking shrinkage into account. The core in the bottom of the keel is enlarged in diameter to take the nut, allowing enough depth to cement over the nut to close the hole in the casting. A core box is made only for the longest core needed, as the molder can break cores off to proper length for the

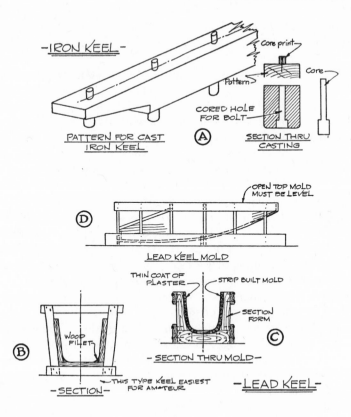

Figure 16–3. *An iron keel must be sand-cast in a foundry, while a lead keel can be cast in a mold at the building site.*

shorter ones. When a centerboard is located in way of the ballast keel, the board's slot must be cored.

The iron casting should, if possible, be given a coat or two of anticorrosive paint such as International 402/414 Steel Epoxy Primer before it starts to rust. First bring the casting to bright metal by sandblasting, or by grinding with 36-grit discs. If fairing is required to achieve a smooth keel, then follow the instructions available from marine paint makers like International, Pettit, or Woolsey.

Lead Keel

When a willing foundry is within a reasonable distance, boatbuilders sometimes make a male pattern for a sand-cast lead keel and let the foundry make the mold and pour the casting. Making the pattern is a relatively easy job as compared to making the sand mold at the boat shop. One firm named Willard solicits this business, either for one-off or production castings of lead. Their address is 101 New Bern Street, Charlotte, NC 28203. Of course, if you have a local foundry that will do the job you are in luck.

Accuracy is particularly important when making patterns for lead castings. Each *cubic inch* of lead weighs about 0.41 pound. As a comparison, cast iron weighs about 0.26 pound per cubic inch.

A rectangular lead keel mold is quite simple to make (Figure 16-3B), as it can be made with planks, with either wood or plaster fillets used to shape the corners when necessary. It must be remembered that the keel will be heavy, and this requires that the mold be strong so that it will not break apart when the lead is poured and that the mold be supported by husky braces and shores. The inside of the mold is given a thin coat of plaster to prevent it from burning. The paster and the mold must be *perfectly dry* before starting, as the lead will spatter if poured into a wet mold and workmen may be burned.

Making the mold for a shaped lead keel (Figure 16-3C) is quite a task and is a good reason to have the keel sand-cast in a foundry. As shown in the section, forms are made to the outside of the keel, plus the thickness of the mold, at stations and half stations. They are then set up rigidly (Figure 16-3D) and the mold is strip-built inside of the forms. As the strips are fitted they are edge nailed to each other and to the forms. The inside is finished to a set of templates representing the finished keel plus an allowance for shrinkage. Gouges and round-bottomed planes are used for this work. The casting will reflect the degree of smoothness of your mold.

Lead, fortunately, has a low melting point, but at the least, you will need a large iron melting pot, supported by bricks so a roaring wood or charcoal fire can be built under it, and several iron ladles. Better still is a melting pot with a pouring spigot or pipe leading over the mold and a metal trough to distribute the molten metal over the length of the keel. The top of the open mold must be level. A centerboard slot can be taken care of by a plank of proper thickness to act as a core. More than enough lead must be on hand to allow for discrepancies, and some of the pigs may be placed in the mold before pouring. Several hands will be needed, because the pouring must be carried on to completion before the top of the lead already in the mold starts to solidify.

Start to pour when the lead in the pot is hot, distribute it in the mold, skim the slag from the top, and puddle the molten lead to prevent the formation of air pockets. Add pigs to the pot as you pour, and they will quickly melt in the hot lead if the fire is kept blazing. Allow at least a day for the casting to cool before removing the mold. The top surface of the lead casting can be smoothed with a woodworking hand or electric plane. The holes for the keel bolts are drilled with a barefoot wood auger or with a twist drill lengthened by welding a rod to the end, preferably used in an electric drill of ample capacity. Either drill must be frequently withdrawn to clear the lead shavings, and kerosene is used as a lubricant. Where necessary, the outside of the keel is smoothed with coats of trowel cement, and the cement is then sanded. The keel casting is liberally coated with thick white or red lead where it fits against keel and deadwood.

Standing Rigging Chainplates

Unless masts are designed to be free-standing, they are kept straight and prevented from breaking by wire rope standing rigging. The mast loads are transmitted to the hull by straps called chainplates. The chainplates must be designed equal to the task, and the designer should show on the construction plan locations and details of the chainplates with the size and number of fastenings.

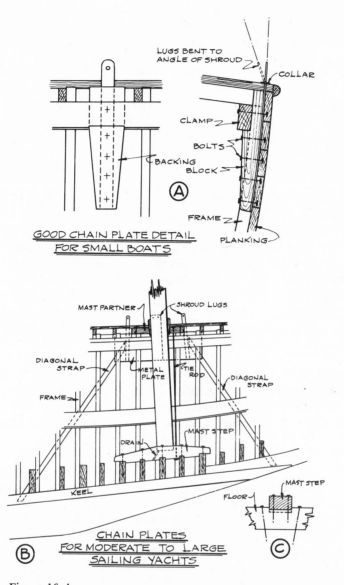

LUGS BENT TO ANGLE OF SHROUD

COLLAR

CLAMP

BOLTS

BACKING BLOCK

(A)

FRAME

PLANKING

GOOD CHAIN PLATE DETAIL FOR SMALL BOATS

MAST PARTNER

SHROUD LUGS

DIAGONAL STRAP

METAL PLATE

TIE ROD

DIAGONAL STRAP

FRAME

MAST STEP

DRAIN

MAST STEP

FLOOR

KEEL

(B) CHAIN PLATES FOR MODERATE TO LARGE SAILING YACHTS

(C)

Figure 16–4.

It is a simple matter to calculate the strength of the metal parts, but their fastenings to the hull can be insufficient. The area of the wood in the hull against which the bolts bear must be equal to the strength of the shroud. Sometimes the chainplates are bolted through the planking and a frame and are located either on the outside of the planking or between the planking and a frame. However, it is better to bolt them to backing blocks between frames that are cut to bear against the clamp. (*See* Figure 16-4A.) Blocks of this type eliminate the necessity of cutting frames with fastenings, which weakens the hull somewhat at that point.

Inside chainplates are to be preferred, as on the outside they will show unless neatly let flush into the planking, and the metal may bleed and discolor the topside paint. It is best to use corrosion-resistant metals such as bronze, Monel, or Type 316 stainless steel for both plates and bolts, because due to corrosion, there have been many cases of chainplates torn out under stress. This may result in a broken mast. There are several types of small boat chainplates peculiar to various classes, and these are shown in detail on the plans for the boats. Referring to chainplates in general, the end of the lug extending above deck should have only slightly rounded edges so as not to reduce strength unnecessarily. To stop leaks, the hole through the deck should be filled with compound or fitted with a metal collar set in compound.

Sailing yachts of the more expensive type with a waterline length upwards of 28 feet are fitted with a rectangular bronze plate between the frames and the planking to which lugs for the shroud turnbuckles are bolted or riveted. Diagonal metal straps extending to the keel are riveted to the plate and screwed to each frame crossed and the keel. This arrangement, shown in Figure 16-4B, distributes the rigging loads over a large area and prevents the distortion of the hull, called hogging, often noticed in the sheerline of old wooden boats. The planking rather than the frames is carefully notched for the straps as each strake is fitted.

Wooden Spars

Traditional wooden sailboats most often have solid wooden spars; the more modern ones have hollow wooden masts and booms to save weight. Otherwise aluminum alloy spars have captured the field. As a result, there are dozens of extruded sizes and shapes from which to select a spar of proper strength.

Wooden spars are preferably made of spar- or aircraft-grade clear Sitka spruce because it is a light, strong wood. This material is stocked by M.L. Condon Co., 250 Ferris Avenue, White Plains, NY 10603; Wicks Aircraft Supply, 410 Pine Street, Highland, IL 62249; Aircraft Spruce & Specialty Co., Box 424, Fullerton, CA 92632; and Pacific Lumber Co., Box 10868, Miami, FL 33101. Clear fir and pine run rather far behind as second choice. Inasmuch as a mast is a column, the maximum sectional area is required at midlength of the longest unsupported panel, so to further save weight aloft, the mast is tapered from the point of greatest cross-sectional area to the head and sometimes to the heel as well. The edges on which sails are set, the top of the boom and the aft side of the mast, are made straight so the sails will set as they should.

When using modern waterproof glue, fastenings in spars are not required or even desirable, as they add weight up high where it is detrimental to the stability of the boat. As a matter of fact, hollow glued spars were in use years before truly waterproof glue was known, water-resistant casein glue being relied upon together with coats of varnish to protect the joints from moisture. Sitka spruce, fortunately, is available in long lengths, and the majority of amateur-built boats will have spars that fall within the range of available lengths. When joining is required, the individual pieces are scarphed on the flat, the length of the joint being made about 10 times the thickness of the piece. Considerable patience as well as sharp tools are needed to make a perfectly fitting feather-edged joint of this type. Theoretically a glued joint is as strong or stronger than the wood, so that splices could be adjacent to each other, but inasmuch as a glued joint will be locally stiffer than the adjoining unjointed pieces, it is best to

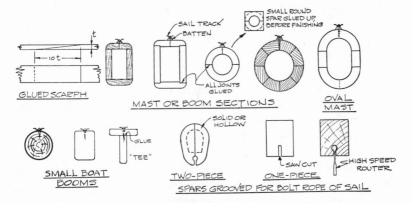

Figure 16-5. *Typical wooden spar sections. Most small craft have rectangular hollow masts and booms.*

stagger the scarphs as much as possible. Figure 16-5 shows a scarph and typical hollow spar sections in use today.

The simplest mast to make is a hollow, rectangular box spar. This section, with the fore-and-aft pieces rabbeted, is preferred by some builders because it is easier to control skidding of the glued surfaces. The section next in simplicity is the round spar made of hollowed-out halves. The larger spars, both the oval section and the round section made of staves, are the most difficult to make and would be quite a job for the amateur. Of the two, the oval is the easier in the smaller sizes, as it consists of two round halves and two tapered side pieces. The wall thickness of oval and round spars is always tapered in the interest of weight saving.

Some of the sailboat classes use a solid mast with a groove routed out for the boltrope on the luff of the mainsail. This groove can be made by first making a saw cut with a circular saw and then routing out the groove in the saw cut, using a very high-speed cutter with a shank narrower than the saw cut. (*See* Figure 16-5.) To make a boltrope groove in a hollow spar made up of two rounded halves, the groove is hand gouged or machine routed on each half before the sections are glued together.

The T-boom is used on smaller sailboats, which also sometimes have solid rectangular booms.

Hollow Rectangular Spars

Probably the easiest way to make a box spar, unless the builder has extensive machine tools, is to order the spar material dressed four sides to the dimensions at the maximum section of the spar. It is desirable to add a slight thickness, say ¹⁄₃₂″, for dressing up and finishing after the spar has been glued. With such material at hand there is nothing to do but taper the pieces in accordance with the designer's detail plans. This is done by laying off the width at the spacing shown on the plan for the spar, fairing the shape with a long batten, and then sawing and planing the edges to the lines. The width layout for the forward and aft pieces is done from a centerline because both edges are shaped. Duplicate sides may be temporarily nailed together

222 MISCELLANEOUS DETAILS

and made at the same time. Be sure to keep the edges square, or else a perfect glue joint with 100 percent surface contact cannot be made. Here again, epoxy adhesives are a boon to the amateur because of their gap-filling ability and minimum clamping pressure.

When only one or two spars are to be made, a makeshift spar bench may be devised by nailing a series of short boards horizontally to a wall or fence, with legs down to the ground to support the outer ends. (*See* Figure 16-6A.) All supports should be level and at the same height, or the top edges shimmed to be so, as upon them will be placed the side of the spar that is to be straight, that is, the aft side of the mast or the top side of the boom.

Shellac has long been the sparmaker's choice for coating the interior surfaces of a hollow spar (though varnish will do the job too). Be careful not to coat the surfaces to be glued. Use a marking gauge to scribe the width of the side pieces on the forward and aft pieces and shellac between the lines. The filler pieces at the ends of the spar and elsewhere as called for by the plans are fitted and shellac is also omitted in way of these. Because solid filler blocks have been known to swell and either split the spar or cause poorly glued joints to open up, some prefer the pad-type fillers glued to the inside before assembly as shown in Figure 16-6B. A long solid filler fitted at the heel of the mast is bound to locally stiffen the mast due to the sudden increase in sectional area. The late Phil Rhodes, one of the great yacht designers, insisted upon a block cut as shown in Figure 16-6C to avoid this situation and also advised running saw cuts longitudinally on the block to allow for expansion. Provide drain holes in all solid fillers except the one at the masthead, so moisture will not collect and start rot.

When everything is ready, mix the glue strictly in accordance with the instructions, paying particular attention to those regarding temperature and working life after mixing. Once the glue is mixed, spread it quickly and thoroughly. Before gluing make sure there are enough clamps at hand; it is surprising how many are needed, as there should be one every few inches or so to apply the pressure required for the glue, particularly resorcinol. Although Figure 16-7 shows a boom that is larger than any that the average amateur would attempt, it is a good illustration of the number of clamps used by a builder to ensure a perfect job. All kinds of clamps may be utilized if their openings are sufficiently wide to clamp the spar plus pieces of scrap used under the clamp pads to distribute pressure and prevent scars. If the number of your clamps is insufficient, you can make satisfactory spar clamps of two husky pieces of oak or ash joined together at the ends with bolts of at least ½″ diameter. (*See* Figure 16-6D.)

The clamps should not be removed for at least 24 hours to allow glue to develop full strength. Finish the spar by scraping the excess glue from the seams, round the corners, and then sand all sides smooth, gradually working down to fine abrasive paper. If a varnish finish is wanted—Sitka spruce has a beautiful appearance when finished clear—apply at least five coats, carefully sanding off or dulling the gloss between coats.

Round Hollow Spars

Even though a boat may have a rectangular mast and boom, the spinnaker pole (Figure 16-6G) will be round, made in symmetrical halves around a centerline. First,

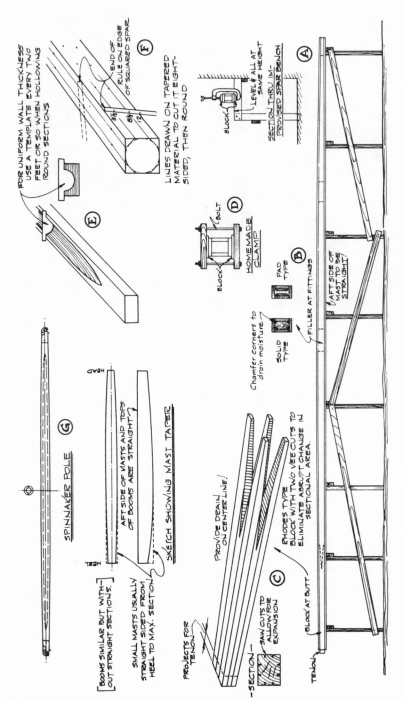

FOR UNIFORM WALL THICKNESS USE A TEMPLATE EVERY TWO FEET OR SO WHEN HOLLOWING ROUND SECTIONS

END OF RULE ON EDGE OF SQUARED SPAR

(F)

(E)

LINES DRAWN ON TAPERED MATERIAL TO CUT IT EIGHT-SIDED, THEN ROUND

3¾

8½

12⅝

BLOCK

LEVEL ALL AT SAME HEIGHT

SECTION THRU IMPROVISED SPAR BENCH

(A)

BOLT

(D)

BLOCK

HOME MADE CLAMP

AFT SIDE OF MAST TO BE STRAIGHT!

(B)

Chamfer corners to drain moisture

PAD TYPE

SOLID TYPE

FILLER AT FITTINGS

SPINNAKER POLE

(G)

HEAD

AFT SIDE OF MASTS AND TOPS OF BOOMS ARE STRAIGHT!

HEEL

SMALL MASTS USUALLY STRAIGHT SIDED FROM HEEL TO MAX. SECTION

SKETCH SHOWING MAST TAPER

BOOMS SIMILAR BUT WITH-OUT STRAIGHT SECTIONS.

PROVIDE DRAIN ON CENTER LINE!

PROJECTS FOR TENON

SECTION

SAW CUTS TO ALLOW FOR EXPANSION

RHODES TYPE BLOCK WITH TWO VEE CUTS TO ELIMINATE ABRUPT CHANGE IN SECTIONAL AREA.

(C)

BLOCK AT BUTT

TENON

Figure 16-6. Spar-making details.

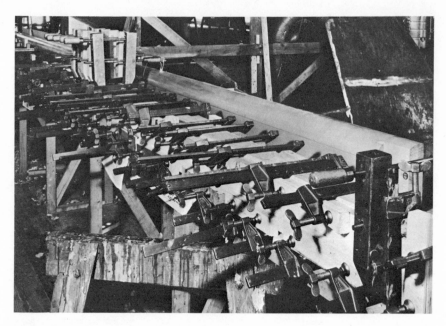

Figure 16–7.

get out two pieces of stock that will be square when clamped together and equal to the diameter of the pole in the middle. Mark centerlines on the mating surfaces of the material; then lay out the inside of the pole, that is, the part to be hollowed. Make hollowing templates, Figure 16-6E, for points every two feet or so apart and constantly use them to check as the wood is cut away. The templates control the wall thickness of the finished spar and guard against ending up with walls that are too thin or not uniform in thickness. The hollow portion is ended in a quick taper, as shown on the sketch, so that pole end fittings will be attached to solid wood.

When the halves have been glued together, the spar must be laid out on the outside, and then the square assembly is tapered. The walls will then be of equal thickness all along the spar's centerline. The next step is to cut the corners off the square and make it eight-sided. This is done by drawing guide lines as done in Figure 16-6F. The following description is an example of how the guide lines might be laid out. At any point along the length of the tapered assembly, the end of a rule is placed even with one corner, and the rule is pivoted until the 12″ mark lines up with the opposite corner. Points are made on the wood at the 3½″ and 8½″ marks on the rule. This is repeated at every foot and a batten is run through the points to draw a line. These figures should be varied to suit differences in the diameter of the spar, because for ease of layout, the rule should be almost square across the spar. The ratio of 12-8½-3½ can be reduced or enlarged to suit any size of spar. For smaller spars of, say, 5″ diameter, the figures can be halved. Therefore, the end of the rule is held on one corner of the spar, and the 6″ mark on the other, with points made at the 1¼″ and 4¼″ marks. When guide lines have been drawn on all four sides, it is a simple matter to make the spar eight-sided with a drawknife and plane and then to round it off to be finished by sanding.

A round mast for a marconi sail will be straight on the aft side, but the method of making it is the same.

Rigging Attachments for Wooden Spars

Not too many years ago almost all masts were round and the upper ends of the standing rigging were spliced in a loop, dropped down over the masthead to the desired location and held in position by shoulder cleats on the mast. With the introduction of the marconi rig and the systems of stays for supporting it came taller masts, and the manufacturers of wire rope started to make what is called strand, a rope consisting of a single wire core with eighteen wires twisted around it. This is known as 1 to 19 construction. It has more strength than any other rope of the same diameter and is logical rigging to use to reduce windage. It is very stiff and difficult to splice and is therefore not suitable for looping around a mast, particularly one with an elongated oval or rectangular section. Consequently, spliced rigging has practically disappeared and the ends of the wire rope are fitted with swaged stainless steel terminals, which are attached to the mast by means of tangs. Most tangs are made of strong sheet metal, like Everdur (silicon bronze) or stainless steel, and are held to the mast by one bolt and a number of wood screws calculated to take the outward and downward stress components of the stay. It is the job of the naval architect to design tangs that are both light and strong, and each tang is usually carefully detailed for the job to be done.

The tangs can be made by a machine shop or a rigging specialist, or the enterprising amateur can tackle the sheet metal work by fitting his bandsaw with a metal cutting blade. Besides making the tangs exactly according to plan, the builder must drill the holes for the tang fastenings with care. Loose holes will permit the tangs to slip, possibly overloading a few of the fastenings instead of letting all of the fastenings do their share of the job. Figure 16-8 shows tangs for double lower shrouds on the main and mizzen masts of a ketch. These particular tangs, designed by the staff of Phil Rhodes, are an example of a simple, strong fitting. They are well made by the builder. The material is Everdur 1010 half hard; the bolts are tubular to save weight aloft. Straps encircling the mast with clips for the heels of the spreaders are found a few inches above the tang bolts.

Fore-and-aft bolts for tangs have nuts on the aft side of the mast that would interfere with the sail track if it were laid directly on the mast's aft face. To get around this, the sail track can be laid on a batten that has been glued on the mast and cut away for the nuts. Battens are also sometimes desirable on booms to prevent sail slides from binding due to contact with the boom at their edges. The screws for the sail track go through the batten and into the wall of the spar. At certain points of extra strain, such as at the extreme ends of a track and at reefed positions of the mainsail headboard, through-fastenings rather than screws should be used.

Mast Step

The compressive load from the mast is taken by the mast step, which is of some hardwood like oak. The step is given a length of several frame spaces to distribute the load over the hull, and in boats of any size it is placed in notches in the floors after first hav-

Figure 16-8.

ing been notched itself. When carefully done, the resulting joint at each floor will prevent movement of the step in any direction, and in addition, it is drift bolted to the floors, Figure 16-4C. The mortise in the step to take the mast tenon should have a drain hole drilled at the low point so that water will not collect and rot the step. A typical step is shown in Figure 16-4B, but like many other boat details, there are other types of steps, particularly in small craft, and details will be found on the plans.

Masts are sometimes stepped on deck or on the cabin roof. The thrust load is then carried down to the hull by a stanchion or by strategically located joiner bulkheads of ample strength.

Aluminum Alloy Spars

The plans for the boat you are building will probably call out the specifications for the parts if the spars are to be made of aluminum alloy. There is now a large choice of sizes of extruded sections for masts, booms, spinnaker poles, and the like, and also a large choice of fittings to complete the rig and make it work. Sailboat rigging is a business of its own and is best left to the experts if you do not have the details of what you need. There are ads in the sailing magazines for many spar suppliers and sailmakers ready to help with your problems if you have decided to use aluminum spars. Among the best-known firms are Kenyon Marine, New Whitfield Street, Guilford, CT 06437; Schaefer Spars, Industrial Park, New Bedford, MA 02745; and Mack-Shaw Sailmakers, Inc., 100 S.W. 15th Street, Fort Lauderdale, FL 33315.

Figure 16–9.

Figure 16-9 is a section through an extrusion for a mast. In this design there is a slot for the sail and a groove for the boltrope of the sail similar to the wooden mast section in Figure 16-5.

Vertical Tie Rod

The forces from the thrust of the mast and the upward pull of the rigging tend to collapse the hull, so that in moderate-size boats it is well to fit a tie rod between the mast step and mast partner as shown in Figure 16-4B. The rod is threaded on both ends for nuts which are set up over washers. Just take up the nuts snugly when installing them, as there is no need to try to pull the deck and step together.

With the advent of plywood bulkheads and well-fitted adjacent parts, the tie rod is no longer as important as it once was.

Types of Rudders

A rudder consists of a wood or metal blade and a stock through which force is transmitted to the blade and around which it pivots. Except for common types of powerboat rudders, it is attached to the hull by hangers called gudgeons and pintles. The location of the rudder is either inboard, meaning forward of the after end of the waterline, or outboard on the transom or sternpost (on a double-ender). Further, the rudder is either unbalanced, with all the blade area abaft the stock or pivot point, or it is partly balanced, with a percentage of the area forward of the stock. In the latter case, the force required to turn the rudder is reduced.

Powerboat Rudders

Modern powerboat rudders are now almost invariably made of metal, although formerly they were often of wood. The most common type has a blade of cast manganese bronze bossed for a rolled bronze or stainless steel stock that is inserted in the head of the rudder. Figure 16-10A shows this type of rudder supported at the top by the rudder port, a stuffing box to prevent leaks where the stock enters the hull, and at the bottom by a pintle riding in a hole in a metal skeg. A spade-type rudder is sketched in Figure 16-10B and is made in the same manner, but is not supported at

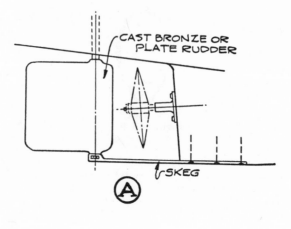

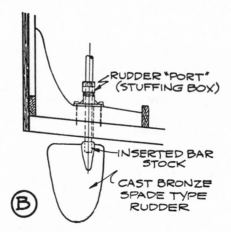

Figure 16–10.

the bottom and is more liable to catch lobster pot buoys and the like. It is a clean design and results from an effort to reduce underwater resistance by cutting away the deadwood, so there is no way of supporting the bottom of the rudder. On twin screw boats a spade-type rudder is used behind each of the propellers and gives excellent steering qualities. The two types of rudders sketched may be purchased in a number of sizes. Spade rudders are now frequently fabricated of welded stainless steel; they are either a single plate blade, or a hollow double blade having an airfoil section.

Small Sailboat Rudders

Small centerboard sailboats have an outboard rudder as shown in Figure 16-11A. The blade may be of one or more pieces, depending upon available material, but in any case it should be doweled with bronze rod to prevent warping, and the grain direction of the wood should be alternated from piece to piece for the same reason. The blade area below the surface of the water is streamlined in shape, as indicated on the

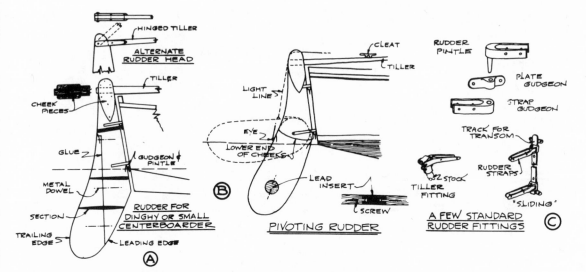

Figure 16–11. *Small sailboat rudders and fittings.*

sections in the sketch, with the maximum thickness being about 25 percent of the blade width aft of the leading edge of the rudder. When the common variety of gudgeons and pintles as seen in any marine hardware catalog is used, the rudder may float up and become disengaged from the boat, leaving the skipper with a tiller in hand but no control over the boat. To prevent this, the rudder may be weighted with an insert of lead heavy enough to offset the buoyancy of the blade, or the upper pintle can be drilled for a cotter pin just below the gudgeon. The tiller is fixed, or preferably made to hinge so it can be raised when tacking.

In shoal water localities the small boat outboard rudder is often made with a pivoting blade so that it may be raised to clear obstructions. (*See* Figure 16-11B.) This is done by pivoting the blade between long cheek pieces riveted securely to a filler of the same thickness as the blade. A lead insert is needed to prevent it from rising due to buoyancy or the forward motion of the boat. A light line is used to raise the rudder while sailing over shoal areas.

Some of the standard fittings available from marine stores are sketched in Figure 16-11C. Besides these, several of the marine hardware manufacturers make sets of fittings for small outboard rudders that prevent the rudder from coming off, yet leave the rudder readily removable from the transom. Rudder fittings should be through-bolted or riveted.

Large Sailboat Rudders

Figure 16-12A shows the rudder for a keel sailboat in which the stock is run down far enough to take a few bolts through the piece of blade next to it. A strap is fitted as shown at the end of the stock to prevent it from bending from pressure of water against the blade when the rudder is turned. At the bottom of the rudder a pintle and gudgeon are fitted for support. Unfortunately, the variety of rudder shapes and

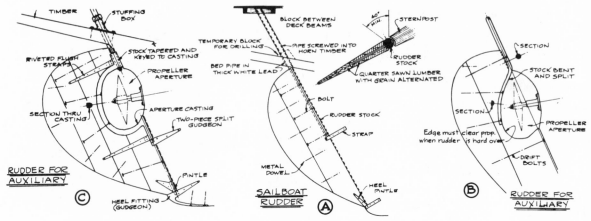

Figure 16-12.

thicknesses is so great that stock fittings are not available and patterns must be made for castings. These fittings are usually detailed by the designer with enough dimensions so that, together with templates made on the hull and rudder, the necessary patterns can be turned out for the use of the foundry. It is inadvisable to use anything but nonferrous metals for rudder fittings. The best materials for rudder stocks are tough, strong Tobin or silicon bronze rod or stainless steel. A rudder is a vital, very important part—*do not skimp on the quality of fittings.*

Larger rudders must be made of pieces that are doweled or drift bolted together as indicated by the plans. The size of dowels and bolts should be shown by the designer and may be decreased in diameter near the trailing edge, where the blade is thinner, so the wood will not be weakened by the fastenings. Dowel holes must be parallel to one another or the pieces cannot be joined together, and all fastenings must be kept in the middle of the blade to prevent their coming through when the blade is tapered. Drift bolts used in heavier rudders do not have to be parallel to each other, and when driven at varying angles, they lock the pieces together. Drifts driven from the trailing edge have a slot cut far enough in from the edge so the head will be hidden, and then a piece of wood is inserted to fill the slot. The enlarged section in Figure 16-12A shows how the blade is tapered. It may be seen that the amount of work required to make a rudder should not be underestimated.

If the builder is fortunate enough to have a thickness planer, some hand labor can be saved by planing each piece to its thickness at the forward edge. Otherwise all tapering is done with plane and spokeshave. The sketch also shows how the grain is alternated in adjacent pieces to prevent or minimize warping, and how the after edge of the sternpost is hollowed out so water will flow past the deadwood onto the rudder with a minimum of disturbance. As mentioned in Chapter 8, the edge of the sternpost is sheathed with copper about 1/32" thick for protection from worms and to eliminate painting, which is practically impossible without unshipping the rudder. The sheathing is carried around the sides by an inch or so and secured with copper tacks. The forward edge of the rudder blade begins aft of the center of the stock so that the rudder can be turned hard over without fouling the sternpost. With the rudder arranged as shown in Figure 16-12A, water is kept out of the hull by screwing a threaded brass or bronze pipe into a hole drilled in the horn timber. The hole must be just the right amount smaller than the pipe so the threads will take hold, and it must be drilled at the correct angle. The best way to start the hole is to cut through a block (shown dotted in the figure) having its face at right angles to the center of the stock. This can be laid out from your mold loft drawings and a drilling guide can be devised to ensure that the hole is drilled at the proper angle.

Rudders for Auxiliary Sailboats

When a sailboat is fitted with an engine and the shaft is on the centerline, there must be a hole or aperture cut in the deadwood and rudder in which the propeller can turn (Figure 16-12B). The aperture should not be larger than necessary, but its size must be such that the propeller blades will not strike the rudder when revolving. The edge of the aperture can be checked on the mold loft floor by setting up a semicircular disc of the same diameter as the propeller on the propeller centerline, and then hinging a piece of thin plywood or heavy cardboard on the centerline of the rudder. The aperture is cut away by trial until the "rudder" can be swung 40 degrees off center and still clear the propeller blades. (*See* Figure 16-13.)

It is not sufficient to end the rudder stock at the top of the aperture: it must either partly surround the opening as shown in Figure 16-12B, or completely encircle it as shown in Figure 16-12C. Sometimes the latter method is carried out by casting the

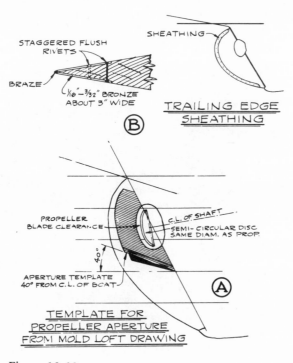

Figure 16-13.

complete stock in one piece from its upper end to the pintle below the aperture, but a long pattern is needed, the casting is not the easiest to make, and quite a lot of machining is required to finish the job. A shorter casting around the aperture, as shown, is hard to beat for strength, and except for grinding rough spots from the casting, the only machining needed is to taper, bore, and keyway the upper end for the stock, drill holes in the blade straps, and turn a pintle or bore for an inserted pintle on the lower end. The blade straps shown are cut from flat bronze and secured with countersunk rivets. The stock, of course, is made from bronze shafting, tapered and keyed to match the aperture casting, and is secured with a pinned nut on the lower end. A rudder made like this may be removed from the hull without digging a deep hole by taking off the two-piece split gudgeon and the stock and lifting the rudder enough to disengage the bottom pintle from the heel gudgeon. A stuffing box is shown on the horn timber. This will very likely be a special job, as seldom can standard fittings be adapted, due to the angle between stock and horn timber. The upper end of the stock of any rudder has a keyway for a standard tiller fitting, or in larger boats for a wheel steerer. There are several varieties of each of these items made by the marine hardware manufacturers.

An expensive and by no means necessary refinement to a rudder is to bronze sheath the trailing edge as illustrated in Figure 16-13B and in the photograph, Figure 16-14. This is made by templating the shape of the trailing edge and bandsawing the sheathing from a sheet of bronze about $\frac{1}{16}''$ to $\frac{3}{32}''$ inch thick, and there is much waste. The edges of the curved strips are filed smooth and laid on the rudder to mark a rabbet that is cut so the sheathing will be flush with the surface of the blade. Fastening is by means of countersunk head rivets as shown, and the trailing edges are brazed

Figure 16–14.

together, then ground reasonably sharp. Sometimes the rudder on a new boat will vibrate so that it chatters considerably, a condition remedied by sharpening the trailing edge somewhat, but the sheathed rudder is perfect from the start and is usually fitted on cruisers and racers of the finest quality.

Steering Controls

There are various means of transmitting directional forces to the rudder, starting with the simple tiller for an outboard rudder shown in Figure 16-11A. When the rudder is inboard, more complicated methods must be used. Some sailboats have an Edson-type steerer with the wheel and gearing attached to the upper end of the rudder stock. These gears must be carefully aligned and securely fastened to the structure. Other sailboats have the wheel farther away from the rudder and use a pedestal steerer connected to a quadrant on the rudder stock with a length of sprocket and chain and wire rope running over sheaves. The Edson Corp., 471 Industrial Park Road, New Bedford, MA 02745, is one of the world's largest producers of sailboat steerers and issues a catalog that is practically a design handbook. A recent Edson innovation utilizes husky push-pull cable steering from a pedestal in lieu of cable-over-pulley connections to the rudder tiller. This greatly simplifies the installation.

There are several types of steerers for powerboats. One method uses a reduction gear steerer at the wheel and chain and wire rope similar to the sailboat pedestal steerer. Others use a gearbox at the wheel or elsewhere in the system and connect to the rudder arm with shafts, solid or pipe. A more modern type of steerer, suitable for small to medium sizes of boats, uses a rack and pinion at the wheel and a heavy push-pull cable from the rack to an arm at the rudder. This is by far the simplest type of steerer and is seen in many boats because it is the least expensive to install.

The fortunate builder has good detail of the steering system on his plans; otherwise he has been left on his own to work it out. The steering should be installed before too much of the interior joinerwork has been built. It is most important that all steering gear parts be securely fastened to prevent movement of units such as the steerer and wire rope sheaves. The latter should be through-bolted and should be carefully aligned to reduce friction and eliminate wear on the wire rope. All parts should also be nonferrous whenever possible.

Due to the high cost of labor, manual hydraulic steering has almost become standard with the stock powerboat manufacturers. This type of steering consists essentially of a pump that is turned by the steering wheel, a hydraulic cylinder, and a reservoir, all connected by three tubes or hoses of small diameter. There can be two or more steering stations—it makes little difference as long as there are no leaks in the piping—so the more the number of stations the more advantageous the system. One drawback, and this is a matter of design, is the great number of steering wheel turns from hard over to hard over of the rudder. In the larger boats, the number of turns can be reduced by introducing a power-driven pump instead of a manually operated one. Two well-known suppliers of hydraulic steering components are Hynautic, Inc., Box 668, Osprey, Fl 33559, and Wagner Marine (USA) Inc., 14326 102nd Street N.E., Bothell, WA 98011.

Fuel Tanks

Due to the danger of explosion and fire, the construction and installation of fuel tanks, particularly gasoline tanks, should not be taken lightly. Both installation and construction are well covered by standards set by the American Boat and Yacht Council, written by people with long experience, and by the U.S. Coast Guard. The standards are only as good as your compliance with them, so heed them well. (*See* Chapter 17 and Recommended Reading.)

The standards specify the all-important matter of tank materials. Monel Alloy 400 remains probably the finest metal from which to make tanks, either for gasoline or diesel fuel, but it is extremely high in cost. Steel remains the most inexpensive material for diesel tanks but must not have a coating of any sort on the inside. A recent development is the approval of certain alloys of aluminum for the construction of fuel tanks. Now tanks can be welded of alloys 5052, 5083, or 5086.

When buying a fuel tank, be sure it bears the label of the manufacturer as called for by the standards and that it shows it was tested. Also, be sure that it has a tab for connection to the bonding system of the boat.

One caution about aluminum tanks concerns the connection of metal fittings, such as metal tubing and metal ends of fuel hoses, to the tank, because the metal may not be galvanically compatible with the aluminum alloy. One way to avoid trouble is to weld half of an aluminum pipe coupling to the tank and then screw a stainless steel pipe bushing into the female threads of the coupling half. The bushing reduces the size of the opening; therefore you must start out with a coupling that is a size or two larger than usual. Fill and vent connections to the tank are normally of hose, and these can be slipped over and clamped to aluminum alloy tubular fittings, either straight pieces or 90° elbows, beaded for hose and welded to the tank.

New in 1986 are fuel line hoses that are not affected by the alcohol-type additives replacing leaded gasoline fuels.

All valves in the fuel piping, including those at the tank for the fuel suction to the engine (and fuel return line in diesel systems), must be of the approved packless type, which do not leak at the stems.

And one final word: openings in the tank for any purpose are not permitted anywhere except on the *top* surface of the tank.

A tank manufacturer that has made hundreds of aluminum alloy fuel tanks for stock and custom boatbuilders as well as for the one-off people is Florida Marine Tanks, Inc., 16480 N.W. 48th Avenue, Hialeah, FL 33014.

Deck Plates for Tank Fills

The location of a fuel fill should be such that any spill or overflow will not drain into the hull or the middle of a self-draining cockpit. Why not the cockpit? Because gasoline fuel could collect here before draining—enough fuel to cause a disaster with the smallest spark. Fuel fills are generally sited on side decks.

There is a large fine in the United States for spilling fuel overboard, and when a boatbuilder becomes a boat owner he must remember that a fuel fill located to protect the boat from spillage does not give him a license for sloppiness.

Use fill plates that are stamped to show the contents of the tanks they serve. This will help prevent, but not guarantee, fuel from being pumped into a freshwater tank or vice versa. As you can imagine, either mistake presents a serious problem!

Fuel Tank Vents

The location of the fuel tank vent is important, particularly in sailboats, in order to prevent sea water from contaminating the tank and thereby causing engine failure or expensive residual damage. Referring to Figure 16-15, we can see that in a common rail-down sailing situation, the vent route shown as drawn is not safe. A horizontal loop (indicated by dashed lines) in the same boat is still only safe to 45 degrees. When the loop is vertical, extending to the underside of the cabin roof, things are better, but can be improved by extending the vent to the centerline of the boat. Heavily ballasted craft may still have positive stability when heeled beyond 90 degrees, so the vent locations warrant close study.

The examples in the figure assume that the tank is located along the centerline of the hull; otherwise, each case must be examined separately.

Through-hull fittings for fuel tank vents are readily available; most come with a flame arrester screen, and are made to connect with a ⅜" I.D. vent hose.

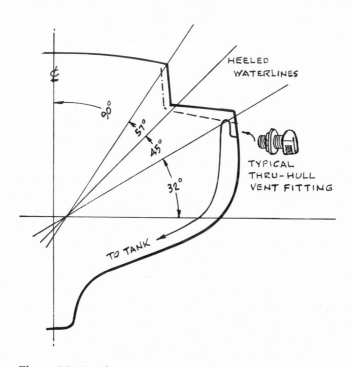

Figure 16–15. *Schematic arrangements of tank vents.*

Tank Capacity Calculation

Figure 16-16 shows tank shapes commonly used in boats and how to calculate their capacity by figuring the volume in cubic inches and dividing by 231 to find contents in U.S. gallons. Boatbuilders seem to always work the capacities from inch dimensions. If dimensions are taken in feet and fractions, the cubic capacity is multiplied by 7.48 for the answer in gallons.

The cylindrical and rectangular tanks A and B are straightforward to figure. Shape C is typical of a tank installed under the cockpit of a sailboat. The sides are parallel but the top and bottom are not, due to hull shape. The cross-sectional area W times H is the average of the area of the ends, or the same as the area at midlength of the tank. Shape D is often used for tanks located under the floor of a cabin, and again the volume is the length times the average of the area of the ends. The W measurements are taken at midheight of the ends.

Propeller Shafts and Bearings

Propeller shafts must be made from strong, non-corrosive material. At this writing two of the best metals, Monel Alloy 400 and the higher strength Monel Alloy K-500, have just about priced themselves out of the pleasure boat market. These are high in nickel content, and this is probably the reason why little people, unlike governments, cannot afford them. A somewhat weaker metal, although "standard" for many years, is Tobin bronze, but this seems to have disappeared (but don't overlook the possibility of finding a used Tobin shaft) and been replaced by various stainless steel shafting materials, notably Armco's Aquamet 17, 18, and 22. If the shaft is going to be turning most of the time, as in commercial boat use, then Aquamet 17 is a strong, suitable metal, but in typical intermittent yacht service Aquamet 22 is a better choice.

If your boat plans do not specify the shaft diameter, American Boat and Yacht Council standard P-6 has charts for selecting the sizes of shafts for the materials mentioned above and also for bearing spacing.

Typical shafts have a keyway machined on one end for the propeller shaft coupling to the engine, while the outboard end has a taper with keyway to match the propeller hub bore and threads for the propeller locking nuts. The tapering must be carefully done so the propeller will fit properly and is best left to a shaft supplier who is set up for this work. Dimensions for machining the shaft end and propeller hub have long been standardized, at least in the U.S., and the SAE data for this is usually tabulated and illustrated in the catalogs of the propeller makers. When setting up the length of your shaft, allow one shaft diameter's clearance between the propeller hub and the strut.

Figure 16-17 shows a longitudinal section at the shaft centerline of a twin screw motorboat. The same section applies to a common single screw motorboat with a keel batten and cutaway skeg. It shows the usual modern arrangement of a rubber-necked shaft log with a stuffing box inboard to prevent water from leaking into the boat around the shaft, and a strut to support the shaft at the propeller. Intermediate struts are used when the shaft is sufficiently long to require additional support.

TANK CAPACITY IN U.S. GALLONS
(DIMENSIONS IN INCHES)

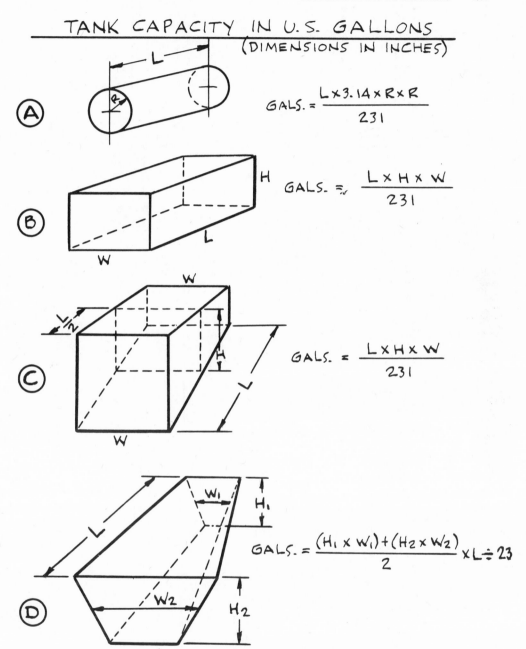

(A) $$\text{GALS.} = \frac{L \times 3.14 \times R \times R}{231}$$

(B) $$\text{GALS.} = \frac{L \times H \times W}{231}$$

(C) $$\text{GALS.} = \frac{L \times H \times W}{231}$$

(D) $$\text{GALS.} = \frac{(H_1 \times W_1) + (H_2 \times W_2)}{2} \times L \div 23$$

Figure 16–16.

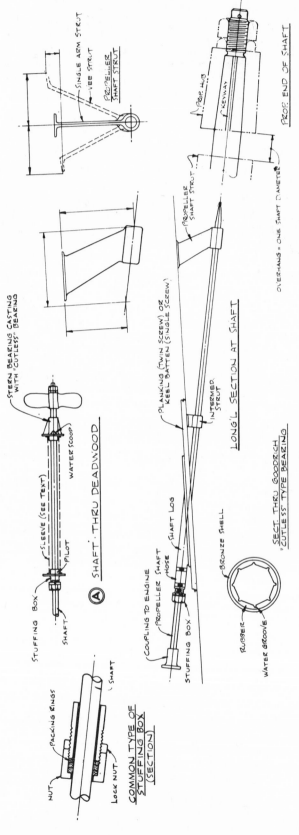

Figure 16-17.

The stuffing box and the shaft log are both of bronze and are connected by a short length of rubber hose secured by clamps. The hose helps to reduce vibration due to minor misalignment of the shaft. Shaft logs are made in the several angles that have proven the most useful for the majority of boats, but they may have to be shimmed with a wedge of wood in your boat to get the correct alignment. The base flange of the shaft log must be made watertight by bedding the flange with a generous amount of bedding compound, such as 3M 5200 or Pettit's Bedding Compound. Wherever possible, the base should be through-fastened with silicon bronze bolts; otherwise wood screws of the same metal should be used.

The shaft hole through the wood should be treated with polyester or epoxy resin, because the hole is difficult to clean and paint later with the shaft in place and is therefore susceptible to worm damage. This precaution is very important indeed.

Some shaft logs are designed with a tube integral with the base. The tube is a lining for the shaft hole and is cut off flush with the outside of the hull. This type of shaft log is rather special and is not used as frequently as the kind that terminates at the base.

Another type of special shaft log is sometimes used in moderate to large size boats where the shaft is quite long in proportion to the diameter and it is desirable to have a bearing between the first intermediate shaft strut and the engine. In this case shaft logs are made that have a short length of bearing. The bearing is housed so the forward end is not exposed to a flow of water; water lubrication is provided by engine cooling water tapped into the log forward of the bearing. The water used is part of that usually piped into the exhaust line for cooling, but the diversion is not detrimental, because only a small amount is sent to the shaft log bearing. This type of shaft log is specially made up and not found in marine supply catalogs.

A part of the propulsion setup that is almost always a special item is the propeller shaft strut. As specified by the plans, these are either the single arm or the v type, and due to the angle of the shaft and the shape of the hull it is nearly impossible to find a stock strut that will fit. There are, however, some adjustable struts on the market that might just do the job. Otherwise, enough dimensions on a sketch as shown in Figure 16-17A or a mock-up must be sent to a strut manufacturer so he can make up one or a pair to fit the boat. I am not advertising anybody in particular, but over the years Columbian Bronze Corp., Freeport, NY 11520 has made thousands of special struts, so they have many patterns that may be adapted with moderate alterations. Most struts are made of cast manganese bronze.

Struts are fastened through the planking and the inside blocking with silicon bronze or manganese bronze bolts. The heads of the bolts should be oval and countersunk and should have a screwdriver slot to keep the bolt from turning while it is tightened. These bolts are best ordered from the strut manufacturer, specifying the length needed.

You might as well have the strut maker install the bearing in the strut. It is hard to beat the Goodrich "Cutless"-type bearing, which is made of rubber bonded to an outer shell of bronze or, if the hull is aluminum alloy or steel, to an optional plastic-type shell. This type of bearing has grooves that channel in water for lubrication and for washing out silt and sand, thus minimizing shaft wear. The shell of the bearing is lightly pressed into the strut and secured with one or two set screws. The bearings are four times the shaft diameter in length when used as the aftermost bearing, and they

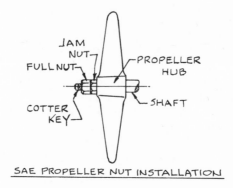

Figure 16–18.

are often reduced to half length in intermediate struts, so that one standard bearing can be cut to make two intermediate ones.

Figure 16-17A also shows a typical arrangement when the shaft of a single-engine boat goes through the deadwood. The stuffing box is inside the hull, the stern bearing outside. The latter has a Cutless-type bearing and a water scoop on each side of the casting for bearing lubrication. The stuffing box can be had "rubber necked," with a piece of hose between the stuffing box and the casting. Both stuffing box assembly and the stern bearing are stock items of marine hardware and are readily available.

Water will fill the hole for the shaft and must be prevented from leaking into the hull through joints in the deadwood structure. This is done by fitting a tube between the stuffing box and stern bearing castings, either a lead sleeve as shown in Figure 16-17A (the lead is easily flanged by hammering) or a bronze tube special-ordered from a supplier like Columbian Bronze. The pilots of the castings can be tapped for the ends of a threaded pipe. The castings should be fastened to the wood with hanger bolts.

The stuffing box packing is square, either waxed braided flax or Teflon-impregnated asbestos braid, and is installed as individual rings, with the joints staggered so they are not all in line, thus preventing leakage.

When you have secured a propeller on the shaft with the thin nut against the hub, followed by the thick nut, don't let anyone tell you it is wrong! Not long ago the Society of Automotive Engineers, which provides the marine propeller bore and shaft taper standards, revised their propeller shaft-end drawing to show the nuts properly arranged. (*See* Figure 16-18.)

Direction of Propeller Rotation

Screw propellers are made either right-hand or left-hand. Looking forward from astern, a shaft that turns clockwise requires a right-hand propeller and a shaft that turns counterclockwise takes a left-hand propeller. It is customary for the propellers in twin screw boats to be of opposite rotation and to turn outboard as shown in Figure 16-19.

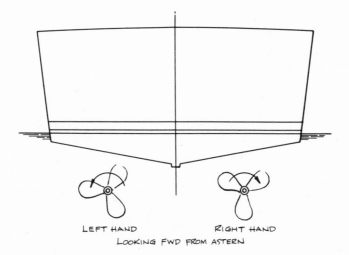

LEFT HAND   RIGHT HAND
LOOKING FWD FROM ASTERN

Figure 16-19.

Aligning Propeller Shaft Couplings

If there is misalignment between the engine and propeller shaft couplings, there will not only be unnecessary vibration when the engine is running but also possible damage to the rear bearing and seal of the reverse gear. The shaft should be installed first and the engine mated to it. If there are only two support bearings for the shaft, the stern bearing or strut bearing and a rubber-necked shaft log, block up the shaft inboard of the shaft log to prevent the shaft from sagging at the rubber neck. Lacking a feeler gauge, test for alignment between the coupling halves by inserting four strips of paper as shown in Figure 16-20. You can tell by gently pulling on the strips whether the pressure, and thus the gap, is the same for all pieces. Hardwood and thin brass shims are used under the engine mounts until the alignment is as perfect as possible. The final test is to tighten down the engine and still have good alignment of the couplings.

Many engines are equipped with adjustable mounts that need but a wrench to lift or lower them a few thousandths of an inch, and some of the larger engines have jacking screws built into the mounts for the same purpose.

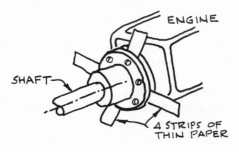

ENGINE

SHAFT

4 STRIPS OF
THIN PAPER

Figure 16-20.

If aligning of the engine is done with the boat out of water, it must be tested again when the vessel is launched because some hulls change shape when water-borne, throwing out the alignment that was done while hauled out.

Pulley Drives

The boatbuilder is often faced with figuring out a v-belt pulley ratio when a bilge pump or extra generator is to be driven from a power take-off pulley on an engine. The formulae below are handy for finding pulley diameter or speed in RPM.

Driven pulley:

$$RPM = \frac{\text{diameter} \times \text{RPM of driver}}{\text{diameter of driven}}$$

$$\text{Diameter} = \frac{\text{diameter} \times \text{RPM of driver}}{\text{RPM of driven}}$$

Driving pulley:

$$\text{Diameter} = \frac{\text{diameter} \times \text{RPM of driven}}{\text{RPM of driver}}$$

$$RPM = \frac{\text{diameter} \times \text{RPM of driven}}{\text{diameter of driver}}$$

Engine Controls

The engine is almost always located some distance away from the steering station of the boat, so remote controls must be installed for operating the throttle, the reverse gear, and an emergency shutdown in the case of some two-cycle diesel engines. This used to be done with complicated linkages of rods, pipes, and bell cranks and was a job of major proportions. One of the greater boons was the advent of the hydraulic reverse gear, requiring but fingertip effort on a small lever on the gear instead of the many foot-pounds of effort needed to operate the old manual clutch. This led to the push-pull cable controls now seen in most boats, a method that drastically reduced the time and cost of installation. The engine control system now consists of an attractive set of levers at the steering station and two push-pull cables running from the levers to the engine, one each for gear and throttle. The control maker usually has kits for each brand of engine for connecting the engine end of the cables to the gear and throttle. These save hours of making brackets for each job.

Control heads of high quality can be furnished by one of the oldest makers, Morse Controls, 21 Clinton Street, Hudson, OH 44236. Another pioneer in control heads is Panish Transdyne, 4806 N. E. 12th Avenue, Fort Lauderdale, FL 33308, an outfit that can give advice from much firsthand experience. A newcomer in the U.S. market with a first class product is Kobelt Manufacturing Co., Ltd., 235 East 5th Avenue, Vancouver, British Columbia, Canada V5T 1H2. The first two mentioned are also sources for push-pull cables, as is Teleflex, Inc., 640 North Lewis Road, Limerick, PA 19468.

The length of cables between control levers and the engine can be almost unlimited, but they should be installed with a minimum number of bends, and the minimum bend radius for the size of cable being used must not be exceeded. Contrary to the opinions of some, it is a mistake to restrict the movement of push-pull cables. They should only be secured sufficiently to keep them from interfering with other equipment. A little time spent planning the cable runs will show which way has the least number of bends. The control manufacturers furnish excellent instructions for making the installation.

A variation of a control head with two levers per engine is the single lever control favored by many operators. Two cables per engine are still required, so the installation is planned the same as when there are two levers.

When two or more control stations are planned and would require long runs of cables with many bends, consideration should be given to hydraulic controls for the throttle and gears. Hynautic, Inc., mentioned earlier in this chapter under Steering Controls, has a system that may do the job for you.

Engine Connections

Water, fuel, and electrical connections to an engine should always have slack so vibration cannot cause premature failure of the lines. Cooling water lines to the engine should be hose, double clamped at each end with stainless steel hose clamps whenever possible. On the other hand, fuel lines should be hose of approved type with threaded end and *never* clamped. The reader should heed the regulations described in the following chapter.

A good number of boats have sunk because exhaust hoses have been inadequately clamped to the adjoining rigid pipes or tubes. Figure 16-21 shows the minimum clamp

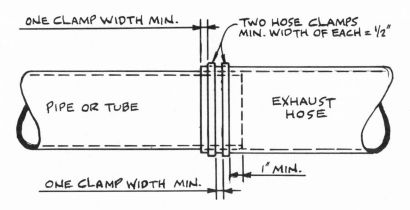

Figure 16-21.

widths and hose overlap permitted by the American Boat and Yacht Council standard on this subject. See the following chapter for additional reference to the ABYC.

Electrical System

Here is a part of modern boatbuilding that can get a builder into a lot of trouble. If he is lucky, there will be only one voltage on board, such as 12 volts direct current. However, more often these days there will also be 115 volts of alternating current from a shoreline connection to operate a charger to keep the batteries topped off and also perhaps to operate the AC side of a dual voltage refrigerator when the engines are not running, and to operate air conditioning while dockside. Progressing further, an AC independent generator on board can be used to provide conveniences such as an AC-powered cooking range, heating or air conditioning, television, etc. And further along the line there can be *two* AC voltages in use aboard, and also *two* DC voltages, such as 12 and 24 or 12 and 32. The complications are endless; in some of the larger yachts there seems to be no end at all. But this has been recognized, and there are American Boat and Yacht Council standards that *attempt* to keep things manageable.

In terms of material, the standards are a guide to the all-important matter of overload protection to avoid fire and to the type of insulated conductors necessary to cope with the various environments aboard a boat. The conductor size is governed by the length of the wire and the ampere load to be carried, and the wires of the conductors should be stranded rather than solid to minimize failure from vibration. Connections must be by approved crimped terminals and should be soldered as well.

The U.S. Coast Guard also has something to say about electrical installations, due to tragic experiences in the past, particularly in boats with gasoline engines. The Coast Guard guideline to safe electrical system installation is listed in the following chapter.

Life is being made easier for the boatbuilder by the appearance on the market of standardized switchboards meeting recognized standards. For years, the only hardware store-type switchboard available to boatmen has been a small 12-volt DC panel having six to a dozen toggle switches and automotive type fuses for circuit protection. Now, there are DC panels and combination DC and AC panels of various sizes, all having approved circuit breakers and meters to show loads and the condition of batteries. There is a sufficient selection of panels and load capacities to take care of the circuits used in many boats, and this often eliminates the necessity of having to utilize custom designed and built switchboards. One of the pioneers in this field is Marinetics Corp., P.O. Box 2676, Newport Beach, CA 92663.

Battery Storage Boxes

The electrolyte in a lead-acid storage battery is very destructive to wood and certain metals, so it is important to prevent spillage. The worst thing that can happen is for an unsecured battery to overturn; therefore the battery, whether it consists of a single or multiple units, must be secured. For small craft there are on the market covered molded plastic cases, with straps and hold-down fittings to keep the thing in place. In

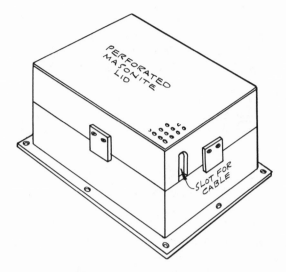

Figure 16-22.

larger boats there might be a bank of two engine starting batteries and a bank of two to eight ship's service batteries, for which custom boxes must be built.

One of the simplest containers is made of plywood, with its interior made acid-resistant by carefully and completely lining the box with fiberglass. The inside dimensions of the box should be about ¼″ larger all around than the battery to provide space for spilled water, which can be removed by suction with an oven baster. A couple of expendable wooden blocks can be used to keep the battery from shifting despite the clearance. The top should be of a material like Masonite, ventilated so that explosive hydrogen generated when the battery is being charged will not be trapped. A top also guards against the possibly dangerous sparking that would take place should a tool be accidentally dropped across the battery terminals.

Figure 16-22 is a suggested battery box.

Freshwater Tanks

Freshwater tanks should be just as carefully built, tested, and installed as fuel tanks. One difference is that there *should* be an opening in the bottom of the tank—the outlet. This is used to drain the tank when a boat is unused or stored in freezing weather. Suitable water tank materials include Monel Alloy 400, superior in quality and cost, stainless steel (Type 316 is the best in salt atmosphere), aluminum alloy, and fiberglass, provided the interior is treated to remove taste and odor.

Plumbing

Copper used to be the ultimate for piping, either salt water or hot and cold fresh water, but it has had drawbacks, such as a tendency to develop pinholes. Now it is costly not only as piping but in the price of the fittings necessary to hook it up. The marine supply stores have good quality hose of other materials: polyvinyl chloride (PVC) pipe, some of which is suitable for hot water, and a polybutylene tubing suitable for cold and hot water that is exceptionally fast to connect with the available fittings.

Where pipes pierce the hull for any reason—toilet connections, cooling water intakes, etc.—up to about a foot above the normal waterline, the "through-hull" fittings should be directly connected to seacocks. These fittings are discussed in detail below.

Seacocks

Seacock is another name for a valve made to close an opening in the hull—an opening for a water intake, or toilet discharge, or the like. A real seacock—unlike an inexpensive, ordinary, residential valve—is made of a corrosion-resistant material other than common brass. The best of them will have a base drilled for bolts through the hull and a backing block or plate; the base is tapped for a threaded through-hull fitting. It is good practice to use seacocks for pipe openings below a line about 12" above the maximum draft of the boat.

The pipe for a marine toilet requires special attention. Installation instructions normally advise the use of a so-called vented loop in the discharge line, and suggest that the loop be at least 6" above the deepest waterline of the boat. Indeed, the vented

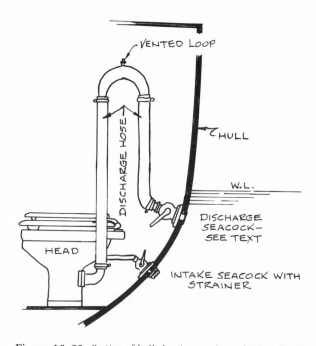

Figure 16–23. *Section of hull showing marine toilet installed below waterline.*

loop is a safe installation that guards against siphoning water back into the boat, but I would modify this to locate the loop *as high as practical* in sailboats, and in the case of rail-down sailing make it a strict rule on board that the seacock be closed except when the head is in use.

The last point brings up another: *all* seacocks *must* be located where accessible. If the seacock has a detachable handle, then a hook or other suitable stowage should be provided adjacent to the valve itself.

Use full-flow seacocks rather than those which, when open, have a flow area less than that of the pipe size.

The toilet piping in Figure 16-23 is only schematic. For example, it may be more practical to mount the loop more nearly 90° to what is shown, that is, mounted along the hull.

Intakes for engine cooling, etc., must have scoop strainers over the opening on the outside of the hull and also good quality intake strainers on the inside of the hull between the seacock and the device pumping the water.

Wilcox-Crittenden and Perko are two manufacturing firms whose seacocks, through-hull fittings, and inboard and outboard strainers are stocked by most handlers. Buck-Algonquin (whose address appears under Bronze Marine Hardware later in this chapter) and Wilcox make vented toilet discharge loops. Gross Mechanical Laboratories, Inc., 7240 Standard Drive, Hanover, MD 21076 makes high quality seacocks and inboard strainers for seawater intakes.

Water Trap Vent

There should be a circulation of fresh air through a boat even when it is otherwise closed up. The vent shown in Figure 16-24 was developed for sailboats at sea some

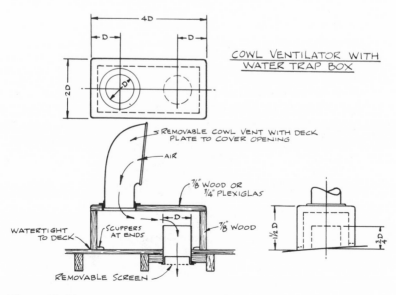

Figure 16-24.

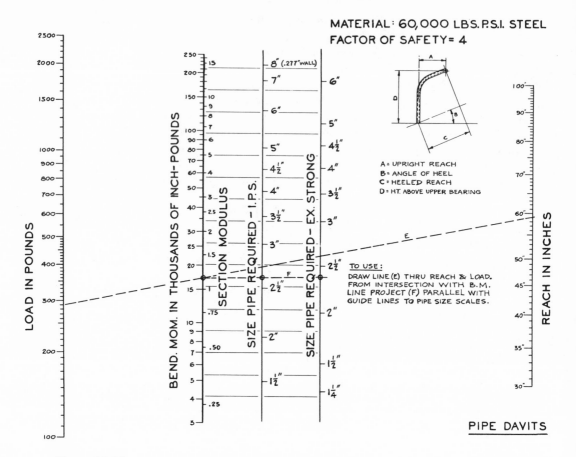

Figure 16–25.

years ago and remains popular and practical for any type of boat, as it permits ventilation while excluding rain and flying spray. The cowl can be turned as desired for best results. The removable screen should not be used unless there are insects, because screens reduce the effective opening by about 25 percent. The cowl can be one of the pliable rubbery plastic kind that bend when a rope crosses it. The tube into the boat can be plastic, aluminum, or copper. The box can be installed either fore and aft or athwartships.

Cure for Bilge Water Traps

While trying to dry a bilge recently, I was reminded of a work task I'd been assigned in a shop that built quality wooden motorboats many years ago. Figure 16-26 shows a section through the keel of one of those boats and is typical of many others, both power and sail, round- and v-bottomed. One drawback to this type of construction is that it creates a pocket which can trap bilge water between frames on each side of the

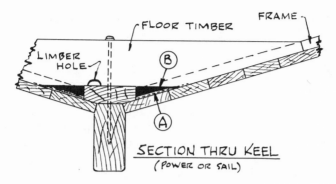

Figure 16–26.

keel batten, as shown in the figure. (Refer also to Figures 8-14A and C.) Accordingly, as soon as a hull was planked (the boats were built upright), the shop foreman gave me a roll of copper insect screening, a pair of shears, and a box of copper tacks. I then tacked a piece of the mesh to the planking between frames (Figure 16-26A); melted a tar-like material in a pot; and filled all of the pockets flush with the top of the keel batten (Figure 16-26B). The bilge water then drained to the low points of the hull through the limber holes in the floor timbers.

I did the tarring very quickly because it was not much fun, but the scheme is still a good one. These days a material other than tar could be used—much healthier for the applicator, and of course more costly.

Davits

Davits are used for handling anchors and dinghies aboard yachts and for other purposes on commercial boats. Aluminum alloy pipe, anodized if possible for protection against corrosion, has become a popular material for davits because of its light weight. This is good when, for one reason or another, a davit must be removed from its socket and stowed and thus needs manhandling. Davits can also be made of stainless steel pipe or tube or of ordinary steel pipe, the latter preferably hot galvanized after shaping and welding whatever fittings are needed on the davit. I worked up the accompanying chart, labeled Figure 16-25, some years ago when scores of small craft going to war were clamoring for davits for all sorts of uses. If you know the load and the reach (dimension A), the chart will give a pretty good idea of the pipe size needed. The chart has a built-in safety factor of four using ordinary steel pipe. A davit is basically a cantilevered beam, so if a load swung outboard will heel the boat much, or if rolling seas are expected, the reach should be increased as noted on the chart. A larger pipe size will then probably be indicated.

Anodized aluminum alloy davits of various capacities, ranging from 150 pounds for anchors and up to 1500 pounds for small boats, are made as stock items and can be had with a tackle arrangement, with a hand-operated winch, or with an electric winch in various voltages. The reach, dimension A in Figure 16-25, is usually limited to six feet. Principal makers of the aluminum davits are Mar-Quipt, Inc., 231 S. W. 5th

Street, Pompano Beach, FL 33060, and Pipe Welders, Inc., 2965 State Road 84, Fort Lauderdale, FL 33312.

Bronze Marine Hardware

Starting about 1970, some sizes of deck fittings and similar gear were no longer made by the large marine hardware manufacturers in the U.S., presumably due to reduced sales. There seems to be no shortage, though, of inferior, die-cast, pot-metal fittings and black cleats and the like that some think good-looking on production boats of peculiar shapes. Take heart; there are still a few firms that make traditional hardware. Here are the names of some that might have the gear you seek:

Rostand R.I., Inc., Box 737, Chepachet, RI 02814.

The Boater's Friend, 1822 Second Street, Berkeley, CA 94710.

ABI Industries, 415 Tamal Plaza, Corte Madera, CA 94925.

Spartan, 204 Middleboro Avenue, East Taunton, MA 02718.

Buck Algonquin, 1565 Palmyra Bridge Road, Pennsauken, NJ 08110.

Grand River Marine, 38387 Apollo Parkway, Willoughby, OH 44094.

New Found Metals, Inc., 240W Airport Road, Port Townsend, WA 98368.

J. Stuart Haft, Box 11210, Bradenton, FL 33507. (This last firm in the list stocks, among other items, windlasses and genuine CQR "plow" anchors.)

Painting

The boatbuilder today has a choice of the finest exterior finishes imaginable, both for protection and appearance, from one-part enamels to the very expensive, long-lasting two-part high gloss polyurethane coatings. There is also a wide choice of varnishes and synthetics to protect and bring out the best natural wood trim.

Underwater there is a wide variety of antifouling paints, usually priced according to life expectancy. Here you must be guided by the length of your season and which paint has proven effective in the areas to be frequented.

The same makers of the fine marine exterior coatings and paint also have material for the interior—where, by the way, there is nothing wrong with using the high-grade latex-base paints, which make cleanup so easy with water.

Marking the Boottop

Nothing looks worse to yachtsmen than a ragged division between the topside and bottom paints. Assuming that the builder has had the foresight to mark the designed waterline at the stem and stern for reference during construction, just about the easiest way to mark the boottop is to first plot the straight waterline at frequent intervals along the hull and then lay off heights to the boottop as scaled from the plan of the outboard profile. Level straightedges are set up at the ends of the boat as shown in Figure 16-27, and then a length of thin, strong cord is stretched tightly between the edges and moved inboard until it barely touches the hull and a point is marked there.

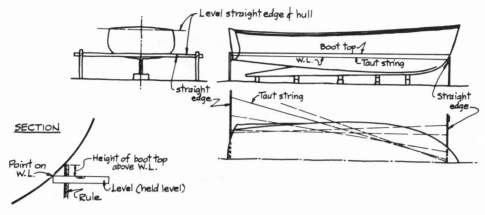

Figure 16-27.

By moving the cord in and out on the straightedges alternately at opposite ends, points on the waterline may be marked as often as desired. Be sure to keep the cord tight, for if it is allowed to sag, the waterline will not come out straight. If the boat is level fore and aft and there is room to work, a builder's level or transit may be used to run in the line. The boottop or stripe is often curved (sheered) for appearance, and offsets above the waterline can be taken from the plans and plotted as shown in the figure. A batten is tacked on the hull to fair the points and mark the line, which is done by scribing with the broken end of a hacksaw blade or similar device or with a so-called race knife made for scribing wood.

Abrasives

The quality of a finished surface depends upon how much time and effort is spent smoothing that surface before the application of paint, varnish, etc. A rough surface cannot be hidden by fillers or topcoats; rather, imperfections become more prominent. Boatbuilders who specialize in providing a high quality "yacht" finish will agree that it takes virtually as much time to properly prepare wood for paint as for varnish.

With regard to sanding wood, don't start with a coarser grit than is necessary before switching to the finer grades. Where to start on the grit scale is quickly learned. If you are making no progress sanding with 180 grit, then you should have started with 100 or even 60 grit. Smooth edges and corners with a sanding block and dust off the work frequently so you can see what you are doing. Don't just blow away the dust—use a brush instead. Also, minimize the clogging of the abrasive by frequently rubbing it with a stick of latex abrasive cleaner (discussed below); this extends the life of the abrasive and therefore saves money, whether sanding by hand or machine.

Figure 16-28 shows a variety of hand-sanding blocks—flat, convex, and concave—which have worked well for me. As dimensioned, these are operated with quarters of standard 9" x 11" abrasive sheets. I use white pine for the blocks and contact cement for the cellular rubber facings.

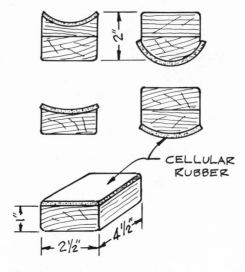

Figure 16-28.

For boatbuilding purposes there really are just two kinds of abrasives to consider for finishing wood. These are *garnet*—reddish in appearance, a mineral with sharp cutting edges, at its best on softwood; and *aluminum oxide*—a synthetic mineral, better on hardwood than garnet. Either one should be marked "open coat" on the back of the sheet. This construction does not clog as quickly as the closed type of abrasive coating.

The finer grade abrasive sheets are made with A grade paper; it takes practice to be able to sand without tearing or wrinkling these sheets. The C and D grade papers are used to make 150 grit and coarser sheets; these are easier to work with when hand sanding.

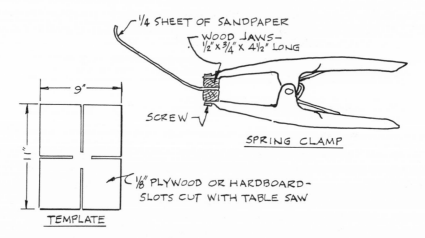

Figure 16-29.

I have two palm-type finishing sanders that each use sandpaper sized 4" x 5½", made by quartering standard 9" x 11" sheets. To minimize the chore of cutting a number of these at one time I place a slotted pattern on a full sheet, run a pencil through the slots to mark the quarters, then cut as many as possible, depending upon the grit, with sheet metal shears. (*See* Figure 16-29.) A similar pattern can be made for marking sandpaper into thirds, sized for orbital/straight-line sanders. To ease the often frustrating procedure of inserting the ends of the sheet into the clamps of the sander, a "kinker"—made by adding wooden jaws to a spring clamp—will turn the edges of the paper into the required curve. (*See* Figure 16-29.)

Many tool catalogs now carry what appears to be a piece of latex about 1½" x 1½" x 8" long, sold as a sandpaper cleaner. This item works, and will save you money. Just stroke it across the paper or hold it against a sander in operation.

Chapter 17

SAFETY

A sound hull is only the beginning of a safe boat, unless it is the simplest of craft like one made to be paddled or rowed. As soon as holes are made in the hull underbody for through-hull fittings or machinery and electrical installations are made, precautions must be taken to prevent leaking, sinking, fire, or explosion. Newcomers to boatbuilding are fortunate in having information available to keep them out of trouble. Not too many years ago this knowledge was not so easy to come by. Many lessons were learned the hard way—sinking caused by a rotted hose attached to a valveless underwater through-hull fitting, loss of fire control from the wrong kind or an inadequate number of fire extinguishers, fire and/or explosion because a fuel line to an engine was installed without slack and broke from vibration, loss of life because passengers aboard a sinking boat could not find the life preservers. These occurrences and others were and are preventable.

The very nature of boats calls for deck levels of varying heights to be accessible by steps and ladders. Risk of injury can be reduced by having an adequate number of hand rails and grabs that are securely fastened in place with through-fastenings whenever possible. Similarly important are the adequate height and fastening of safety rails and lifelines around the edges of all decks accessible to those aboard.

American Boat and Yacht Council

This non-profit council was formed in 1954 by members of the boating industry concerned with safety. Over the years dozens of members have served countless hours in the preparation of standards for safe practices in the general areas of hull, equipment, machinery, electrical, and engineering standards. Ample time has been given for comment and criticism of the standards before they have been approved; therefore the standards do not represent one-sided opinions.

Membership in the ABYC is open to all and includes: a complete set of standards, copies of new standards as they are developed, and revisions to existing standards. For further information, contact the Secretary, American Boat and Yacht Council, P.O. Box 806, Amityville, NY 11701.

There are numerous and detailed standards in each of the council's general divisions mentioned above. If membership is not desired, the ABYC standards are for sale on an individual basis. It may well prove less expensive, though, to join up and receive them all. Following is a list of standards that should be of interest to boatbuilders:

Project	Title	Project	Title
	HULL DIVISION		MACHINERY DIVISION
H-1	Visibility from the Helm	P-1	Exhaust Systems
H-2	Ventilation of Boats—Gasoline	P-6	Propeller Shafting
H-3	Hatches and Doors		
H-4	Cockpits and Scuppers		ELECTRICAL DIVISION
H-5	Boat Load Capacity		
H-7	Metal Fastenings in Vessels	E-1	Bonding of Direct Current Systems
H-8	Buoyancy in the Event of Swamping	E-2	Cathodic Protection
H-13	Glazing Materials	E-3	Wiring Identification
H-15	Hull Opening Between Water Line and Sheer Line	E-4	Lightning Protection
H-17	Thermal & Acoustical Insulation, Sheathing Materials, etc.	E-8	A.C. Electrical Systems
H-22	Bilge Pumps	E-9	D.C. Electrical Systems under 50 Volts
H-23	Potable Water Systems		
H-24	Fuel Systems—Gasoline		EQUIPMENT DIVISION
H-25	Portable Fuel Systems	A-4	Fire Fighting Equipment
H-26	Powering of Boats	A-5	Ground Tackle
H-27	Seacocks, Thru-Hull Connections, etc.	A-9	Distress Signals
H-30	Hydraulic Systems	A-16	Navigation Lights
H-32	Ventilation of Boats—Diesel	A-17	Life Saving Equipment
H-33	Fuel Systems—Diesel	A-20	Battery Chargers

ENGINEERING STANDARDS DIVISION

S-7	Boat Capacity Labels
S-8	Boat Measurements and Weight
S-10	Hull Identification Number (HIN)
S-11	Outboard Motor Dimensions
S-12	Outboard Motorboat Transom and Motor Well Dimensions
S-14	Sailboat Inboard Well Dimensions
S-15	Sailboat Auxiliary Horsepower
S-17	Compass Installation

Note that standards H-24 and H-33, pertaining to gasoline and diesel fuel systems respectively, specify acceptable fuel tank materials, minimum material thickness, etc., as well as procedures for testing the entire fuel system (not just the tanks) for leaks.

Federal Safe Boating Regulations

Poor design, construction, and equipment installations that resulted in explosions, fire, and loss of life have inevitably led to the enactment of laws in the U.S. governing gasoline fuel systems, electrical systems in boats with gasoline-fueled engines, safe loading and safe powering, and level flotation in case of swamping. The American Boat and Yacht Council, under contract to the U.S. Coast Guard, prepared "compliance guidelines" to ease the burden of the boatbuilder, whether he be a manufacturer or backyard builder, to determine whether his product will meet the regulations. In my opinion, the standards required by law are the same as the practices recommended by the ABYC.

Copies of the following booklets may be obtained from your nearest U.S. Coast Guard District Office or from U.S. Coast Guard, Office of Boating Safety, Washington, DC 20590:

Electrical System Compliance Guideline—applies to all inboard or inboard/outboard gasoline-powered boats and boats that have gasoline auxiliary engines such as generators.

Fuel System Compliance Guideline—applies to all boats powered with gasoline engines (except outboard engines), all boats with gasoline auxiliary engines, such as generators, and to *gasoline fuel tanks* that are permanently installed in inboard and inboard/outboard boats.

Level Flotation Compliance Guide—applies to monohull boats less than 20 feet in length. It does not apply to sailboats, canoes, kayaks, or inflatable boats.

Coast Guard publication CG-466, *Safety Standards for Backyard Boat Builders*, is a boon to the home builder and includes directions as to how to work up the safe loading calculations for boats under 20 feet long to which the law applies. In addition, it tells how to go about attaching a "capacity label" and a "certification label" to the hull, and how to obtain a hull identification number for your boat.

It is hoped that all these things will not discourage a would-be backyard builder; a careful study of the safety regulations will show that their intent is good.

Many government regulations seem to consist of endless pages of solid text, making them difficult to read; not so the guidelines put out by the Coast Guard. These clearly illustrate with simple line drawings what is acceptable and what is prohibited.

Product Testing

A step for safety beyond mere words has also been taken. Manufacturers can now have their products tested for compliance with American Boat and Yacht Council standards and so labeled when the product meets the requirements. The agency that does the testing is the marine section of the well-known and respected Underwriter's Laboratories (UL), which succeeded the pioneering Yacht Safety Bureau.

The UL label on hardware and other items of equipment assures the purchaser that the material has been tested and found suitable. Underwriter's Laboratories, Inc. is located at 12 Lab Drive, P.O. Box 13995, Research Triangle Park, NC 27709.

Shop Safety

Woodworkers have ample opportunity to cut themselves. Machine tool guards, in general, are seldom used as they should be—many woodworkers actually regard these devices as safety hazards. So they work at their own risk, and some are lucky. At the very least, there should be a good first aid kit on the premises.

Many builders are lax about eye protection, while others are careful to wear either a face shield or safety glasses; both items are readily available from hardware stores, lumberyards, and mail order catalogs. Hearing protection is also fairly easy to find; so too are dust masks for working with wood and other materials.

Rough lumber and plywood provide plenty of splinters—some species and some glues can produce a rapid infection. Take the time to slip on a pair of gloves.

Many fumes are toxic to internal parts of the body as well as to the skin. Beware of petroleum distillates and other harmful ingredients in paint thinners and removers, brush cleaners, adhesives, solvents, etc. These call for wearing a respirator and latex (or heavier) gloves for protection. Always check containers for warnings from manufacturers; sometimes the print is quite small.

Professional boatbuilding shops are regulated for safety by state and federal agencies and by their own insurance carriers; the amateur's shop is not. But any builder who engages in boat construction in any material should become aware of hazards to himself and to any helpers.

Remember: volatile materials should be stored outside the work space when not in use; the shop should have adequate ventilation; a fire extinguisher should be at hand; extension cords should be unplugged when work stops for the day.

This manual began with the assumption that the reader has come to boatbuilding having completed, at a minimum, basic training in woodworking. In the end this book can do no more than urge the reader—the builder—to exercise caution and common sense in a work environment which can never be made completely safe.

RECOMMENDED READING

Boatbuilding One-Off in Fiberglass, by Allan H. Vaitses, 1984. Written by an old hand who thoroughly discusses the pros and cons of the optional one-off methods. International Marine Publishing Co., 21 Elm Street, Camden, ME 04843.

Boatbuilding with Plywood (Second Edition, 1978) and *How To Fiberglass Boats* (1974), both from Glen-L Marine Designs, 9152 Rosecrans, Bellflower, CA 90706. Because plywood remains one of the most inexpensive hull planking materials, the instructions in these books for handling and fiberglass covering plywood are particularly useful.

Boat Buyers Guide, published by *Yachting* Magazine, Box 1200, Cos Cob, CT 06807. An annual directory of boat equipment and a list of naval architects offering plans from dinghy-size right up to too big for most of us to consider building, and in all materials.

Build the New Instant Boats (1984) and *Build the Instant Catboat* (1986), both by Harold H. ("Dynamite") Payson. Relatively easy-to-build plywood planked small craft, both sail and power. Worthy of study by the newcomer or veteran lover of small craft. International Marine Publishing Co.

Building Classic Small Craft, Volume 1 (1977) and Volume 2 (1984), by John Gardner. Brought together in one book are instructions for building a number of classic wooden boats. International Marine Publishing Co.

Cold-Moulded and Strip-Planked Wood Boatbuilding, by Ian Nicolson, 1983. Stanford Maritime Limited, London, England. Distributed in the United States by Sheridan House Inc., Dobbs Ferry, NY.

Fiberglass Boatbuilding for Amateurs, by Ken Hankinson, 1982. Good coverage, including lots of details of interest. Available from Glen-L Marine Design, address above.

Finishing, by Walter J. Simmons, 1984. This tells what he has learned from his predecessors and from his own long experience. Available from the author at Duck Trap Woodworking, R.F.D. 2, Cannan Road, Lincolnville Beach, ME 04849.

Lapstrake Boatbuilding, by Walter J. Simmons. A book specializing in the art of building wooden boats with clinker planking. Originally published by International Marine Publishing Co. in 1980. (Reprint published by the author; see address above.)

Modern Boatbuilding Materials and Methods, by Steve Sleight. The latest information on new materials and the best techniques for using them. International Marine Publishing Co., 1986.

Modern Wooden Yacht Construction: Cold-Molding, Joinery, Fitting Out, by John Guzzwell. One of the best books on boatbuilding from start to finish. Well illustrated with photographs and line drawings. The technique of cold-molding is described in depth. International Marine Publishing Co., 1979. (Now out of print, but available in libraries.)

National Fisherman, 21 Elm Street, Camden, ME 04843. A monthly newspaper loaded with news, pictures, and plans of commercial fishing boats.

Practical Small Boat Designs, by John Atkin. Designer and surveyor John Atkin is the son of William ("Billy") Atkin, and this volume continues in that fine tradition. International Marine Publishing Co., 1983.

Safety Standards for Backyard Boat Builders, U.S. Coast Guard Publication CG-466, available from nearest Coast Guard District Office. Best described by the booklet foreword: "This pamphlet . . . (CG-466) is a simplified explanation of Federal recreational boat construction requirements and is intended for the use of the non-professional individual builder. The primary objective of these requirements is to avoid certain safety hazards which have been found to be the cause of boating accidents."

Safety Standards for Small Craft, American Boat and Yacht Council, Inc., Box 806, Amityville, NY 11701. Industry standards for boat construction and the installation of equipment. This is of great value to the boatbuilder, especially the parts on electrical wiring and circuit protection. See Chapter 17.

Ship and Aircraft Fairing and Development, by S.S. Rabl, 1941. A good old book with clearly illustrated details of some lofting techniques. Cornell Maritime Press, Centreville, MD 21617.

Steel Boatbuilding, Volume 1 (1985) and Volume 2 (1986), by Thomas E. Colvin. Much experience is the background of these books. Available from International Marine Publishing Co.

Wood: A Manual for Its Use as a Shipbuilding Material. Department of the Navy, Bureau of Ships, 1957-1962. (Reprint: Teaparty Books, Kingston, Massachusetts, 1983.) A superb source of information, including specifications and storage of wood for boatbuilding, moisture content, structural design of parts, wooden boat repairs, etc.

Wood Handbook (Handbook No. 72), Forest Products Laboratory, USDA Forest Service. Available from Superintendent of Documents, U.S. Government Printing Office, Washington, D.C. 20402. Contains much basic information about woods of interest to the boatbuilder. The address of this very cooperative agency is One Gifford Pinchot Drive, Madison, WI 53705-2398.

WoodenBoat, a bi-monthly magazine for wooden boat lovers and builders. WoodenBoat Publications, Inc., Box 78, Brooklin, ME 04616.

EQUIVALENTS

Linear

1 in. = 25.4 mm = 2.54 cm
1 in. = 0.083 ft.
1 ft. = 12 in. = 30.48 cm
6 ft. = 1 fathom
1 statute mile = 5280 ft.
1 statute mile = 1.6093 km

1 mm = 0.03937 in.
1 cm = 0.3937 in.
1 m = 39.37 in. = 3.2809 ft.
1 fathom = 1.8288 m
1 nautical mile = 6080 ft.
1 km = 0.6214 statute mile

Area

1 sq. in. = 6.4516 sq. cm
1 sq. ft. = 144 sq. in.
1 sq. ft. = 0.0929 sq. m

1 sq. cm = 0.1550 sq. ft.
1 sq. cm = 0.00108 sq. ft.
1 sq. m = 10.764 sq. ft.

Volume

1 cu. in. = 16.39 cu. cm
1 cu. ft.= 1728 cu. in.
1 liter = 61.017 cu. in.
1 cu. ft. = 7.481 gal. = 0.0283 cu. m = 28.32 liter
1 pt. = 0.4732 liter
1 qt. = 0.9464 liter

1 gal. = 0.1337 cu. ft. = 3.785 liter
1 cu. cm = 0.061 cu. in.
1 gal. = 231 cu. in.
1 liter = 0.03531 cu. ft.
1 liter = 2.113 pt.
1 liter = 1.057 qt.
1 liter = 0.2642 gal.

Note: The gal. above = U.S. gal., and 1 pt. = ⅛ gal.; 1 qt. = ¼ gal.

Weight

1 oz. = 28.35 gr	1 gr = 0.03527 oz.
1 oz. = 0.02835 kg	1 kg = 35.274 oz.
1 lb. = 16 oz.	1 oz. = 0.0625 lb.
1 lb. = 453.6 gr. = 0.4536 kg	1 kg = 2.2046 lb.

Pressure

1 lb. per sq. in. = 0.0703 kg per sq. cm
1 kg per sq. cm = 14.223 lb. per sq. in.

Miscellaneous

1 Imp. gal. = 1.2 U.S. gal.
1 ft. high column of water = 0.434 lb. per sq. in.
1000 watts = 1 kilowatt = 1.34 horsepower
1 horsepower = 746 watts
1 long ton = 2240 lb. = 35 cu. ft. of sea water
1 cu. ft. fresh water = 62.5 lb.
1 cu. ft. sea water = 64 lb.
1 knot = 1 nautical mile per hour = 1.85318 km per hr.

Decimal and Millimeter Equivalents

Inches		Decimals	Millimeters	Inches		Decimals	Millimeters
	1/64	0.015625	0.397		33/64	0.515625	13.097
1/32		.03125	0.794	17/32		.53125	13.494
	3/64	.046875	1.191		35/64	.546875	13.891
1/16		.0625	1.588	9/16		.5625	14.288
	5/64	.078125	1.984		37/64	.578125	14.684
3/32		.09375	2.381	19/32		.59375	15.081
	7/64	.109375	2.778		39/64	.609375	15.478
1/8		.1250	3.175	5/8		.6250	15.875
	9/64	.140625	3.572		41/64	.640625	16.272
5/32		.15625	3.969	21/32		.65625	16.669
	11/64	.171875	4.366		43/64	.671875	17.066
3/16		.1875	4.762	11/16		.6875	17.462
	13/64	.203125	5.159		45/64	.703125	17.859
7/32		.21875	5.556	23/32		.71875	18.256
	15/64	.234375	5.953		47/64	.734375	18.653
1/4		.2500	6.350	3/4		.7500	19.050
	17/64	.265625	6.747		49/64	.765625	19.447
9/32		.28125	7.144	25/32		.78125	19.844
	19/64	.296875	7.541		51/64	.796875	20.241
5/16		.3125	7.938	13/16		.8125	20.638
	21/64	.328125	8.334		53/64	.828125	21.034
11/32		.34375	8.731	27/32		.84375	21.431
	23/64	.359375	9.128		55/64	.859375	21.828
3/8		.3750	9.525	7/8		.8750	22.225
	25/64	.390625	9.922		57/64	.890625	22.622
13/32		.40625	10.319	29/32		.90625	23.019
	27/64	.421875	10.716		59/64	.921875	23.416
7/16		.4375	11.112	15/16		.9375	23.812
	29/64	.453125	11.509		61/64	.953125	24.209
15/32		.46875	11.906	31/32		.96875	24.606
	31/64	.484375	12.303		63/64	.984375	25.003
1/2		.5000	12.700	1		1.000	25.400

1 mm = .03937"   .001" = .0254 mm

Index

Abeking & Rasmussen, 33–34
ABI Industries, 250
Abrasives: garnet, aluminum oxide, backing paper, grit, 252; dividing sheets, abrasive cleaners, 253
Adhesives: water-resistant, waterproof, one-part, two-part, 74–75; sources, 76; *also see* Epoxy resin
Adjustable Clamp Co., 26
Aircraft Spruce & Specialty Co., 76, 220
Airex foam core, 50
Aladdin Products, Inc., 50
Alaska cedar: description, strength vs. weight, 34; design stresses, 35
Alcoa Almag, 35, 213
Aluminum alloys: hulls, 52; spars, 226–227; fuel tanks, 234; fresh water tanks, 245
American Bureau of Shipping (ABS), 35
American Boat & Yacht Council (ABYC), 234, 236, 244, 254–256
American Plywood Association: U.S. Product standard PS 1-83, 37
"Anchorfast" nails, 61, 66–69, 164
Arc-bottomed hulls, 2, 6
Armco Aquamet propeller shafting, 236
Ash, white: description, 33; strength vs. weight, 34; design stresses, 35
Atkin, John, 15
Atlantis Manufacturing Co., Inc., 212

Backbone, 109; bolting 119
Back rabbet, 105, 108

Ballast keel, 122, 216–218
Balsa core, 50, 53
Baltek Corp., 50
Bandsaw, 18
Baseline, 86
Bates, Fred, xii, 166
Battens, 111–112; spiling, 148–149
Batten seam planking, 162–164
Battery storage boxes, 244–245
Bearding line, 105–108
Bedding compounds: Dolfinite 2005N, 106; Boatlife, 106, 160; 3M 5200 sealant, 106, 160, 239; Pettit's, 239
Bevel board, 111–112
Bevels, 107, 110–113, 159–160
Bilge stringers, 141
Board foot of lumber, 30
Boaters Friend, The, 250
Boatlife caulk, 106
Body plan, 80; sections, 90
Bolts: screw bolts, drift bolts, 58–60; carriage bolts, fin head bolts, 60–61; bolt threads, 61; hanger bolts, 65
Bomar, 197
Boulter Plywood Corp., 36–38
Brass fastenings, 55, 61, 71
Breasthook, 173
Bristolcomp, 100
Broad strakes, 151
Bronze marine hardware, 250
Buck-Algonquin, 247, 250
Building: upside down or right side up?, 122; building under cover, building

upside down, 123–124; building outdoors, building right side up, 125–127

Bulkhead, 178–179, 202, 204

Bulwark rail, 192–193

Buttock, 78

Butts, butt blocks, 146–147

Cabin sole, 210

Cabin trunk, 189–192

Cabosil, 155, 184

Cannell Boatbuilding Co., William, 71

Castings: patterns, 213–214; molding, 215–216; cores, core print, core box, 215–218; ballast keel, 216–218

Cast iron: ballast keel, 216; weight, 216, 218

Caulking: cotton wicking, grommet, 106; carvel planking, caulking tools, cotton, 154–157; seam, 186–187

Caulking seam, 145, 150, 161

Cedar, Port Orford, Western red, 32; Alaska, 34; veneers, 41–42

Ceiling, 208–209

C-Flex planking, 46

Chine, 2–3, 5, 7, 82–83, 109 (Figure 8-8), 184

Circular saws, 18

Clamps (structural), 140

Clamps (tools), 17–18

Clinch ring, 59

Cockpit: coaming, 189; watertight self-bailing, 198–199; seats and lockers, 199

Cold-molded: wooden hull, 41; veneer sources, 42; cold-molded planking, 168

Columbian Bronze Corp., 116, 239, 240

Companionway closure, 194

Computer-aided lines fairing, 100

Condon, M.L. Company, 37, 42, 220

Contourkore, 50, 53

Copper: fastenings, 56, 65–67; worm sheathing, 118, 230

Copper Nail, The, 71

Cordless tools, 21

Core materials: cellular foam, end-grain balsa, 45, 47, 50; closed cell polyvinyl chloride foams, 50

Craftsman Wood Service Co., 26

Crook, natural, 33, 105, 173, 178

Cure for bilge water traps, 248–249

Curved transom development, 95

Cuprinol, 42, 147, 158

Cypress: description, 32; strength vs. weight, 34

Davits, 249–250

Dean Company, The: veneers for cold-molded wooden hulls, 42

Decay, wood: causes, prevention, preservatives, 42

Deck beams: camber, 175; headers, half beams, 176

Deck framing, 172–179

Deck joinerwork: general, 188; finishing, 188–189

Deck: plywood, 179, 182–183; tongue and groove, 180; strip-built, 181–182; canvas covered, 183; fiberglass covered, 184; laid, caulked, 185–187

Deck rails: toe, bulwark, 189–192; monkey, 193

Deck tie rods, 177

Deep keel sailboat, 6

Defender Industries, Inc., 45

Deft Clear Wood Finish, 214

Delta International Machinery Corp., 18–19

Developable surface, 6

Diagonal, 78

Diagonal hull straps, 220

Diagonal planking, 170

Dolphin Paint Co., 161

Double diagonal planking, 170–171

Douglas fir: description, 31; strength vs. weight, 34; design stresses, 35; veneer, 42

Drawer construction, 204–207

Drill press, 21

Drills: electric, 19–20; bits, 19–20, 63; augers, 20; countersinks, counterbores, tapered and brad point bits, 63–64

Duck Trap Woodworking, 71

Dynel wood sheathing, 43, 45

Edson Corp., The, 233

Electrical system, 244

Electric plane, portable, 21

Electric screwdriver, 21

Electrolysis, 57

Elliptical transom development, 97

Engine: beds, 144; controls, alignment, 241–242; connections, 242–243

Epoxy resin: additives, caution to users, 75–76; sources, 76; adhesion, 184

Everdur bronze: *see* silicon bronze

Exotic materials: graphite fiber, S-glass, Kevlar, Nomex honeycomb, 53

Fairing: battens, 89, 92; diagonals, long line endings, 92

Fastenings: galvanized iron, 54–55, 61, 74; brass, 55–61; silicon bronze, 55–56; Monel, copper, 56; stainless steel, 56–57, 64–65; bolts, 58–59; lag screws, hanger bolts, copper wire nails, rivets, 65–66, 70–71; galvanized boat nails, 66–67; threaded nails, 67, 69; miscellaneous, 71–73; machine screws, 71–72; staples, 72–73; "pop" rivets, 73; metric, 73
Fastening metal fittings, 74
Faying surfaces, 106
Federal Safe Boating Regulations, 256
Ferrocement hull, 52
Fine Tool Shops, The, 26
Fine Woodworking , 257
Fiberglass: hulls, 6–7, 9; wood sheathing, 43–45; female molds, 45–46; molded hulls, 45, 102; fresh water tanks, 245
Fin keel sailboat hulls, 116
Flat bottomed hulls, 2, 6
Flat transom development, 93
Floor timbers, 138–140
Florida Marine Tanks, Inc., 234
Forest Products Laboratory, U.S. Department of Agriculture, 35
Frames, 2–3, 6; v-bottom, 131; bent, 132–133; sawn, 133; steaming, 133–134; bending, 135–136; cold-fitted, 136–138
Framing: transverse, longitudinal, 131
Freshwater tanks, 245
Fuel tanks: construction, piping, 234; fills, 234–235; vents, 235; ABYC standards, 256
Fuller, W. L. Co., 64, 119

Galvanized boat nails, 66–67
Galvanic corrosion, series, 57–58, 74; fuel tank fittings, 234
Garboard strake, 150
Genwove U.S. Ltd, veneers, 42
Glen-L Marine Designs, 15
Glue: Weldwood Plastic Resin, urea resin, aliphatic resin, Weldwood Carpenter's, Titebond, resorcinol resin, 74; Weldwood Resorcinol Waterproof, 75; urea-formaldehyde resin, Aerolite Glue, 76; *also see* Epoxy resin
Goodrich "Cutless" bearing, 239
Gougeon Brothers, Inc., ix, 40
Grand River Marine, 250
Grid, the, 86
Gripe and horn timber, 118

Gross Mechanical Laboratories, Inc., 247
Guards: sheer, lower, 200
Gudgeon, 227, 229, 232

Hackmatack: description, 33–34; strength vs. weight, 34; stem, 105
Haft, J. Stuart, 250
Hand tools, 16
Hanging knees, 177–178
Harbor Sales Co., The, 36–37
Hatches: sliding, 193–194; deck, 195–197; aluminum, 197–198; flush, 198
HDI, Inc., 204
Headers, 176
Headliners, 211
Herreshoff, L. Francis, 60; Halsey C., 100; Manufacturing Co., 161
Highland Hardware, 26
H & L Marine Woodwork, Inc., 212
Hobbs, William G., xii
Hollow wooden spars, 220; rectangular, 221, round, 222–225
Honduras mahogany, 34–35
Huckins, Pembroke, 134
Huckins Yacht Corporation, ix
Hull: flat bottomed, 2, 6, 115; v-bottomed, 2–3, 6; round bottomed, 2–3, 6; arc-bottomed, 2, 6, 115; fiberglass, 6–7; kit boat, 9; steel, 50–52; aluminum alloy, 52; ferrocement, 52–53; exotic materials, 53
Hullforms, Inc., 100
Hull lines: sheer, deck line, profile, waterlines, buttocks, diagonals, sections, body plan, abbreviations, 78–82. *Also see* Lines plan
Hynautic, Inc., 233, 243

Icebox, 211–212
Imperial Marine Equipment, Inc., 198
Independent Nail, Inc., 54, 67
Interior joinerwork: description, finish, materials, 201–205
International Marine Publishing Co., 15
International Nickel Co., 68
International Paint Co.: 1026 Wood Sealer, 36; 402/414 Steel Epoxy Primer, 217

Jamestown Distributors, 71, 106, 156
Jig saw, portable, 19
Jointer, 21

Kargard, Ray, 167
Keel and centerboard sailboat, 6, 118
Keel, deadwood, keelson, 114–118
Kenyon Marine, 226
Kerwin, Justin E., 100
Kevlar, 45
Kit boats, 9
Klegecell Corp., Klegecell foam core, 50
Kobelt Manufacturing Co., Ltd. 243

Laminating wood and plywood, 39
Larch: *see* hackmatack; as plywood, 37
Lauer-Leonardi, Boris, ix, xi
Lead: weight, 216, 218; ballast keel, 217
Lines plan: profile, half-breadth plan, centerline, baseline, stations, sections, body plan, table of offsets, 78–83; grid, 86; chine, Figure 7-4
Lloyd's Register of Shipping, 35
Locker door catch, 207
Lodging knees, 177
Lofting: mold loft floor, 77; mold loft, 83; template paper, lofting tools, 84–85; battens, 85, 91; the grid, 86; pick-up sticks, 90; transom development, 93, 95, 97–98, computer, 112
Longitudinal strength members, hull: stringers, clamps, shelves, inwales, engine stringers, 140–143
Lower guard, 200
Lumber, sawing of, 27; plain sawn, quarter sawn, 28; rift, vertical, edge-grain boards, seasoning, moisture content, 28–30, 42; slash grain, 27, 29; flat grain, 28; air drying, kiln drying, 29–30; board foot measurement, 30; oven dry, moisture content meters, summer cutting vs. winter cutting, strength vs. weight, 34; flitches, "boat boards," round edge or "live edge" boards, *see* white cedar, 31; lumber sources, 41; veneers, 41–42; decay and preservatives, 42
Lumber support rollers, portable, 24

Machine screws, 71–72
Mack-Shaw Sailmakers, Inc., 226
Mahogany: *see* Philippine "mahogany," 32–33; Mexican, Honduras and African mahogany, *see* Other Mahoganies, 33
Marinetics Corp., 244
Marine surveyor, 14

Marinium, 74
Marking the boottop, 250–251
Mar-Quipt, Inc., 249
Masonite hardboard, 105, 245
Mast partners, 177
Mast step, 227–228
Metric measurements: plywood panel thickness, 38; fasteners, 71, 73
Metric & Multistandard Components Corp., 71
Mold loft, 77, 216, 231
Mold, female, 102
Molded hulls: cold-molded wood, 41–42
Molded hulls: fiberglass, wooden plug, female mold, 45–46; "one-off," C-Flex, 46; sandwich core, 46–47, 50
Molds: sectional, 101; hull thickness deduction, 103; spall, 105; spacing, 113; *photos*, 128
Monel: fastenings, 56, 58, 60–61, 66–69, 72, 74, 216, 220; fuel tanks, 234; propeller shafts, 236, fresh water tanks, 245
Monkey rail, 193
Montfort, Platt, 50
Morse Controls, 242
Motor Boating & Sailing, 15
Mr. Z's Products, 59

Nails: "Anchorfast" 56–61, 66–69, 164; galvanized boat, 66–67; copper, 56, 65, 70–71; threaded, 67; "Stronghold," 68–69; unusual, 70–71
National Fisherman, 9, 41
Natural crook, 33, 105, 173, 178
New Found Metals, Inc., 250
Nevins, Henry B., 161, 207
Nomex honeycomb core, 53

Offsets, 83
"Oil" finishes, 158
Oregon pine: *see* Douglas fir, 31

Pacific Lumber Co., 220
Painting: hull, bottom, 158
Panish Transdyne, 242
Patterns for metal castings, 213–214
Patterns: garboard strake, 150; for foundry castings, 213–218; patternmaker's tools, 214–215; core print, 216
Patterson, Andy, xi
Payson, Harold H. ("Dynamite"), 15
Perko, Inc., 247
Pettit Paint Co., 217, 239

Philippine "mahogany:" description, 32-33; strength vs. weight, 34

Pintle, 227, 229, 232

Pipe Welders, Inc., 249

Plank fastenings, 153-154

Planking: procedure, carvel type, 148; spiling, spiling batten, 148-149; hollowing and rounding, 152-153; stealer planks, 153-154

Planking: strakes, carvel planking, 145-146; butts, butt blocks, 146-147; caulking seam, 145, 147, 150; sheerstrake, 148-151; bottom planking, turn of the bilge, shutter plank, 148; broad strakes, 148, 151; smoothing, 156; lapstrake (clinker), 156-160; double, 160-161; batten seam, 162-164; strip, 164-167; plywood, 167-168; cold-molded, 168-170; double diagonal, 170-171

Planking scale, 151-152

Planksheer, 184-185

Plans, 10; for boats carrying passengers for hire, 14; sources, 18

Plastiglide Manufacturing Corp., 204

Plug, male, 102, 122

Plumbing, 245-246

Plywood panels: description, Douglas fir, grading, marine, exterior, U.S. Product standard PS 1-83, medium density overlay (MDO), 35-37; marine grade panel sizes, 37; foreign marine grade panels, 37-38; inch vs. millimeter thickness, 38; foreign brands, teak-faced panels, simulated teak laid decking, 38; sawing panels, 38-39; bending and laminating panels, 39-40; scarphing panels, 40-41

Polyester resin, 184

Polypropylene wood sheathing, 43, 45

Port Orford cedar: description, 32; strength vs. weight, 34

Powerboat keels, 116

Powerboat transoms, 98

Power tools, 18-19, 21-23

Product testing, 256

Profile, 80

Profile and rabbet, 89

Projected transom, 93

Propeller: rudder aperture, 231-232; shafts and bearings, 236-240; stuffing boxes, shaft log, 236, 239-240; shaft alignment, 241-242

Pulley drives, 242

Quarter knees, 173, 175, 178

Rabbet, rabbet line, 105, 108, 116, 118

Ready-made woodwork, 212

Red meranti veneer, 42

Red oak, 30

Resin: epoxy, 43-46, 74-75; polyester, 43-46; *also see* Epoxy

Restoration of old boats, 14

Rhodes, Philip L., vii, ix, xii, 167, 222, 225

Ribbands, 101, 125, 127-128

Rivets, copper, 65, 70-71; "pop," 73

Roberts, Bruce, 15

Rostand R. I., Inc., 250

Round-bottomed hulls, 2-3, 6, 115

Rudder stock, 227, 229, 231-232

Rudder, The, xi, ix

Rudder: types, 227-233; pintles, gudgeons, blade straps, trailing edge sheathing, propeller aperture, 231-232; steering controls, 233

Rules for Building and Classing Reinforced Plastic Vessels, 35

SAE: *see* Society of Automotive Engineers

Safety, 254-257

Sanders: disc, belt, 22; finishing, 23, 253

Sandpaper, 156. *Also see* abrasives, 252-253

Saws: circular, band, 18; portable, 18-19; jig, 19; hole, 20-21; plywood, 38-39; scarphing attachment, 40-41

Scantlings: definition, 42

Scarphing lumber and plywood, 40-41; use of "Scarffer," 40, 119-121

Scarphs, 40, 119-121

"Scarffer," 203

Schabo, Joe, xii

Schaefer Spars, 226

Screws: wood, 61-65, lag, 65

Scrive board, 90

Scuppers: deck, 192-193; cockpit, 198-199

Seacocks, 246-247

Sea rails, 203

Sears Roebuck & Co., 24, 26

Sections: body plan, 78; stem, non-vertical, 107-108

Seemann Fiberglass, Inc., ix, 46

Setting up, 122

Seven Corners Ace Hardware, Inc., 26

Shaft log, 116

Sheer guard, 200
Sheerline, 7, 78
Sheerline and deck line, 86–89
Shelf, shelves, 172
Shellac: double planking, 161; patterns, 214, hollow spars, 222
Shrinkage: metal, 214, 216, 218; rule, 214
Sikaflex, 160, 162
Silicon bronze (Everdur): fastenings, 55, 58, 60–61, 65, 74, 216, 225, 239; rudder stock, 230
Simmons, Walter, 17–18, 26, 158
Sitka spruce: description, 32; strength vs. weight, 34; design stresses, 35; veneer, 42; spars, 220, 222
Skilsaw, 18
Sliding hatch, 193–194
Small Boat Journal, 41
Society of Automotive Engineers: propeller hub and shaft end standards, 240
Spartan Co., 250
Spiling, 148; spiling batten, 148–149
Spruce: *see* Sitka spruce, Northern white spruce, 32
Stainless steel: fastenings, hardware, rigging, 56–57, 74, 220; bolts, 60, 239; wood screws, 64–65; machine screws, 71; rudder stock, 230; propeller shafting, 236; freshwater tanks, 245
Standing rigging chainplates, 218–220
Stanley Tools, 160
Staples, 71–72
Star Class sloop, 2
Steel hull, 50–52
Steering controls, 234
Stem and rabbet, 105
Stephens, Olin, xi
Str-r-etch Mesh, 50
Sternpost: description, 119; worm sheathing, 118, 230
Stopwaters: 106 (Figure 8-5), 109, 116, 119
Strawbery Banke, Inc., 71
Stringers: bilge, 140–141; engine, 142, 143 (Figure 10-12)
Strip planking, 164
"Stronghold" nails, 61, 66, 68–69

Tamarack: *see* hackmatack
Tangs, standing rigging, 225
Tank capacity calculation, 236–237
Tanks: fuel, 234; capacity calculation, 236; freshwater, 245; standards, 256

Taunton Press, Inc., The, 257
Teak: description, 33; strength vs. weight, 34; design stresses, 35; plywood, 38; deck, 185–187
Templates: stem, 105–106; rabbet, 107–108; keel, 116; bulwark rail, 193; interior joinerwork, 203–205; ballast keel, 216, 218; hollow spars, 224; rudder, 230, 232
Tenon, 121
Termanto foam core, 50
Texas Dory Boat Plans, 15
Thickness planer, 21–22, 230
Tobin bronze: bolts, 216; rudder stock, 230; propeller shafting, 236
Toe rail, 192
Toe space, 203
Teleflex, Inc., 243
Termino foam core, 50
Tools: hand, layout, 16–17; clamps, 17–18; power, 18–24; cordless, 21; sources, 24–26
Torin, Inc., ix, 50
Transom: stern board, 93; development of, 93, 95, 97–98; tumblehome, 100; bevels, construction, 113–114
Tremont Nail Co., 71
Trend-Lines, Inc., 26
Types of rudders: inboard, outboard, balanced, powerboat, 227; spade, 227–228; small sailboat, 228–229; large sailboat, 229–231; auxiliary sailboat, 230–233

Underwriter's Laboratories (UL), 257
U.S. Coast Guard regulations: for passenger-carrying boats, safety, 14; electrical systems, 244
U.S. Product Standard PS 1-83: specifications for plywood manufactured in the U.S., 37

V-bottomed hulls, 2–3, 6–7, 9; frames, 110; setting up, 130; planking, 162–164
Veneer: *see* Douglas fir, 31; plywood, 36; species and sources, 41–42
Ventilation, 207–208
Vertical tie rod, 227

Wagner Marine (USA) Inc., 233
Waterline, 78, 86
Water trap vent, 247–248
Weldwood: Plastic Resin Glue, Carpenter's Glue, Resorcinol Glue, Resorcinol Waterproof Glue, 74–76

Western red cedar: description, 32; strength vs. weight, 34; veneers, 41

Westlawn School of Yacht Design, ix

Wetzler Clamp Co., Inc., 26

White ash: *see* Ash, white

White cedar, Northern and Atlantic: description, 31; strength vs. weight, 34

White oak: description, 30–31; strength vs. weight, 34; design stresses, 35

White pine: description, 31; strength vs. weight, 34

Wicks Aircraft Supply, 76, 220

Wilcox-Crittenden, 247

Wiley, Ralph, 166

Willard (ballast keel foundry), 219

Wittholz, Charles W., 15

Wood: A Manual For Its Use As A Shipbuilding Material, 34

Wood: for boatbuilding, 27–42; seasoning, 28–30; moisture content, 28, 42; kinds of, 30–34; summer cutting vs. winter cutting, strength vs. weight, 34; ABS design stresses, 35; laminating, 39; veneers, 41–42; decay prevention, 42; fiberglass and other sheathing, 43–45

Woodcraft Supply Corp., 26

WoodenBoat, 15, 41, 178

Wooden spars, 220–225; rigging attachments, 225

Wood Handbook, 35

Woodlife, 42, 147, 158

Wood preservatives, 42, 119, 158

Wood screws, 61–64

Woodworker's Supply of New Mexico, 25–26

Woolsey Paint Co., 217

YDI Schools, ix

Yellow pine, longleaf: description, 31; strength vs. weight, 34; design stresses, 35